THE LEAST
OF THESE

THE TRAGIC STORY OF DUBLIN'S
FOUNDLING HOSPITAL

MARK B. ROE

THE LEAST OF THESE

THE TRAGIC STORY OF DUBLIN'S FOUNDLING HOSPITAL

MARK B. ROE

First published 2022

The History Press
97 St George's Place, Cheltenham,
Gloucestershire, GL50 3QB
www.thehistorypress.co.uk

British Library Cataloguing in Publication Data.
A catalogue record for this book is available from the British Library.

ISBN 978 0 7509 9876 5

Typesetting and origination by The History Press
Printed and bound in Great Britain by TJ Books Limited, Padstow, Cornwall.

Trees for Life

'Inasmuch as ye have done it
Unto the least of these little ones,
Ye have done it unto me.'

Matthew 25:40

Inscription over the western fireplace,
Foundling Hospital Chapel[1]

To Moira, Niamh and Lia

Contents

Acknowledgements

I am grateful to the following for assistance in preparing this work: The National Library of Ireland, Trinity College Dublin, the National Archives, Marsh's Library (Dublin), Dublin City Library and Archive, the Irish Architectural Archive, the Public Record Office of Northern Ireland, Queen's University Belfast, University College Dublin, the Heritage Centre at the Royal College of Physicians of Ireland, Westmeath County Library, the National Archives, UK, the Bureau of Military History, and the Irish Georgian Society. Thanks also to my editors Nicola Guy and Ele Craker, and particular thanks to Moira, Niamh and Lia for their endless patience.

Prologue

The walls stretched for some 400ft along James's Street. At their base ran a muddy footpath, separated from the street by a patch of waste ground.[1] To the left of the gates a narrow doorway was set into the wall. It was through this doorway that the five visitors were admitted by the porter, William Kellet.[2] The date was Tuesday, 11 April 1797.[3]

Inside the walls, dozens of windows looked down on the visitors, from ranges of plain, barrack-like buildings stretching to left and right. At the centre stood a vast hall, whose towering arched windows dwarfed the visitors. Built in the old-fashioned style of the previous century, the hall had a steeply pitched roof on which were perched six tiny dormer windows, high above the level of the street. Its entrance was a grand and imposing doorway, itself as tall as a two-storey building.

Within, the cavernous bare hall, lit by its soaring arched windows, had the look of some utilitarian cathedral. On each windowless end wall was a great fireplace – bleakly empty of any warming flame. Over the left-hand, eastern wall hung the huge painting of a plump and satisfied-looking cleric. This was Archbishop Hugh Boulter, who had been central to the creation of the Foundling Hospital generations before. Now his portrait looked down on rows and rows of long wooden tables that filled the hall and could accommodate a thousand children.[4]

On the far side of the hall a doorway led outside, where more ranges of prison-like two- and three-storey buildings enclosed a vast courtyard.[5] Away in the distance, the long building that formed the rear boundary of the yard had once been called 'Bedlam'. There the insane had been sequestered, far from the street, where their cries could not be heard. Because of its scale, the whole complex had been likened by one observer to a walled town lying on the edge of the city – a world unto itself.[6]

Although vast, the buildings had barely space enough to contain the dormitories and schoolrooms needed. Many of the dormitories, particularly those on the upper floors, were felt to be cramped and overcrowded with beds. These were bunk beds, crammed together without space between them. Such was the crowding at some periods that two or three children slept in each bed.[7]

However, it was to the infant infirmary that the visitors proceeded with some urgency, for they had been dispatched specifically to investigate conditions there. The infirmary they found to be a 'black and gloomy' chamber.[8] (Either there were few windows, or their light had been deliberately obscured.) In the gloom they made out five 'filthy cradles'. It's likely in fact that these were simply modified bedsteads of the heavy wooden type.[9] On each bedstead were laid three or four infants side by side – eighteen in total. The infants were noticeably underdressed to cope with the cold, given the 'inclement season' and the lack of adequate heating from any fire. What's more, the clothing they did have was 'filthy and dirty'. It later emerged that sick infants, on being transferred from the nursery to the infirmary, had their clothes removed and replaced with old clothes taken from babies on their arrival at the Hospital. The newer clothes were then returned for use elsewhere in the Hospital. What's more, the 'cradles' were lined with straw – which was difficult to keep free of infestations – and the infants were covered with cast-off blankets, no longer good enough even for use elsewhere in the Foundling Hospital. These too were dirty and the cradles 'swarming with bugs'.[10]

To look after these eighteen babies, or whatever number might be in the infirmary, throughout the day and night, day in and day out, there were but two women – Catherine Maquean and Esther Wiggan.[11] Given the intense demands of their duties, and in keeping with the practice of the times, it is likely that these women slept in the same room as the infants, on mattresses on the floor, or on settle beds, which could be rolled or folded away during the day.[12] They may have taken their meals in the same room, or left for short periods to eat nearby, since the infirmary had its own small kitchen, far removed from the main kitchens or the great hall. Perhaps the two women alternated shifts, with one sleeping during the day, the other at night – this might be one explanation for the darkness of the chamber. Each of the women was paid £4 per year (plus board and 'lodging') – little more than the lowest rank of maidservant. As was the norm for the time, they were completely untrained.[13]

By now the visitors were sufficiently alarmed to send for Mrs Hunt, the matron. Confronted by what was later described as 'inhuman neglect' and perhaps spurred into defensiveness, Mrs Hunt spoke with a candour that she would later appear to regret. 'Those children,' she said, were 'just laid there to die.' Having spoken to her, the visitors concluded (in their report to the governors, which was later submitted to parliament), that 'no human efforts are ever made use of to save the lives of the children, except administering to them the common food, bread and milk or bread and water'. And 'when weakly, infants are sent into this place of death … all are indiscriminately treated: bread and milk or bread and water must sustain them or they perish'.[14]

Surprisingly, in a visit to a room containing eighteen poorly fed infants, the visitors failed to mention any crying from the infants. However, Catherine Maquean later gave the most likely explanation for why noise makes no appearance in the report of the visitors. For despite the lack of medical attendance, there was one medicine that *was* in plentiful supply – 'the Bottle', which Maquean 'supposed it a composing draught, for the Children were easy after taking it for an hour or two'.[15] By this she meant a sleeping draught and in the eighteenth century these invariably contained opium.[16]

In their report the visitors pulled no punches in describing the 'miserable situation' of the children and in lamenting that the matter had 'a complexion of more than savage cruelty'. It was later to emerge that here in this one room, in the quiet and semi-darkness of the infant infirmary, away from the great hall and the other buildings, 5,215 infants had died during the course of the previous six years.

This book examines how this came about, and what happened subsequently. In doing so it will look at the origins of the Foundling Hospital as a workhouse and the radical decision to change it to a repository for infants in 1730. It will follow the progress of the institution as it struggled with its new role, and, above all, it will attempt to uncover the fate of the roughly 127,000 infants who entered its doors, 100,000 of whom died or disappeared from the records.

1

Foundations

During the Williamite War, which swept Ireland from 1688 to 1691, an observer
described seeing a 'crowd of forlorn and famishing outcasts' who had been dis-
placed by the fighting. 'So dreadful was their destitution,' he wrote, 'that a morsel
of garbage was a feast, and they flocked as ravens round the putrefying and black-
ened carcasses of dead horses which lay rotting in the summer sun.'[1] Recurrent
episodes of warfare and famine in the 17th century set multitudes on the move
in a desperate attempt to survive. Many of them gravitated to the capital.

In 1695, Dublin city governors complained of a 'great number of sturdy
beggars, both men and women … with their children, which they send in the
night to beg at the doors … [of] particularly the most considerable persons,
crying at their doors at unseasonable hours in the night'.[2] One concern of the
burgesses was that these 'idlers and vagabonds' would take advantage of the
distraction caused by their 'troublesome children' to 'rob and plunder houses'
(a ruse that, if it had been used, had been well and truly rumbled by the time
it was denounced in the council chamber).

Stables, barns, haylofts, outhouses, communal latrines in courtyards, ruins,
abandoned houses and those under construction – these were the places the
poor could find shelter in a city. Warmth could be obtained from cow sheds
and dunghills, which were common throughout the city, and even in 'anneal-
ing yards associated with the glass manufactory'.[3] But these spaces may have
been already occupied by the luckier urban poor, in which case the 'foreign'
beggars may have slept in the fields near the city and tramped in at night to
beg, when there was less chance of being accosted by local paupers.

The city of Dublin had long struggled to cope with its poor. To the indigenous
paupers of its crowded streets and lanes were added the vagabonds and beggars who flocked to the city in times of crisis. Formal legal provision for the
indigent was limited. A 1542 Act allowed alms to be raised for the 'deserving'
poor and the punishment of the 'undeserving' poor, who could be whipped

and returned to their place of origin.[4] This law was, in fact, a transcription of English legislation and took little account of actual conditions in Ireland. For example, it referred to administrative units such as 'hundreds' and 'wapentakes' that had never existed in Ireland. What's more, the brutal warfare, dispossession and plantation that characterised this era made these provisions purely theoretical when they were introduced.

It was to be nearly a century before the next legal development – a 1635 Act under which each county was to have its own house of correction with 'mills, working cards and other necessary implements' to set the poor to work.[5] This act was another hasty transcription of English legislation – so carelessly drafted that it wrongly assumed that the Elizabethan poor law of 1601 applied in Ireland and that effective local poor relief was in operation.[6] However, the implementation of this act was delayed, and its measures were never fully to take effect.

In 1640 a new bill included provision for poor orphans, including binding them as apprentices, and setting the poor to work.[7] However, this legislation too was stymied in its later stages, before ever coming into operation. Thereafter, government relied on proclamations to address temporary and local crises. These were reactive and lacked the authority and longevity of legislation.[8]

Throughout this period, a fundamental distinction between the 'deserving' and 'undeserving' poor was made. The 'undeserving' poor – also called 'vagabonds' and 'sturdy beggars' – were considered able to earn their living but simply too idle or too feckless to do so. However, the definition of this class was conveniently wide and could, for example, include unregistered priests and defeated Irish soldiers. Imprisonment in houses of correction or ordinary gaols, deportation to the American or Caribbean colonies, or even summary execution was their possible fate.[9]

The 'deserving' poor, including invalids, the 'superannuated', and women with dependent children, were considered more worthy of charity. However, as we have seen, there was little or no legal or formal provision for this. What's more, as one historian notes, as time went on, 'the dichotomy between the "deserving" and the "undeserving" poor became more closely aligned with the fundamental ethnic and sectarian division of Irish society'.[10]

The Anglican Church of Ireland parishes formed the main organ of local government.[11] The Church acted as an arm of the state, with the appointments of senior clerics determined by government and the parishes collecting alms for the relief of the poor. In theory, responsibility for the deserving poor lay with them. However, their narrow population base and limited acceptance left the parishes unable, and probably unwilling, to engage in relief on the scale that was required. What's more, unlike England, on which practices were loosely based, no legislation had been put in place to underpin this role.

However, in 1665, the St Andrew's Act was introduced, allowing 'for the relief of the poor and putting out child apprentices'.[12] It enabled the parish to raise money specifically for the poor. Although it applied to the Dublin parish of St Andrews only, it nevertheless established a precedent that other parishes followed.[13]

Other sources of relief for the deserving poor were charitable individuals and town corporations. Both sometimes ran small-scale poorhouses, often continuations of institutions run by Catholic monasteries before their suppression in the 1500s. Given the small scale of these poorhouses, entry was highly selective and often reserved for relations or dependents of influential citizens.[14] Examples in Dublin included St John's Poorhouse, on Thomas Street, and St Stephen's Poorhouse, near St Stephen's Green.[15]

From time to time the city governors made attempts to address the problem. The King's Hospital, or Blue Coat Hospital, which opened in 1670, was originally meant for the relief of aged and infirm poor but was subsequently used as a school for the sons and grandsons of 'decayed' freemen. Then, in the 1680s, the city acquired some land on its outskirts, and in 1688, enclosed the site with a wall and began 'the foundation of [a] workhouse and infirmary'.[16] However, little progress was made, due to lack of funds. According to the city records, from time to time the site was used 'to gather the poor people together to clear the city of mendicants' – it is not clear whether they were gathered and held by force.[17] The location of the site was significant since it lay just outside St James's gate, the main access point to the city from the west, from which it was presumed many of the wandering poor came. Thus the site on James's Street had an early association with the poor. But no further advances were made in establishing a workhouse before the country was engulfed in the Williamite War – yet another in a long series of conflicts that devastated the country.

When it came to the 'deserving' poor, as we have seen, in the absence of comprehensive legislation or formal measures, individuals could undertake their own charitable efforts. One such individual was John Collis, creator of a workhouse in Dublin that was subsequently 'lost' to history. In 1690, Collis, a Dublin merchant, printed his *Proposals for the Taking in Boys into the King and Queens Work-House in Strand-street near Capel-street, Dublin, agreed on by the Master, Officers, and Senior Workmen of the said House.* The parishes had, at least in theory, an obligation to orphans and impoverished children. As we have seen, the 1640 bill included provision for 'binding' these children as apprentices. The problem was that potential masters were often reluctant to accept such apprentices, believing they inherited habits of idleness. And parents, even though impoverished, also could object to potential masters, fearing ill-treatment, exploitation, or worse.[18] In addition, in this era before industrialisation, employment opportunities for unskilled children were rare.[19]

Collis set out to address this problem by establishing a workhouse specifically for this type of apprentice (although it would also take in non-pauper apprentices, depending on capacity and the demand for places from the parishes). Collis's Workhouse was intermediate between the old system under which parishes struggled to find places for poor children in the general apprenticeship market, and the later development of large-scale workhouses – which would become fashionable a few years later.

Collis's document, *Proposals*, sets out arrangements for entering boys into the Workhouse for an apprenticeship of seven years. They must abide by the rules of the house or otherwise be 'dealt with as sturdy Beggars and Vagrants'.[20] The service did not come cheap. Firstly, each place had to be secured by an auction process, where the 'Disposers' would bid for each place, starting at a minimum of £5. Furthermore, each boy who obtained a place had to be provided with 'three new suits of apparel' as well as three hats, six pairs of stockings, six pairs of shoes, six cravats, six handkerchiefs and six shirts. Also required were a Bible, a knife, a comb, a thimble, 'a porringer or like dish, and a penner'. In addition, each boy was required to bring 'a piece of plate to the value of twelve shillings, at least'.[21]

Collis was an independent-minded original thinker with a clear financial acumen. His hard-nosed, up-front demands probably indicate pragmatism and a desire for his undertaking to succeed, rather than any greed. He believed strongly in the importance of workhouses in addressing poverty in Ireland. In April 1697 he made a proposal to the Board of Trade in London to establish one in every county. His proposal was considered over the course of four months, and he made numerous visits to the Board's meetings, before his suggestion was finally rejected.[22]

Nevertheless, he did succeed in establishing a workhouse in Dublin. In his work *A National Credit for a National Use*, printed in Dublin and submitted to parliament in February 1706, Collis relates how:

I have spent near 30 years, with great expense and labour, to endeavour the settling a public Work-house for the poor: and because the City did not endeavour any such thing, I undertook the enterprise at my own charge; and in order thereto, I built a house to hold 60 poor, to diet, lodge, and work in, and I furnished the said House with working-tools and took in some poor, and they are now at work there.[23]

But while Collis had been pursuing his goal of a resolutely solvent workhouse, Dublin Corporation had resumed its efforts at establishing an institution on a much larger scale. In 1697 it passed a resolution to lobby the government for funding to build a 'house' to 'put idlers to work in' and if necessary to approach parliament.[24] Within a few weeks the Recorder, William Handcock, who was also an MP for the city of Dublin and acted as something of an intermediary between Dublin Corporation and parliament, placed a bill before parliament 'For the erecting of a public workhouse in Dublin'. However, the bill failed to progress.[25]

What's more, the land intended as the site for the new workhouse, and on which the city had spent so much money, enclosing it with a wall in the 1680s, had become entangled in a complex legal situation. This was due to forfeitures – the confiscation of land from the Catholic supporters of the defeated James II. However, the Corporation finally managed to reacquire the land in 1703 and set about the project in earnest. A committee was formed, to meet regularly to consider how to proceed, and to lobby parliament. The meetings were to be at the Tholsel, the seat of the Dublin city assembly. The result was the presentation to parliament, again by the Recorder (now John Forster) in October 1703 of a new bill, which this time was approved by parliament.

John Collis's smaller workhouse was now to be overshadowed, and ultimately thwarted, by a development on a much larger scale. This time, in addition to Dublin Corporation, the movement was supported by senior figures such as the Duke of Ormonde (the head of English government in Ireland) and his wife, Mary. This new workhouse, Collis wrote ruefully, would achieve all his aims and 'be in all future ages to [their] immortal praise and memory, though it accidentally has eclipsed and frustrated mine, to my great loss, and almost ruin, as is well known to most of the inhabitants in Dublin'.[26] Collis was right about being 'eclipsed', for his workhouse was to disappear from memory, and no mention of it is to be found in any of the annals of Dublin's history.

The legislation underlying the new Dublin Workhouse had its origins in the London Corporation of the Poor of 1647.[27] Incorporation involved bestowing certain functions of the numerous city parishes onto one body corporate and granting legal status to that body. This facilitated central management of some civic functions – where before each parish had operated as an individual entity. Another advantage was that its legal status allowed the new organisation to receive and manage charitable bequests in perpetuity.[28] Although the London Corporation of the Poor became defunct, the idea of incorporation was revived in the 1690s by a Bristol merchant, John Cary,[29] and became the legal basis for the Bristol Workhouse.[30] In turn, this legislation with minor changes was subsequently applied to fourteen English cities, establishing workhouses, in fourteen separate Acts of the English parliament, between 1696 and 1712.[31] It's clear that this legislation was adapted by the Irish parliament for Dublin in 1703. Comparing, for example, the Exeter Corporation Act passed in 1698, and the Dublin Workhouse Act of 1703, there are clear similarities, including almost identical wording in the preamble.[32] In addition, a carefully transcribed extract from Cary's book on the subject, published in 1700,[33] is found in the papers of Lord Lanesborough.[34] Lanesborough, along with his wife, was one of the largest individual donors to the Dublin Workhouse building fund, further supporting the influence of the Bristol example.[35] Nevertheless, the Dublin Act did contain indigenous features, such as the use of revenue from the carriage trade to finance the Workhouse, as we shall see.

Those supporting the new workhouse included, in addition to the Duke and Duchess of Ormonde, the Anglican Archbishop of Dublin, William King, senior aristocrats Lord and Lady Lanesborough, and others.[36] In a religious era it was important for regimes to bolster their legitimacy through acts of 'godliness' and 'righteousness'.

Another factor that contributed to the opening of a workhouse in Dublin was the existence of reform societies in the city in the 1690s. Reform societies were religiously motivated associations targeting immorality, such as 'profane language' (although these often ended up directed against the poor and marginalised).[37] In England, Corporation Acts were enacted in cities with a strong reform society presence.[38] There may have been a similar connection in Ireland. There was considerable movement between Dublin and London at the time, many Protestant Dublin merchants having fled to London between 1688 and 1690, returning when hostilities had ceased. Further indirect evidence linking the Dublin reform societies to the Workhouse comes in the person of Sir Richard Bulkeley, who was prominent in the reform society movement in Dublin[39] and an early advocate of workhouses.[40] He was one of only four people individually named in the Dublin Workhouse Act as a governor (among a large number of unnamed 'ex-officio' governors).[41]

This combined activity culminated in 1703 in 'An Act for erecting a workhouse in the city of Dublin for imploying and maintaining the poor thereof'.[42] The legislation decreed that from 1 May 1704 'there be and shall be a corporation to continue forever within the county of the city of Dublin' to be known as 'the Governors and guardians of the poor of the city of Dublin'. This Corporation was to consist of senior government officials and senior clergymen as well as the Lord Mayor and aldermen of the city of Dublin and a number of other named individuals – to a total of approximately one hundred. The largest groups were the twenty-four aldermen and forty-eight sheriff's peers of Dublin city council. In addition, any person donating £50 could be made a governor, subject to election by the existing governors.

The governors were to vote annually, to elect from among themselves a 'Court of Assistants' of seven governors, and a treasurer, who would look after the operations of the Workhouse for the following year. This Court of Assistants was required 'upon the first Thursday in every month to keep a court or assembly', which could make bye-laws and regulations. The governors were to set to work 'all vagabonds and beggars, which shall come within the city or liberties' and were given the power to detain 'all idle or poor people begging or seeking relief' within the city, or poor people in receipt of parish alms.[43] Vagabonds might come from anywhere in Ireland, but the Workhouse was also to cater for the 'parish poor' – people dwelling within the parishes of Dublin who were destitute and dependent on parish alms. In addition, any children above the age of 5 who had no means of support could be taken up. These children could be placed in bonded servitude to 'any honest person, or persons, being protestants' until the age of 21 in the case of females, and 24 in the case of males.[44]

Surprisingly, given that it led to the building of such an iconic structure, the legislation did not specify the nature of the building to be provided, merely referring to 'such hospital or workhouses as be hereafter erected'.[45]

The Act stated that the governors 'shall have the care of the maintenance of the poor of the said city and liberties' – a sweeping responsibility. But in effect the only provision the Act made to discharge that responsibility was the erection of a 'hospital or workhouses'. The governors were given 'full power to examine, search and see what poor persons' were in the city and to apprehend any 'idle vagrants and beggars'. These were then to be incarcerated in the workhouse(s) for up to seven years. Any existing almshouses were excluded from the governors' remit.

There were to be two main sources of income for the Workhouse (and in addition it was hoped the work of the inmates would generate profits). The first was a tax on 'any hackney coach or coaches, carts or cars (crude carts with solid wooden wheels) … chairs or sedans' plying for hire within the city. This tax consisted of a licence fee called a 'fine' as well as an annual tax. These were costly – £5 to licence a coach (equivalent to the cost of twenty full days of hire) and 40s for the annual tax – equivalent to eight full days' hire. Notably, coaches and chairs not for hire in private ownership (mostly of the wealthy) were not to be touched. The Act also specified the rates coach- and chair-men could charge their customers.

One reason for using this source for funds was that taxing the carriage trade was already within the purview of Dublin Corporation, and had been ring-fenced to finance a workhouse as early as 1681.[46] However, some may have felt it was a form of poetic justice. Jonathan Swift, later Dean of St Patrick's Cathedral, complained that pedestrians like himself and his 'brother walkers' bore the brunt of demands from beggars, while 'as to persons in coaches and chairs, they bear but little of the persecution we suffer, and are willing to leave it entirely on us'.[47]

The second source of income was a tax on houses, at 3 per cent of their (rate-able) value per annum. This was to be collected by churchwardens, in keeping with the practices of the time whereby, as we have seen, the Anglican Church had a significant role in the administration of the state. The churchwardens were then to turn the proceeds over to the governors.[48] A twenty-one-year term was set on the operation of the Act – a not uncommon measure to ensure that legislation with revenue implications was reviewed.

At the same time as it passed the legislation founding the Workhouse, the Irish parliament, controlled by the Anglo-Irish victors of the Williamite War, passed further anti-Catholic laws, refining what were already unjust and repressive legal instruments. The latest addition was 'An Act to prevent the further growth of popery'. This was premised on the assertion that 'papists', because of their 'hatred and aversion to the … true religion', were daily endeavouring 'to persuade and pervert [others] from the Protestant religion' 'by cunning devices and contrivances' 'to the destruction of the Protestant interest in this kingdom'.[49] Any 'papist' found guilty of such an offence was to suffer the penalty of 'premunire' – the loss of all civil rights, forfeiture of lands, goods and 'chattels', and indefinite imprisonment 'during the royal pleasure'. Furthermore, previous laws having forbidden Catholic children from obtaining an education in Ireland, the new Act now included detailed restrictions to prevent 'popish families' from sending their children abroad to be educated. In addition, if the eldest son of a Catholic was to convert to Protestantism 'such popish parent shall become, and shall be, only tenant for life' on what would now become the son's property. 'No person of the popish religion' could be the guardian of a child 'or have the tuition or custody of, any orphan, child or children, under the age of twenty one years'.

Furthermore, 'every papist' was 'hereby made incapable to buy and purchase … any manors, lands, tenements or hereditaments'. No Catholic could take out a lease of more than thirty-one years. A Catholic who had land was not entitled to make a will. Rather, if all his children remained Catholic, on his death he was obliged to divide his land in equal shares among all his sons, and the land shall 'in like manner from such respective sons, being papists, descend to and be inherited by all and every the sons of such sons, share and share alike'. Within a few generations the land of any Catholics would be reduced to small uneconomic allotments that could then be easily purchased by non-Catholics (Catholics being forbidden to buy land).

It was in this context that, in the wake of the new workhouse Act, the first meeting of the governors of which we have record was held on 9 May 1704, just eight days after the legal establishment of the Corporation of Governors.[50] The new governors set about raising fresh funds for the project in earnest.

2

'Such Useless Ancient Poor'

On 12 October 1704, a mere five months after the first meeting of the governors, a party of dignitaries gathered at the chosen site for the new Workhouse. This was at the very edge of the city, just within the legal city boundary, at the end of James's Street, where the city petered out to be replaced by fields. The site was bounded to the west by Cut-Throat Lane, perhaps called after a family named Cothroit, said to have had land in the area in medieval times.[1] It included, to the south, an area known as 'the pipes', through which ran a watercourse that was the city's principal, though rudimentary, water supply. Across the river the Royal Barracks was taking shape – eventually to become the largest military barracks in Europe.

Although lying at the edge of the city, the site was far from undesirable. In fact it was elevated and airy – at a time when fresh air was considered essential to good health. Nearby, fields sloped steeply down to the River Camac, then rose to another elevation on which stood the Royal Hospital, the beautiful and prestigious building created by Charles II for retired soldiers. Indeed, when the Workhouse was finished, the two buildings, which shared a similarity of design, must have formed a harmonious pair.

Afterwards the group was lavishly entertained, probably in the Tholsel, the city hall. Sir Francis Stoyte, a silk merchant,[2] as Lord Mayor for that year, was effectively chairman of the governors and would play a leading role in the building programme. The Recorder, John Forster, who had helped initiate the legislation in the Commons, was also present. The presence of the Duchess of Ormonde, wife to the Viceroy (who was abroad), indicated approval at the highest level of government. In her own right, she would go on to play a significant role in fundraising for the project and in offering to solicit support at the English court.[3]

The heavy workload, or enthusiasm, of the new governors can be glimpsed from a petition by Mary Semour, a servant who was paid for the upkeep of the

Tholsel. In 1705 she requested an increase in her fee, because 'she is obliged to keep two servants to clean the stairs and rooms of the Tholsell, by reason of the continual number of people that attend the Governors of the Poore House'.[4]

The next detailed account we have of the activities of the governors comes in a report printed in June 1705 by Francis Stoyte.[5] And it indicates progress at an astonishing speed. By then there were 'erected two large buildings, of three hundred foot long, and twenty foot broad in the clear; two stories high, besides garrets, (with one large vault) proper for stores, and setting the poor to work in, and the same are finished except the glazing. The buildings for lodging of about six hundred poor, are raised to one story high. Two kitchens [are] ready for roofing. The Great Hall is going forwards, and the vaults under the same almost finished.' The buildings were likely to be completed by Christmas, the report said – as long as the money held out.

The project had by then received, or been pledged, around £5,000 from various sources – mostly voluntary contributions.[6] The Duchess of Ormonde raised £900, the Lord Mayor £341. Lady Lanesborough personally contributed £200, and her husband £100. Not everyone contributed in monetary form – Thomas Burgh, the Surveyor General, who probably designed the building and supervised the building work, donated 'a pile of stone-work at his own cost at the entrance into the Workhouse'.[7] This probably refers to stone gate piers. (By reason of his office, Burgh was also a governor, and took some part in the financial management of the Workhouse, being a member of the Court of Assistants, at least in 1706.)[8]

As to the city's bequest, in an ominous portent of things to come, only £10 of the expected £408 due from the tax on houses – on which the Workhouse would have to rely for part of its income – had been paid. And, from the tax on carriages, £183 out of £778 was also outstanding. It was projected that a total of £10,500 would be needed to finish the building, including £2,500 for furniture and manufacturing equipment, and £2,000 for 'an apartment for lunatics'.[9]

It's likely that the reasons Stoyte went to the trouble of having this report printed were threefold. Firstly, to reassure contributors about the use of their money; secondly, to encourage those who had pledged money, but not yet paid, to do so; and thirdly, to encourage more pledges. He promptly sent two copies to Archbishop King, who was visiting London, with the specific request to pass them on to the Duchess of Ormonde, also in England, so that she could use her influence at court to secure further support.[10]

However, there was trouble with the building works from the start. A handwritten document lodged in Marsh's library outlines a petition to the governors by a Mrs Dorcas Peters.[11] She claimed to be part-owner of a quarry at nearby Dolphin's Barn. According to the petition, workmen on the new building had 'by strong hand and with great force and violence' taken 'all or most part of the stones that were [used] in the building of the said Workhouse', from her quarry, and in addition had sold 'a great many loads of stones to several persons for ready money' and had 'refused to make any satisfaction for same'. To add insult to injury they had 'almost destroyed … the herbage and grass … of about 20 acres of land' next to the quarry 'by the many horses and carrs that went daily to the said quarry for stones for the said Workhouse' amounting to 'commonly 4 or 500 loads on a day'. Peters, 'finding herself likely to be ruined by this oppression made application to Sir Francis Stoyte … and the [governors] who at their several meetings instead of ordering satisfaction to the said [Peters] gave her only fair promises to no purpose'. Peters was forced to take the matter to 'the High Court of chancery', which proved 'very expensive almost to the ruin of her and her family'. The unfortunate Mrs Peters never received any satisfaction – eventually the matter was referred to arbitrators 'who never made any end of the said matter'.

However, the building must have proceeded at breakneck speed for, according to a later document 'the House was finished by 1 February 1706'.[12] This was at a time when comparable buildings often took much longer. Nevertheless, the Workhouse was finally open for business.

Another document outlines what happened next: '… all vagrants found in several streets were apprehended & sent to the Workhouse.'[13] There were 124 of these, the document relates. The Act allowed them to be incarcerated and 'set to work' for up to seven years.

Then in October 1707, 'the several Churchwardens pursuant to a proclamation of the [Act] brought to the Workhouse their parish poor in number 180'.[14] These were the settled residents of the various Dublin parishes who had fallen on hard times and were being supported at the expense of the parish. In addition there were 'twenty boys', who from the very start were on the books of the Workhouse. Their origins are not explained. Quite possibly these were boys from John Collis's now superseded Workhouse, and they may have helped in the construction of the new building.

This brought the total number of inmates to 324, 'which number of 324 continued in the Workhouse two years notwithstanding that sixty boys and girls were in that time [apprenticed] to trades by indentures, and some died, all whose places [were] constantly filled up by fresh objects of charity which daily fell charge on the several parishes'.[15]

Another category catered for in the early years of the Workhouse was the mentally ill. William Fownes was a prominent merchant of the time, who was active in the early years of the institution. He was one of the seven members of the Court of Assistants in 1705 and became Lord Mayor in 1708. In a letter to Jonathan Swift he later recalled that 'when I was Lord Mayor I saw some miserable lunatics exposed to the hazard of others as well as themselves. I had six strong cells made at the Workhouse for the most outrageous, which were soon filled; and by degrees, in a short time, those few drew upon [us] the solicitations of many, till by [1727] we had in that house forty and upwards. The door being opened, interest soon made way to let in the foolish, and such like, as mad folks.'[16]

However, in the first sign of trouble in the Workhouse's long history, a handwritten note from 1710 refers to debts incurred by the governors, both through the building of the Workhouse and providing for the poor in it – debts that the governors simply could not repay.[17]

The governors 'having no way to pay the said debts but by reducing the … poor in the Workhouse, and so lessening their charge, for a year no poor have been admitted into the Workhouse except 3 or 4 [lunatics] … so that the number at present [is], by old persons dying and some being taken out for servants, reduced to 280'.[18] In other words, after a mere three years in operation, a freeze had to be placed on admissions.

This is where the plans of the Workhouse supporters began to unravel. The philosophy underlying the Workhouse was that the idle – those sturdy vagrants and idle poor – would be taught the virtue of labour, and even earn some material reward, so that by the time they left they would be converted to the merits of honest toil and become useful members of society. This presupposed that 'idleness' was a lifestyle choice, rather than being forced upon the individual through economic conditions. In addition to the beneficial effects on their souls, it was assumed that through the labour of the inmates the Workhouse would become economically productive and thus become wholly or partly self-financing.

But the poor, it seems, had different ideas. For when the parishes were directed to send in their poor, it appears that many 'pretending to find means to maintain themselves … did not go into the House'.[19] It's likely only the very incapable – the helpless, the sick, the old and the very young – who had not the resources to fend off admission, ended up inside.

One clue as to why this might be so is contained in one of the governors' own reports: 'Beating of hemp has been a constant work, the terror of which drove out great numbers of beggars and vagrants from the city,' the governors reported.[20] The beating of hemp was a laborious repetitive task, often used as a punishment in jails and bridewells.

Another clue is provided by W.D.Wodsworth, who had access to the minute books of the governors and describes the accommodation for the poor in these early years. This consisted of 'the vaults and other convenient places' under the hall of the Workhouse.[21] According to Wodsworth, 'These vaults, or cellars, are specified as having been 240 feet long by 17 wide, with an "airy"' sunk at the outside of the building for the purpose of affording light and to carry off the rain water, and they were to have a double row of beds two [tiers] high to admit of sleeping 100 men and 60 women, and also to be used for their working and day accommodation.' 'Anyone fond of calculation,' he goes on, 'can form a good idea of what the sanitary aspect of these low pitched, dark, damp, and dreary lodgings must have been.'[22]

As we have seen, 124 vagrants had been rounded up in the first sweep. But it seems that when the Workhouse rapidly ran into financial difficulties these were the first to be let go, probably as being the most troublesome and the most able to fend for themselves. Preference was shown to keeping on those less able to support themselves – the old and the sick. The only problem with this was that the financial model on which the Workhouse rested required the young and fit to labour to support the others. Was it to be a self-supporting and profitable prison factory, or a bloated almshouse that would always need a large subsidy?

The harsh economic reality of the time is touched upon by the governors when they reported that in the city at large outside the Workhouse 'the most able [spinners] who work above 16 hours in 24, cannot earn 2d per diem'.[23] This reality went to the heart of the concept of the Workhouse. The governors were running up against a truth they had not foreseen, and perhaps still did not see – that the causes of poverty did not lie within the poor themselves. It was not idleness nor fecklessness, nor even 'popery', that caused them to be destitute and no amount of reform would cure them.

Even though the governors reported that they spared no effort to find suitable work for the inmates, they felt they were either too old or too young for productive labour, and so could only earn just enough to 'defray the charges of the instructors, and pay for the tools for working'.[24] And therefore, they complained, 'by the charge of such useless ancient poor, the house must become … for the most part an alms-house, instead of a workhouse'.[25] In fact, the governors argued that separate almshouses should be established to relieve them of this burden.

The governors even claimed that they offered to hire out the inmates at a rate of a half-penny a day – one quarter of the reported going rate – for the first three months (thereafter to increase by a half-penny each quarter until it reached 2*d* per day), and to provide clothing, food and lodging. All the employer would have to provide was the materials. But even this was not enough, and the governors found any employers reluctant to take on the inmates 'when they had examined their incapacities'.[26]

Despite all this the governors still maintained that the Workhouse was 'of no small benefit to the public' since it would raise its child inmates in the Protestant religion, 'considering most of these children are … of popish parents'.[27] The governors emphasised the Protestant instruction all inmates received: 'They have prayers twice a day, the children instructed in the catechism, reading and writing at certain hours, by turns, as they are capable.' Therefore, they argued, even if the Workhouse was costing more to run than anticipated, it was worth it.

'A Murdering-House'

Sadly, few shared enterprises are undertaken with complete unanimity of purpose, and so it proved with the Workhouse. Early in its history John Vernon, after briefly serving as 'secretary' to the board, became embroiled in a bitter dispute with the governors. And it is thanks to this that we have valuable insight into its early years.

Vernon first came to prominence in 1695, when he initiated a notorious legal case. A few years earlier a Colonel Edward Vernon, owner of Clontarf Castle, on the outskirts of Dublin, and considerable lands in the area, had died, leaving two daughters, Eliza and Maria. Vernon, who was a first cousin of the colonel, sued for possession of the estate, alleging that it had been kept in trust for him by the colonel. Through an Act of Parliament in 1698, Vernon won the case and Maria was dispossessed of her inheritance. Not content with this, a number of years later, the litigious Vernon sued the Corporation of Dublin, claiming exclusive rights over 195 acres of strand between the shore of Clontarf and the North Bull.[1] Around the same time that he initiated the dispute with the Corporation, Vernon was also in yet another clash – this time with a fellow Dublin merchant, John Rogerson, who when building his eponymous quay, ordered stones from a John Vernon of Clontarf. When these were delivered they were seemingly of the wrong size, but Vernon refused to take them back, presumably because of the cost of moving them. Instead he dumped them in the River Liffey, and they subsequently had to be removed at the city's expense.[2]

In 1716 Vernon published a detailed and scathing attack on the Workhouse, *Remarks on a paper, entituled, An Abstract of the State of the Work-House, for maintaining of the poor of the city of Dublin,* which commented on a governors' report, castigating both the way in which it had been set up and its day-to-day running ever since. Firstly, he alleged that the original charitable donors had been 'induced' to subscribe on the false premise that 500 poor would be 'immediately' housed and that eventually that number would rise to 1,600.[3] In addition, Vernon poured scorn on the claimed annual contribution of £100 from the rent of lands donated by the city. He claimed, firstly, that the lands only achieved an annual rent of £94; secondly, that out of this was payable an annual charge of £33 'to the Lady Susana Belasis'; and thirdly, that part of the land had been conveyed to Sir Mark Ransford, alderman and one of the governors closely involved with the Workhouse – leaving less than £50 per annum for the poor.[4]

He also argued that beating hemp was grossly unsuitable work for the old and for children, being too arduous. He pointed out that 'the aged and feeble have been over-pressed with unreasonable labour exacted from them, and undue correction inflicted on them' in the Workhouse 'so that some have not spared to call it a Murdering-House'.[5] The severity of their treatment, Vernon maintained, only served to scare away the healthy beggars and vagabonds, who would 'find all means they could to excuse themselves from coming under their lash' – thereby defeating one of the primary aims of the Workhouse.

One of the main ideological aims of some supporters of the Workhouse was the reform of 'dissolute persons' by Christian teaching, and by rewarding work with financial gain. No doubt the majority of supporters were happy if the number of beggars on the streets was reduced, regardless of whether it was due to their reform, or due to simply scaring them away through fear of incarceration in a prison factory. But since it was largely the latter, this resulted in 'filling the house with superannuated beggars and young children able to do little work'.[6] As we have seen, one disadvantage of the lack of healthy inmates of working age was that the whole financial model of the Workhouse was undermined.

However, although beggars may have fled from the clutches of the Workhouse, they did not disappear from the streets of Dublin. The city 'is so far from being eased or freed from beggars, that their number is rather increased', claimed Vernon. Indeed conditions in the country 'have been such as have compelled the poor to come a-begging for relief to this the metropolis of the kingdom, to which as a fountain the distressed continually resort'.

Vernon contradicted the argument of the governors that viable paying work could not be obtained for the inmates. While, as we have seen, the governors had maintained that the hardest working and most capable spinners in the city could not earn as much as 2*d* per day, even if working sixteen out of every twenty-four hours, Vernon argued instead that 'an able spinner will spin two balls per week, and earn 10*d* per ball' – in other words just over 3*d* per day; and that 'other spinners in finer work' will make 5 or 6*d* per day, while spinning linen yarn could make up to 8*d* per day. And even children, 'after 14 days or a month's instruction', could earn from 2 to 4*d* per day 'for quill-winding' (that is, winding the yarn around the bobbin, leaving it ready to feed into the loom) 'and tending the twisting mill'.[7] However, like the governors, he provides no evidence to support his claims. In fact, in an earlier document Vernon had made the staggering claim that, if properly set up, the linen manufactory could bring in nearly £4,000 a year.[8]

Another error the governors made, he claimed, was to employ 'smart boys' in the spinning of wool, which he describes as 'work proper for old women and girls'. The boys became so discouraged by this, he claimed, that they 'made all the shifts they could among their friends' to get out of the Workhouse.

The governors were proud of their record in having 'one hundred youth of both sexes … put out apprentices' between 1706 and 1710, but Vernon pointed out some problems with the process. He maintained that a 20*s* clothing allowance, which was given up front to the master who was to take on the apprentice, attracted unscrupulous employers. Then, having received the allowance, they would simply abandon the would-be apprentice as soon as convenient.

Vernon, predictably, railed against the quality of the religious education in the Workhouse. He demanded to know, as proof of its quality, whether any of those so instructed were competent to officiate at the 'several necessary services', or to take over any clerical posts, thus reducing the need to pay the salaries of chaplains. This was setting an impossibly high standard – expecting the Workhouse to be able to turn vagrants and beggars into clerics. Vernon also slated the Workhouse officers for allowing 'infamous persons [fit] for Newgate or Bridewell' (both notorious prisons) to be admitted, and to fraternise with the other inmates, and become 'tutoresses to the children which brought an ill name on the House and might well [he's being unusually equivocal] discour-age any sober persons from taking up their lodging among them'.[9] According to Vernon, the governors had even had the idea of recommending that the Bridewell be moved to the Workhouse from its then location – something that did eventually happen, but not until 1729.[10]

Vernon perhaps gives some insight into the elusive lives of the children who would come to be products of the corrupt and abusive system he describes. He paints them as 'turned prodigals, rambling on the mountains, or vagrants in the streets, for want of … due care' by the Workhouse in their upbringing.[11]

Incidentally, the document casts an interesting light on the origins of some of the inmates. The movements of the British Army were believed to contribute significantly to the number of impoverished women and children in the Workhouse. The governors reported in *An Abstract of the State of the Work-House* that 'the many recruits and new regiments which have come into this city of late years, also the rolling of the regiments to do duty in Dublin [have] brought and left here great numbers of women and children, who have no places of abode to go to, their husbands being abroad in the Service'.[12] The presence of a standing army in Britain was considered an unacceptable threat to civil liberties. A solution was found whereby the army was largely quartered in Ireland – at the expense of the Irish exchequer.[13] The military recruited heavily in England during the War of the Spanish Succession (1702–15) and many of these regiments were stationed in Ireland and would have passed through Dublin on their way to the Continent or in rotation to country barracks.[14] The men were paid directly, even when abroad, with little or no provision for their wives or children, who were often left destitute.[15]

Vernon goes on to make a direct accusation of corruption when it comes to the issue of raising taxes to support the Workhouse. There are, he notes, 'not less than 400 brick, stone, lime, and sand carts that ply for hire in the city of Dublin', which he says were liable for tax under the Act. This tax was not being levied, he claimed. The matter had been 'considered, debated, consulted, counsels' opinion [obtained], resolutions [made] thereon, and directions given for the taking them up … but the power of their purse hath prevailed … to stifle it … to the prejudice of the Workhouse' – a loss that he put at £200 per annum.[16] (Presumably he had some knowledge of the cost of transporting building material, given his dispute with Sir John Rogerson and the city authorities already mentioned.)

It is perhaps not surprising, given his character, that after a short time as secretary – probably less than a year – and before even a single inmate had been admitted to the Workhouse, Vernon had fallen out with the governors. The cause isn't clear, but an aggrieved Vernon alleged that 'their inferior court' (that is, the Court of Assistants) 'hath disgracefully thrust me out, and by violence, taken away the books and papers committed to my charge' – a claim that conjures up the ludicrous image of a physical tug-of-war with the Workhouse ledgers.

Pugnacious as ever, it seems that Vernon made a formal complaint to a general meeting of the governors in July 1710, and even complained to the 'chief Governors of this kingdom and chief magistrates of this city'.[17] He had the last word though, publishing his *Remarks* in 1716, still maintaining that he had never been 'legally discharged' from his post as secretary. He is also careful to direct his criticisms to the Court of Assistants, rather than the governors as a whole, since to do otherwise would be to antagonise the entire upper echelon of Irish society.

✱   ✱   ✱

In 1716, in a sign that oversight of the Workhouse was not functioning as it should, legislation was passed under which the Court of Assistants of seven and quorum of five were increased to nine and reduced to three respectively – because of the difficulty in getting a quorum of five together on the first Thursday in every month 'whereby the necessary business of the said Workhouse is very much delayed'.[18]

Little documentary evidence survives regarding the operations of the Workhouse between 1716 and 1725. We have to wait until the latter year for a parliamentary enquiry to shed some light.[19] It's likely that the governors submitted petitions to parliament on a regular basis and these sometimes prompted parliament to enquire more deeply into the Workhouse's affairs. At this time, parliament sat for a session of a few months only every two years.

There was considerable political turmoil in Dublin during this period. The Rage of Party – that intense conflict between Whigs and Tories in England, which centred on the legitimacy of the succession to the throne – spilled over into Ireland. There was 'a complete breakdown in city government in 1713–14', with violent scuffles at the Tholsel leading to one fatality.[20]

Another fault line within the ruling class existed between supporters of the 'English interest' – who, loosely, believed that local interests should be firmly subordinate to those of England – and supporters of the 'Irish interest', who favoured the interests of native-born colonialists (in so far as the interests of the two could be disentangled).

The arrival of Archbishop Hugh Boulter from England in 1724 to take up the post of Primate of All Ireland ensured a considerable boost to the 'English interest'. This was not just an ecclesiastical post. Boulter was a senior member, and at times head, of the government in Ireland. Boulter opposed Irish-born candidates for senior posts, in government and in the Church, in favour of English-born ones, and he energetically pursued the interests of the English crown in Ireland.[21] This put him at odds with the

Archbishop of Dublin, William King, who was closely involved with the Workhouse in its early years. Boulter would have had considerable influence on the 1725 enquiry into the Workhouse, and its findings should be considered in that context.

By the time this committee began its enquiry it was already, according to the members, 'notorious that the Workhouse had not answered the end of its erection'. To understand why, the committee 'examined several of the Governors and Officers of the said house, and inspected the books'.[22] There they found evidence of 'a very great neglect and mismanagement'. This may have been due to the political turmoil of the preceding decade. On the other hand, it's possible that the criticisms levelled by the enquiry were simply a means of damaging political opponents. In any event, they found that the practice of the governors of meeting in the Tholsel – the main meeting place for the city assembly, which also functioned as a centre of business – deprived them of a close acquaintance with the Workhouse (half-an-hour's walk away) to the detriment of its management. Incredibly, they found that the Court of Assistants, the subgroup of seven and then nine governors chosen to manage day-to-day affairs 'had not, for about eleven years last past, met to execute those powers intrusted with them'.

They also found that one Higgisson 'was appointed Master of the Workhouse, without any security given by him, and is since gone off, as your committee was informed … with about three thousand pounds of the Workhouse money'. (There seems even to have been some confusion over Higgisson's identity, since a blank is left for his Christian name in the report.) Higgisson is likely to have had expertise in linen manufacturing, the principal industry of the Workhouse – perhaps he ran a linen business before his appointment. He would have been recommended by one or several of the governors and his appointment confirmed by the Court of Assistants or a general meeting of the governors (had they been meeting). An appointment like this would be an example par excellence of the system of patronage that dominated life in the eighteenth century.[23] Thus this disaster was a considerable embarrassment to the governors. It's not known how long Higgisson worked as master, but his ability to accumulate and misappropriate such a large sum of money is questionable. On the other hand, it would not be the last time in the Workhouse's history that a fraud was taken advantage of to account for a multitude of unrelated deficiencies in the Workhouse books.

At the time of the 1725 enquiry there were 229 inmates in the Workhouse – 95 boys and men and 134 girls and women. The preponderance of females is a feature that recurs throughout the history of the Workhouse, and no doubt tells us something of the social and economic value attributed to girls and women at the time.

Of these 229, the committee found 'but few of them are capable of, or are employed in working', and those that were, were 'generally employed in knitting stockings'. Knitting stockings, as we have seen, was treated as one of the least skilled tasks associated with the textile trade, and as it also required little physical strength, it was often carried out by children.[24]

By the time of the enquiry the management of the Workhouse had been taken over by Alderman Porter (probably John Porter), who seemingly reintroduced the beating of hemp – the arduous physical labour that deterred many able-bodied poor. Porter also informed the committee that he believed the root of the problems of the Workhouse lay in 'a false step' made in its first year when it took in far more poor than it was able to support, and thus fell into debt that it was never able to repay. Nevertheless, the committee found that from 1 May 1704 to 11 June 1725, the Workhouse had taken in £38,323 and spent £38,266. Despite all the criticisms, the committee concluded that the continuation of the Workhouse would be of benefit to the public, provided the management was changed. Significantly, the committee made no mention of the fact that the taxes on houses, and transport, which were to be levied by the original act for twenty-one years, were due to expire within months. If this was allowed to happen the consequences for the Workhouse would be dire.

In a further investigation the following year, 1726, the House of Commons found that the annual tax on houses and on wagons, carriages and sedan chairs was worth a total of £1,762 to the Workhouse.[25] However, there were perpetual difficulties in collecting this money. For one thing, the brewers and owners of drays and cars disputed their liability and refused to pay, amounting to an annual loss of £114. Worst of all, the collection of house tax was completely dependent on churchwardens, who owed their allegiance to the parish they worked for, not the remote, central Workhouse. Even with the best of motivation, collection of this tax must have been difficult. Sure enough, the MPs found that the churchwardens often failed to collect the tax, or failed to pass it on to the Workhouse, so that at the time of the enquiry it was owed a huge £2,675 from this tax.

But by far the most devastating information contained in the report was that the entire tax income of the Workhouse, whether from houses, carriages or sedan chairs, had 'ceased to be collected, or paid, ever since the 25th day of December 1725, at which time the said funds, appointed by the said act, did expire'. Inexplicably, parliament had failed to renew the legislation.

At the end of that year a great storm struck the city. Amidst gales and sleet, the Liffey overflowed its banks and thirty-seven horses were drowned in the city stables. Several houses were swept away, and ships driven ashore with the loss of all aboard.[26] The poor, the disabled, the old and the sick in the Workhouse can hardly have been unaware of the precariousness of their situation.

A possible reason for the failure by parliament to renew the legislation was the apparent tension between it and Dublin City Corporation over the running of the institution – rivalry that was to continue for the next century. In December 1725 parliament had proposed a bill that would have reduced the representation of the City Corporation on the board of governors from seventy-five to just eight (the Lord Mayor, two sheriffs and five aldermen). The Corporation, mindful of its role in establishing the institution, not least by its donation of part of the site, the rental interest in several properties, and the revenue from the licensing of the carriage trade, jealously guarded its stake.[27] It lobbied against the proposed bill, even in Britain. There the legislation was amended by the English Privy Council – a means of scuppering it – and returned to the Commons, where the bill was subsequently dropped in February 1726.[28]

Parliament had failed to get its way in drastically reducing the influence of Dublin City Corporation on the Workhouse. Whether this was the reason that it failed to renew the legislation that provided the Workhouse's income remains conjecture. For whatever reason, parliament went into recess in March 1726, still without having taken any steps to restore funding, leaving the fate of the inmates hanging in the balance.

Remarkably, a complete list of the inhabitants of the Workhouse in March 1726 survives.[29] There were 222 inmates in total, from 82-year-old Elizabeth Muckleroy, of St Paul's parish, described as 'bedrid', to 5-year-old Alice Lyons from St Bridgets. None of the adults are healthy; all are either 'mad', 'bedrid', 'infirm', 'a cripple', 'a foole', 'hath fits', having 'the king's evil', or 'superannuated'. Fourteen-year-old Lettice (Letitia) Lester, also from St Paul's, is recorded as blind, but most of the child inmates appear to have been without a significant illness or disability. Some family groups are apparent, such as 44-year-old Catherine Nowlan ('infirm'), along with 8-year-old Stephen Nowlan and 9-year-old Mary Nowlan, all from St Audeon's parish. Ann Williams (St Michael's parish), age 40, although an inmate, is described as 'a nurse', while Mary Moore, age 48, 'washes' – which probably meant that she worked as a washerwoman for the institution.[30] From the same parish as Mary, and perhaps related to her, were Arthur Moore, 61 ('blind'), and Alice Moore, 13. The dual roles of Ann Williams and Mary Moore – as both inmates and 'staff' – demonstrate the precarious separation of some occupations such as washerwoman and nurse from pauperhood.

By 6 April, the number of poor in the Workhouse had dropped to 211. But by then the governors had already made a grave decision: the financial situation made it impossible to continue without an income. In an act of brinksmanship, or desperation, or both, the governors pledged to maintain all the poor in the Workhouse only until 1 May. After this they would be returned to the care of their parishes – unless the parishes stumped up a monthly allowance to support each individual from their area in the Workhouse. This would amount, the governors calculated, to 1*s* 9*d* per person per week for food, and an additional, optional, 4*d* per person per week for clothing.[31]

The reason the governors were acting now, they said, was because they hoped to preserve what little funds were left, since they thought it 'especially incumbent upon them to subsist as many of the lunatics and such sort of poor as are the most miserable and helpless [who] if turned out, would be most inconvenient to the public'.[32]

It appears there was little response from the parishes, perhaps indicative of their view of the value of the Workhouse. As a result, the governors had no choice but to act on their threat. And so, by May 1726 'there only remained in said Workhouse the number of 43 of said poor'.[33] From the idealism and high expectations attending the founding ceremony twenty-two years earlier, the Workhouse had sunk to its lowest point.

From Sir William Fownes's letter to Jonathan Swift written a few years later, it appears that most of the dwindling number left in the Workhouse in 1726 were 'lunatics'. His letter goes on to describe their fate: the Governors 'got rid of most of these by death or the care of friends and came to a resolution not to admit any such for the future and the first denial was to a request of the Earl of Kildare which put a full stop to all farther applications'.[34] And so, with parliament in recess, things were left to lie – the Workhouse without an income and its few remaining, insane inhabitants dying one by one, or being taken into 'the care of friends'.

Parliament did not sit again until November 1727. When it did so, it finally got around to addressing the crisis. A new act was passed[35] technically abolishing the old corporation, and establishing a new one with a new name.[36] A compromise seems to have been reached. This time, instead of parliament slashing the number of aldermen on the Board of Governors, there was a smaller reduction, but their influence was diluted by greatly increasing the number of other members. The multitude of governors was augmented by adding many peers, 'lord bishops', MPs and other prominent figures to the numbers, as well as 'the minister of each and every parish in the city and suburbs of Dublin'. According to Jonathan Swift, the new corporation was 'near

three times' the size of the old, by reason of inclusion of 'all the city clergy …
beside a great number of squires'.[37] In fact, the number of governors increased
from an already unwieldy 100 to an even more impractical 146, with the
representation from Dublin City Corporation reduced from seventy-five to
just twenty-seven.

But the Act contained other measures, one of the most important of which
was to allow for the appointment of a full-time, salaried treasurer with an
income of £60 per annum. Before then, the no doubt gargantuan task of
administering the accounts of such a large organisation, not to mention
overseeing the collection of taxes on hundreds of vehicles, and ensuring
churchwardens from all the various parishes handed over the money from the
tax on houses, fell to the particular governor (usually in the early days at least,
an alderman), who was elected for that year to carry out the task in a part-
time, unpaid capacity. This would appear to be the type of situation in which
corruption flourishes. There is no doubt that many of the governors who were
engaged in trade also did business with the Workhouse, supplying goods and
services and therefore creating what we would see today as a huge conflict of
interest. At the time this would not have been regarded as corruption – just
as many of the wealthier governors would have seen it as perfectly natural to
use their influence as governors to, for example, fill posts with followers. But
allegations of outright fraud against governors are few. On the other hand,
Swift was almost certainly referring to the Workhouse when he wrote: 'Yet I
confess I have known an hospital where all the household officers grew rich,
while the poor, for whose sake it was built were almost starving for want of
food and raiment.'[38]

In general, Swift was disdainful towards the changes brought in by the new
Act. By reason of his position as Dean of St Patrick's Cathedral, Swift had
automatically been one of the governors from the early years. He felt the great
increase in number of the governors rendered 'so good a design not only useless but a grievance instead of a benefit to the city'. He particularly objected to
the inclusion as governors of persons who lived outside Dublin, who 'cannot
possibly have the least concern for the advantage of the city'. He seems to have
attended few board meetings and when he did he claimed 'very little was done'
since he 'found the court of assistants usually taken up in little wrangles about
coachmen or adjusting accounts of meal and small beer'. He noted ironically
how Dublin was more 'infested' with 'strollers, foreigners (i.e. non-Dubliners)
and sturdy beggars … since the establishment of the poor house than it was
ever known to be … before its first erection'. Since it was paid for entirely
by the inhabitants of Dublin, he found it 'absurd' that it was 'misemployed

in maintaining foreign beggars and [the] bastards or orphans of farmers'. He claimed that half the revenue of the Workhouse 'if employed with common care and ... common honesty' would have been enough to achieve its ends.[39]

The new Act also allowed for the appointment of a register – a senior administrator subordinate to the treasurer – at a salary of £25. In addition, the governors were given 'full and absolute power and authority to inspect into and regulate the management of the gaol or house of correction, commonly called Bridewell, near the city of Dublin'. And in 1729 the Bridewell was moved to a building constructed for the purpose at the front wall of the Workhouse, just as Vernon had alleged the governors had wished back in 1716.[40]

Most importantly, the Workhouse at last had its source of funding restored. The new Act reinstated the tax on coaches and sedan chairs, and on houses, for another twenty-one years. These were to be collectable from 1 May 1728. The legislators also finally got around to clarifying the law on the taxing of 'carts and cars' carrying 'stones, bricks, sand or gravel for building' – an issue that John Vernon had drawn attention to more than ten years earlier. They justified this by pointing out that 'the city of Dublin and suburbs thereof have very much increased ... and consequently the poor, which may be supported in the said Workhouse are now more in number than formerly'. However, in a development that must have been unwelcome to the Workhouse, some 25 per cent of the revenue on vehicles was to go to the Blue Coat Hospital, the older charity now exclusively dedicated to the education of Protestant boys.

The Act also made provision for poor children who were too young to be admitted to the Workhouse (now, those under 6). Each parish was to appoint at least two 'overseers of the poor', who were to engage nurses for these children and inspect them quarterly. The money for the upkeep of these children was to be raised as an additional tax on householders within each parish. Crucially, each parish would set and collect the amount of tax required, and would have control over its spending, unlike the tax that they had to collect for, and hand over to, the Workhouse.

But it was the drastic failure of this section of the Act, as we shall see, that was to have profound consequences for the future role of the Workhouse.

4

Children of the Parish

In September 1728, Elizabeth Hyland was hired as parish nurse by the church-warden of St John's parish, Dublin.[1] The old parish of St John's sloped steeply down to the Liffey from the foot of Christ-Church Cathedral. Small in area, but densely packed, with steep narrow alleyways and courtyards, its huddled houses seemed to prop up the ancient, ramshackle cathedral and stop it from sliding down the hill into the river.

Hyland was employed by the churchwarden, Charles Fisher, at a rate of £3 per annum. Her role was 'to take up foundling children' in the parish. Foundlings were children abandoned by their parents and found by others – often in doorways, sometimes on waste ground. When abandoned they became the responsibility of the parish in which they were found – and an expense on its accounts.

By December 1729, Hyland had, by her own account, 'taken up' twenty-seven such children in that one parish. Eighteen of the twenty-seven infants were 'lifted to other parishes' – that is, secretly brought by her to another city parish and abandoned there in order to relieve St John's of the cost of rear-ing them. For example, one was 'left at the door of Mr Green, a surgeon in St. Paul's parish'. Another was left 'at Mr Tilson's in the same parish'. St Paul's was, in comparison to St John's, a sprawling parish, located on the north bank of the Liffey, on the western outskirts of the city. Its most notable feature was the huge and dominating military barracks with its attendant services such as brothels and taverns.

But the traffic of foundlings to St Paul's was not all one way. One infant – whom Elizabeth Hyland had left at a Mr Worthington's door – was discovered by St Paul's very own parish nurse. She, with considerable acuity, returned the child directly to Hyland, who promptly consulted the churchwarden, Charles Fisher. He upbraided her, telling her 'she should not go too often to one place'. Taking this message to heart, Hyland promptly 'lifted' the child to St Anne's parish and abandoned it there, its subsequent fate unknown. A contemporary inquiry found that seventeen of the eighteen infants 'lifted to other parishes' by Hyland had been trafficked to one parish – St Pauls.[2] On investigation, however, fewer than half of these children could be traced, leading to the conclusion that the remainder had perished.

Later, Hyland was to recall that she 'frequently found diacodium' in the mouths of the children 'by which they were stupefied'. Diacodium, or syrup of poppies, was an opium solution made by apothecaries from the deseeded heads of the poppy, *papaver somniferum*. These were steeped in water and boiled for many hours before the resulting liquid was strained through a cloth. A sweet syrup was then added to make the opium palatable – a feature that, it was thought, made it particularly suitable for children. Being a liquid, diacodium could not have been identified by Hyland in the mouths of the infants but for the fact that it had a distinctive dark greenish colour.[3] Hyland was adamant 'she never put any into their mouths herself'. Nevertheless, by her own account, seven of the twenty-seven children had died in her own hands.[4]

The seven who died were buried – without baptism – on Fisher's orders in the churchyard on the slope below the Church of St John the Evangelist, among the tilting gravestones, where the fragile bones of the newborns would dissolve quickly in the soil.

Like other Dublin parishes, St John's was not only the source, but also the recipient, of 'lifted' babies. One example occurred in June 1729, when a boy and a girl were found abandoned in the parish.[5] The day before, the same children had been seen in the custody of the bell man of St Luke's parish. In fact, it was customary throughout the city for Church functionaries, with the knowledge of the clergy, 'to convey foundling children from one parish to the other'.[6] Quite how often this happened was soon to emerge.

Not all Church officials were happy about the practice. As long as six years previously, in February 1723, William King, Archbishop of Dublin, had written to his clergy in the city.[7] His letter spoke of 'the dropping of children, and carrying them from parish to parish by clandestine means, by which, as it is alleged and seems probable, a great many are destroyed'.[8] Knowledge of the practice was seemingly widespread among the congregation, for King described it as 'a wicked practice, which I find makes a great noise, and is in every body's mouth'. He clearly identified churchwardens as the culprits – acting 'to ease their own parishes and burden their neighbours'. King called on the 'ministers in their pulpits', 'churchwardens, and all good Christians' to end the practice, and hoped the churchwardens would 'call on the constables, and the watchmen in the several parishes to give their assistance to discover and prevent this evil'. Sadly, King's admonitions seem to have fallen on deaf ears, since, as we have seen, the practice was still rife six years later.

By 1729, however, concern was mounting about the practice. The issue was even raised in the House of Lords. A committee of inquiry was formed whose 'lordships have power to send for persons, papers and records'.[9] Thus it was that Elizabeth Hyland was duly summoned to appear 'before the bar' of the House to be questioned by their Lordships. We can only imagine how unnerving this must have been for a woman near the bottom rung of the social ladder. Hyland was interrogated about her activities as parish nurse, giving rise to the information outlined above.

Her fear would surely have been heightened by the fact that, a few years previously, in July 1722, a Mary Allen had reportedly been burned to death at Stephen's Green for 'drowning one of St James's parish children'.[10] Hence her protestations that although she had seen diacodium in the mouths of children, she had not placed it there. This is as close as one can get to a crime without actually being involved. She probably feared being prosecuted for murder.

She was not helped by the evidence of Balaam Dempsey, the churchwarden who had taken over from Charles Fisher. Churchwardens were laymen of the parish, usually men of standing, appointed annually, in a voluntary capacity, to help manage the affairs, particularly financial, of the parish. Dempsey 'produced a book, with an account of the times when the said children were found, and when they were lifted by the said Hyland'.[11] Dempsey explained to the Lord's committee that he had received the book from Hyland's husband, and had kept it in his custody ever since.

But there were similar goings-on in other parishes. Patrick Aylmer also testified in the House.[12] He was the former churchwarden of St Mary's parish, on the same side of the river as St Paul's. When he had taken up the post he had asked the beadle for a list of the 'parish officers and servants'. On the list he had found that 'there was a person by the name of a lifter'. This was a woman called Joan Newenham. The seemingly naive Aylmer sent for her and questioned her about the nature of her employment. When she identified herself as the parish nurse, Aylmer at first assumed she meant a wet nurse, except 'that from her years and appearance, he believed said Joan incapable of giving suck'. In any event, 'the said Joan informed the deponent, that [wet-nursing] was none of her business' for she 'was employed to take care of foundling children, and lift them out of that parish into other parishes'.[13]

Newenham had informed him that in order to avoid detection she sometimes kept the infants for a night or two, and that to prevent their crying she gave them diacodium – there is no evidence that she ever fed them – 'and by the assistance of a man who used to go with her, left the said children at gentlemen's doors in other parishes'. She did not know what became of them after this, for 'after she had parted with them, she had done with them'. At one time Newenham had been paid 4s 9d per child by the parish, but this had been changed to an annual rate of £4 10s. Aylmer claimed that he admonished Newenham for her 'wickedness' and dismissed her and 'hired a wet nurse to take care of the Foundling children until such time as they could be provided for'. Yet this sounds like a suspiciously neat resolution. For if St John's parish was anything to go by, St Mary's would have easily had twenty foundlings a year to care for. Yet one wet nurse could surely feed no more than two children satisfactorily at a time until they were weaned.

The beadle of St Mary's parish, John Watson, also gave evidence, confirming some of Aylmer's testimony. However, contrary to Aylmer's evidence, he revealed that the replacement parish nurse, Catherine Mathews, did in fact 'lift' abandoned children to other parishes, and wasn't acting merely as a wet nurse – although he denied any knowledge of whether or not she used diacodium.

Following its enquiry the committee of the House of Lords ordered the prosecution of Charles Fisher but did not recommend any specific action in relation to Elizabeth Hyland or Joan Newenham. However, since 'attested copies' of the report and examinations were to be forwarded to the Attorney General to facilitate prosecution of Fisher, it's possible that further action was also taken in relation to the women. The only other recommendation the Lords made was to have the report printed – which meant that, unlike much material generated by the House, it survived in the parliament's *Journals* to allow us to read it today.

Since, by its nature, abandonment of children is a secretive affair, we have little information on the background of the infants, their parents, or the events leading up to their abandonment. Some clues, however, might be gleaned from one historian's survey of infanticide for this period.[14] Infanticide represented an alternative to abandonment, being at the extreme end of the spectrum of choices faced by the expectant mother in crisis. So it may offer insight into the cases that concern us. In the cases of infanticide where the information was available, it was found that the vast majority of mothers were unmarried.[15] Most were from the lower socioeconomic half of society and the largest represented social group was that of servant.[16] There was little information on the social status of fathers. Servants were the most vulnerable, due to the sharing of a household with unrelated males, and the possibility of exploitation of dependency by masters.[17] These cases, if discovered, usually ended in dismissal.[18] It was not uncommon for an unmarried pregnant woman to be ejected from her lodgings, 'sometimes with fatal consequences'.[19] A pregnancy could be concealed until quite late, and it was possible for the mother to give birth in secret in her employer's home. The penalty for infanticide was severe under the 1707 Act 'to prevent the destroying and murthering of bastard children'.[20] The penalty was death, which for women often meant burning, as outlined above. Infanticide must, in some cases, have been influenced by fear of discovery, or lack of opportunity to abandon the infant alive.[21] Undoubtedly a preferable course was abandonment, with at least the hope that the child would be raised by others.

Research on France and England in the eighteenth century has found that the vast majority of women in urban centres coming to the attention of the authorities for giving birth to illegitimate children were female domestic servants.[22] However, in contrast to the above, these were found not to be necessarily as a result of master–servant liaisons.[23] In fact, in these surveys most illegitimate births resulted from relationships between couples of relatively equal status, and very rarely from relationships between master and maid.[24]

While the enquiry by the House of Lords had been proceeding, simultaneously, in what was hardly a coincidence, moves had begun in the Commons to significantly alter the legislation governing the Workhouse and dramatically change the nature of that institution by adding to it the role of foundling hospital.

As this new legislation wended its way through the two Houses of Parliament, and the Irish and then the English Privy Councils, a remarkable pamphlet was published anonymously in Dublin: *The Case of the Foundlings of the City of Dublin*. This was a closely argued and persuasive document of eight pages that seemed to echo some of the findings of the Lords' committee. It's worth quoting from, since it seems to outline the rationale of the legislators and many of the issues raised in it were subsequently reflected in the legislation.

The pamphlet drew attention to the practices already outlined, while pointing out that there were wide divergences in the approaches of different parishes, with some having 'vast numbers' of foundlings to maintain, while others 'who are more careful' had very few. By 'careful' the author meant the cynical disposal of infants in order to save money. The writer bluntly relayed how diacodium was used to 'daze and stupefy them, that they may not by their crying, alarm their neighbours, and detect [betray] the lifters'. And 'by this means, children are often poison'd to save charges' (i.e. costs). The writer also claimed that in one year to 25 December 1729, seventy-three children were abandoned in St Michan's parish alone. Of these, twenty-eight had died 'within the year' and it may be surmised that many more of them would die in subsequent years, so that there were only sixty-eight foundlings (under 5 or 6 years of age) from that and previous years, still alive in the parish. Whereas, if seventy-three had been average for a year, and if all foundlings had survived to 5 or 6, the number should have been about 365. The survival of only sixty-eight suggests an attrition rate of 85 per cent. But St Michan's was a 'good' parish 'where they honestly provide for their foundlings'.[25] The writer believed St Michan's contained roughly one eighth of the city's houses.[26] But he did not believe that the seventy-three children abandoned there in the year represented one eighth of the annual total of foundlings since he believed 'many of these have been lifted out of other parishes into St Michan's'. The passing of infants from one parish to another makes it impossible to calculate their total numbers for the city as a whole.

According to the author, 'this method of running or lifting of children is no new practice, there have always been in most parishes some persons more careful to save expenses to the parish than to preserve the lives of the poor children'. In order to 'make it cease to be the interest of any parish to lift their foundlings into another' the writer makes a radical proposal: to have them 'sent to one common house of reception, where they may be all maintained by one common fund'.[27]

The writer concedes that 'to build such a house of reception for so many infants would be a matter of time and expense, and difficulties would arise in appointing Governors and overseers … to avoid which it is humbly proposed, that they may all be taken into the Workhouse, and placed there under the conduct and inspection of the Governors thereof'.[28]

The author addresses the possible objection that the Workhouse would not be large enough to contain the foundlings by pointing out that it had been 'always reputed to be capable of receiving 700 persons' and that there were currently only 400 inmates there, and besides 'such havock and destruction has been made of the poor foundlings all over the town, they would not be more than enough to make up the complement of 700 persons'. The author concedes that the scheme, if successful, would lead to the survival of more infants, but does not make the figures explicit. However we can calculate that, based on his own figures, if St Michan's *were* representative, and if only half the infants survived, within five years there would be 1,500 children to maintain.[29] It is, perhaps, understandable that the pamphleteer chose not to emphasise this fact.

But in future, he argued (assuming it was a man), if there was not enough room in the Workhouse 'may not sheds be erected by the walls …, at a very small expense, which would be sufficient to receive vast numbers of them?' If this were not sufficient 'there is the infirmary at the Blew-Coat Hospital, a large and capacious building, never yet made use of'.[30]

When it came to paying for the foundlings' upkeep, he suggested doubling the tax on houses that was already being paid to the Workhouse, i.e. from 3 to 6*d* per rateable pound according to the valuation of the house. Under the existing legislation parishes were already obliged to set and collect an additional cess, or tax, to maintain any surviving infants (up to age 5 or 6) – hence the reason for the 'lifting'. The writer argued that the 3*d* per pound extra tax would not in fact be greater than the cess already being collected. He did, however, accept that those parishes that had been most nefarious in their treatment of foundlings would end up paying more, but that the reason they were paying less now was in effect because of their murder of infants. Or as he put it 'where they have been burthen'd least, they have lifted most'.[31] And, he added, 'what money is now given for secret services to beadles, parish-nurses, and such sort of vermin for lifting and destroying children will now be saved'.[32]

However, he does concede that the *future* maintenance cost will exceed the taxation proposed – because more children would be likely to survive – but this cost cannot be calculated at present due to the uncertainty over the num-bers. Meanwhile, he argued, until the costs are established more certainly, the tax should be set for a short time only. But he advises that any future overruns in cost can be made up by donations raised at 'Charity-Sermons all over the city' and 'it is not to be doubted, but that pious and charitable persons will contribute to so charitable a work, or bequeath legacies at their deaths'. Finally he argues 'in a case of this nature we must not leave providence out of the scheme, nor must we doubt but that God, who feedeth the young ravens that call upon him, will one way or other provide for these innocents'.[33]

There is no doubt the author is passionate in his desire to prevent 'the ruin and destruction of so many infants … thousands of [whom] have been destroyed in this city'. 'One would think', he argues, 'that we need not use many words to persuade men and Christians to [take] any measures to prevent the effusion of blood, the blood of poor children; especially in a kingdom where people are wanting, and every hand is money-worth to the nation.'

But if further persuasion is needed, the author appeals to the sectarian spirit then prevailing among the ruling elite: 'It may be considered that these children will be bred up in the Protestant religion, which also, in a political view, will be a strength to the Protestant interest.' He argued that under the current haphazard system, any children that survived could be 'taken off by their mothers, and so bred papists'. It's interesting to note, that then and later, it was assumed that the foundlings were born of Catholic parents, despite the probable Protestant majority in the population of the city at the time. Separately, parliament had recently resolved on the even harsher implementation of the anti-Catholic laws it had so carefully devised, citing what was perceived as the 'insolence' of 'papists'.[34]

The alternative fate of the foundlings who survived infancy, if not taken back by their mothers and 'bred papists' was that 'as soon as they are able, they are turned to beg, or become shoe-boys, or vagabonds; and, as they grow up, turn thieves or whores, being unaccustomed to work in their childhood; for churchwardens are glad to ease themselves of the burthen of maintaining them as soon as they can'.[35]

The writer clearly envisaged the children being nursed in and growing up in the Workhouse. Apart from the main benefit – removing the incentive from parishes to conspire in the deaths of these children – raising them in the Workhouse would also be cheaper, since one woman could nurse multiple children 'especially when they beg[a]n to run about'. And it would also solve the alleged problem of women abandoning their children and then presenting themselves to the parish as wet nurses, thereby, somehow, managing to be paid for rearing their own child – a crime both against morality and the finances of the parish. This is an accusation that recurs throughout the history of the Workhouse, and in the history of foundling hospitals in other countries.

The writer reveals how difficult it is for the parishes to obtain wet nurses 'by reason that nurses are scarce and the salary allowed but small, being seldom more than forty shillings a year'. He seemingly does not foresee this as being a problem for the Workhouse, however, arguing that 'it will provide also for great numbers of poor women who must be employed to look after them, and who would otherwise beg or starve', thereby addressing two problems at once.

The Case ends with an entreaty: 'Hither therefore these poor innocents fly as to a sanctuary, they implore the protection of the Governors, and they hope by the goodness of the Parliament to be preserved from the cruelty of parish beadles and parish nurses.'[36]

It's worth considering why the author thought it important to go to the trouble of publishing his paper when parliament had already held an enquiry into the matter,[37] and legislation had already been initiated. The answer may lie in a passage on page six of the document, where the writer declares 'we must break through many objections, and that speedily, (for delay is cruelty) where the lives of so many poor innocents … is so immediately concerned'. In addition to ensuring the legislation was passed 'speedily', there must have been some anxiety whether it would be passed at all, since there were many stages involved, and much legislation fell at the various obstacles. However, the Act was finally passed in April 1730.[38]

As we have seen, the 1727 Act had, for the first time, made provision for abandoned children under the age of 6. The parish was obliged to care for them locally, and was allowed to raise a local 'cess' or tax on houses to pay for their upkeep. Two or more 'overseers of the poor' were supposed to be appointed yearly by each parish. These overseers were to arrange for the care of foundlings and inspect them regularly and report to the parish. But, if they were ever appointed, there is no evidence of any activity by these overseers in the parishes covered in the enquiry. And a mere two years later, the entire 1727 legislation, which obliged the parishes to raise money locally for the care of abandoned children, was scrapped.

According to the new 1729 Act, 'to avoid the said expense, it is notorious that a wicked and detestable practice hath been carried on in some parishes, if not throughout the whole city, of lifting or running from one parish to another the said foundlings, to the utter ruin and destruction of them'. From 25 March 1730, under the new Act, all abandoned children under the age of 6 at that time in the care of the parishes were to be handed over by the churchwardens to the governors of the Workhouse, whose responsibility they now became. Thereafter children were to be handed up as they came into the custody of the churchwardens. And instead of a separate tax being raised at the discretion of each parish to pay for their upkeep, the tax on houses was to be doubled and the entire amount handed over to the governors annually. This would remove any incentive to 'lift' children. As recommended in *The Case*, this tax was imposed for a short period to allow assessment of its adequacy. Interestingly, the Act makes absolutely no mention of where, or how, the infants are to be cared for. It does not, for instance, order them to be brought up in the Workhouse, as the author of *The Case* had envisaged.

It is worth investigating what precedents inspired advocates of the Foundling Hospital. *The Case*, for example makes no mention of any. There was no precedent in England. When Thomas Bray had published a pamphlet in 1728 or 1729 calling for the opening of a foundling hospital in London, he had taken his example from the Paris foundling hospital.[39] And when the London institution eventually opened in 1741 it took its lead from the Paris and Lisbon foundling hospitals and the orphanage in Amsterdam.[40]

Foundling hospitals were relatively common in Catholic countries. Most texts date the earliest orphanages or foundling hospitals to the one founded in Milan in 787. However, there may have been precedents in Constantinople in the fourth century,[41] followed by Roman equivalents organised by the papacy in the seventh century based on the Constantinople model.[42] By the Renaissance period they were present in many Italian cities and other Catholic European countries. With the colonisation of the new world, foundling hospitals were opened in Mexico in 1529, Lima in 1597 and Bogota in 1642.[43]

However, foundling hospitals were not a feature of Protestant or Protestant-ruled countries. Notwithstanding a short-lived venture in installing a revolving basket at the orphanage in Hamburg (1709–14),[44] according to one writer, foundling hospitals did not get underway in the German-speaking world until the 1760s.[45] The London Foundling Hospital did not open until 1741 and, according to the same source, was the first to be established *successfully* in a non-Catholic country.[46] If this is correct, then the Dublin Foundling Hospital appears to have been one of the earliest to have been created in a Protestant or Protestant-ruled country.

In any event, it is clear that there was enthusiastic support at the highest level of government for the new role of the Workhouse. Hugh Boulter, the Archbishop of Armagh and primate of all Ireland, at this time was head of the government in Ireland. In May 1730 (although not referring to the Foundling Hospital), he wrote 'the great number of papists in this kingdom, and the obstinacy with which they adhere to their own religion, occasions our trying what may be done with their children to bring them over to our Church'.[47] On 30 October 1730 he chaired a meeting of the governors of the Workhouse, which 'ordered that a turning wheel or conveniency for taking in children be provided near the gate of the Workhouse that at any time by day or night a child may be lay'd in it to be taken in by the officers of the said house'.[48] There are a number of implications to this decision. Firstly, the clear precedent was the large foundling hospitals of the Continent, particularly those in Italy, and we must conclude that such an operation was what Boulter intended to emulate, with the addition of a proselytising function.[49] Secondly, this decision meant that all infants would be accepted without question. And since no enquiry was made regarding the origins of the child, children from all over the country and not just Dublin could be taken in.[50] A turntable was accordingly installed to the left of the gates, which opened into the porter's lodge.[51] A new era had begun for the Workhouse.

A Suicide and an Explosion

To start with, the Workhouse struggled to fulfil its new role as a foundling hospital. The first year of operations under the 1729 Act saw the new 'foundling side' take in 263 abandoned children.[1] Numbers increased rapidly, so that by the third year the annual intake had risen to 533. As we have seen, the new Act was remarkably vague as to how the infant foundlings were to be cared for. The governors therefore had to improvise. They decided that the majority of the infants would be handed over to poor women, who undertook to wet-nurse them in their own homes for a number of years at a fee of 40s per annum. At a suitable age (usually 6 years old) the child was to be returned to the Workhouse to live – a process referred to as 'drafting'. There they would live until ready to be 'apprenticed out', usually at the age of 12 or 13.

This was the most common approach adopted by foundling hospitals on the Continent for the care of infants. The usual method of feeding was by wet nurse, either on site or in the nurse's own home.[2] To put this in context, in the wider population wet-nursing appears to have been relatively common, at least among the wealthier classes.[3] For example, one of the earliest books on midwifery in English,[4] *Speculum matricis hybernicum* (which translates to *The Irish Midwives' Handmaid*), written by the Cork-based physician James Wolveridge in 1670,[5] assumed that the infant would be fed by a nurse and included detailed advice on selecting one.[6] This advice originated with writers in ancient Rome and Greece, and was based on the belief that the nurse's personal characteristics could be transmitted to the child through her milk. It was to be repeated as more or less standard doctrine until the middle of the eighteenth century.[7] At the same time, Wolveridge briefly advised that it would be best for the mother to nurse her own child, and described how a well-to-do woman could manage this conveniently – with the help of servants.[8]

There are other examples from the period that indicate both that the practice was relatively common, and also that there was a growing awareness of its disadvantages. The works of the English physician Walter Harris (1647–1732) were in circulation certainly as late as 1742.[9] Although much of his advice was of dubious quality, nevertheless Harris did raise concerns about the widespread practice of wet-nursing. It was particularly common as a source of income for poor women in country areas adjoining cities, and the mortality rate for the infants was high. Harris recorded being told by the rector of a parish in Kent that 'his parish ... was, when he first came to it, filled with suckling infants from London, and yet, in the space of one year, he buried them all except two'. But they were soon replaced, 'the same number of small infants being soon twice supplied ... from the very great and almost inexhaustible city'. However, the replacements fared no better for 'he had committed them all to their parent earth in the very same year'.[10]

Harris highlighted the alleged practices that put the children at such risk. These included nurses surreptitiously giving suckling infants in their care 'wine and brandy perhaps with sugar ... to still their crying and procure ease to themselves ... whence dreadful symptoms arise from hidden causes'.[11] Another hazard was the giving of opiates by nurses to their charges. He also warned about nurses who themselves 'guzzle down a great quantity of strong beer and burning spirits ... and thereby... spoil their own milk'.[12] What's more, they also gave spirits 'to the tender infants committed to their care', especially to infants suffering 'gripes which [the nurses] have occasioned by their improper diet or intemperance', thereby piling one evil upon another.[13]

Contemporary writers like Harris, who tended to ascribe all the blame to the wet nurse, may have been guilty of exaggeration – perhaps in part due to gender and class bias, and in part due to keenness to discourage the practice. Modern historians have interrogated these accounts more closely and, while their findings are inconclusive, they point to multiple factors, apart from the supposed ignorance of the wet nurses, that may have contributed to the high mortality rates.[14]

The monumental task of recruiting hundreds of wet nurses every year, by a single organisation, had never before been undertaken in Ireland.[15] This, combined with the startling growth in in the numbers of infants taken in – doubling in the first three years – placed considerable strain on the nascent

foundling hospital. Compounding these difficulties was the institution's perennial challenge of procuring sufficient funding. It was perhaps these or other
difficulties that lay behind a tragedy which befell the Workhouse in 1734, as
outlined by the following newspaper notice:

> Thursday last [8 Aug 1734] Mr Charles Sprainger, Treasurer of the Work-
> House of this City shot himself through the head, most people imagine, thro'
> a consciousness of a Deficiency in his accounts, he having been taken notice
> of to appear dejected of late.[16]

The tragedy occurred in the Workhouse itself, in Sprainger's own apartment.[17] The treasurer was the senior manager of the Workhouse, reporting
to the governors, who of course were part-time volunteers meeting, at best,
weekly to oversee the organisation. The unfortunate Sprainger had been
treasurer for just eleven months at the time of his death, but it seems the
Workhouse accounts were already in considerable disarray.[18] Perhaps his suicide should have been a warning to anyone considering filling his shoes.
But if so, it was a warning that the 62-year-old French Huguenot Nicholas
Grueber, merchant and manufacturer of explosives, failed to heed.

Grueber had been born in Lyon but had left France at the age of 11 with
his family as part of the Huguenot exodus. On fleeing France, his father had
established a gunpowder manufacturing concern in Kent, England, and this
became the family business. By 1698 Nicholas, now an adult, had moved to
Ireland, where he took advantage of the thriving French Huguenot network
in Dublin to establish himself in business. In 1703 he married a Marguerite
Moore in the French Church and together they had at least six sons and
two daughters.

In 1716 Nicholas petitioned the Irish parliament for the right to manufacture gunpowder in Ireland.[19] His petition was successful, despite opposition
from the British East India Company, which objected to interference in its
trade.[20] By 1723 Grueber had erected powder mills and other buildings at
Clondalkin, Dublin, and was planning to erect another mill.[21] From 1724 on
he received over £1,000 a year for supplying 300 barrels of gunpowder to the
government.[22] At some point, Grueber had moved into a house on Ormond
Quay, where he raised his large family a stone's throw from the commercial
heart of the city. Here the busy markets often overflowed onto the quays,
obstructing the path of pedestrians, sedan chairs and carriages alike. Yet from
the upper floors the view was airy and south-facing, extending across the river

to the elegant Old Customs House – higher than even the tallest masts of the sea-going ships tied up in front of it – and taking in the busy Essex Bridge, the main crossing point in the city. But in 1733, disaster struck Grueber. A massive explosion ripped through his complex of gunpowder mills, forcing a temporary halt to the milling at Clondalkin.[23]

Whether or not Grueber was now short of money is unclear. Delivery of gunpowder resumed the following year, and Grueber continued to be paid by the government.[24] But no doubt the overheads were high and cash flow could have been problematic. The gunpowder business was no guarantee of wealth. After all, the family business in England, now run by Nicholas's brother Francis, had faced bankruptcy in 1728.[25, 26]

It was under these circumstances that Grueber took over the role of the tragic Charles Sprainger, as treasurer of the Workhouse, a position with a salary of £40 per annum.[27] Perhaps mindful of the strains of the post following Sprainger's death, the governors had created the post of assistant to the treasurer, paid for from the treasurer's salary. Grueber managed to have his son George appointed as his assistant at a salary of £20. Neither of these salaries was large for a person of their rank, and there must have been a considerable sense of disappointment within the family at the course of events.

As we have seen, as treasurer, Grueber was, in effect, the senior manager of the Workhouse, accounting directly to the governors for the spending of the considerable funds paid to the institution. The treasurer was obliged to attend meetings of the Court of Assistants[28] – the small sub-group of governors who met regularly to oversee the running of the Workhouse – or any general meeting of the governors to which he was summoned. Grueber's other responsibilities were to 'buy provisions, clothing, utensils … and to keep an account of same. To examine the several books of the Butler and House-keeper, and to see that the provisions and clothing distributed by them were justly accounted for. To examine all accounts delivered to him for payment, and see that the several articles are properly priced … To attend daily at his office either by himself or his clerk (Sundays excepted) from nine of the clock in the morning until three in the afternoon.'[29]

It is easy to imagine that Grueber's skills in gunpowder manufacturing and business did not well equip him to manage an institution responsible for the lives of hundreds of children and impoverished and vulnerable adults. In any event, whether worn out by the difficulties of his lifetime's enterprise, or too busy with other money-making schemes, Nicholas left most of the day-to-day work to George.

✳   ✳   ✳

At first, all the children under 2 years old brought to the Workhouse and foundling hospital were given to wet nurses outside the Hospital to be nursed, while all older children were retained within its walls. The governors, however, seemingly became unhappy with this arrangement of 'farming out' the younger children, believing their charity was being taken advantage of by mothers who, 'exposed their children, in hopes of being employed and paid as their nurses'.[30] According to the governors, these women conveyed their child to the Workhouse, and then presenting themselves as wet nurses, cunningly contrived to be paid for the rearing of their own offspring.

Whatever the truth of this allegation, as we have seen, it is a charge that surfaces again and again in relation to foundling hospitals, not just in Dublin, but as they were later to develop in other countries.[31] A moment's reflection will reveal how uncertain an undertaking this would be for a mother – for how could she be sure that she would receive her own child back and not some other foundling? Would a mother, realistically, not care about the possibility that she was giving up her own child in order to raise another? Perhaps in desperate times, but the governors were explicitly stating that the mothers were retrieving their *own* children after conspiring to abandon them. Such an operation could only succeed with inside help. In the case of the Dublin Foundling Hospital, such a situation would be particularly troubling to the governors, for it would mean government funds being spent on the rearing of Catholics.

Whether or not the accusation was groundless, within three months of the Gruebers' arrival, the governors decided on a drastic course of action. All children being brought to the Workhouse, including those under 2, were from now on to be 'retained' in the Hospital and reared 'by hand'.[32]

Although 'hand-feeding' of infants was an ancient practice, it was even more fraught with risk than wet-nursing. The finding of clay feeding vessels from 2000 BC or earlier provides evidence of the use of animal milk in the practice. Medieval prints show the use of cow's horns as feeding vessels and these were still in use in the eighteenth century. One example is described as 'a small polished cow's horn … The small end of it is perforated, and has a notch round it, to which are fastened two small bits of parchment, shaped like the tip of the finger of a glove, and sewed together in such a manner as that the food poured into the horn can be sucked through between the stitches.'[33] However, given the difficulties of obtaining fresh uncontaminated supplies of milk, particularly in cities, more common was feeding with 'pap' or 'panada' by 'boat' or spoon. There were many recipes for both and considerable overlap between the two, but 'pap' tended to be made of milk, flour and various flavourings, while 'panada' tended to be made from broth, breadcrumbs and flavouring, such as sugar or spices.[34]

Medical authorities later in the eighteenth century were aware of the risks. Sir Hans Sloane calculated the mortality rate in hand-feeding at 53.9 per cent compared with 19.2 per cent for breast feeding.[35] William Cadogan (1711–97), a more authoritative source, estimated the survival rate at no more than one in three. Another put the survival rate at no more than one in eight.[36] However, in the period under discussion, the practice was little discussed in the literature, and what advice was given was contradictory.[37]

Nevertheless, from 22 November 1734 to 25 March 1736 at least 700 infants who arrived at the gates were kept in the Hospital and not sent out to nurses.[38] We do not have separate mortality figures covering this precise period but the increased death toll is likely to have been high. A later investigation simply notes that the experiment was 'unsuccessful'.[39]

Not content with this, in 1735 legislation was introduced to address another preoccupation of the ascendancy (as it was later to be called).[40] As in earlier years, the governors and parliament were of the opinion that the majority of children found abandoned in the streets of Dublin and Cork were 'of popish parents'. They were convinced that these children were being contacted within the Workhouse and being influenced by 'their parents and popish relations, who notwithstanding all possible care to prevent it, find means to converse with them'.[41] By this means the children were being 'prevented from embracing the Protestant religion'.[42] Once more the Lords spiritual and temporal and the Commons intervened. The resulting new Act declared that:

> For remedy thereof … it shall and may be lawful for the Governors of the workhouses of the city of Dublin and Cork to exchange the children, which they shall have in their respective workhouses, or to send foundling children from one of the said workhouses to the other, as often and in such manner, as the said Governors shall agree upon and find convenient.[43]

Children were to be exchanged between the Dublin and Cork workhouses in order to sever any ties with their parents.

According to Wodsworth, who had access to the minute books and other records of the Workhouse, a committee was formed to implement this directive. As he notes, such a distance, in that era, for poor people, was 'tantamount to nearly absolute separation'.[44] As a result, the children who survived the journey in open wooden carts, over many days, would be prevented from ever seeing their parents again. But parliament's wishes were frustrated by the delay in establishing the Cork foundling hospital, which did not open until 1747. By that time, it appears, the statute had been forgotten.

By 1736 it was clear that the experiment of keeping all the infants in the Workhouse and feeding them 'by hand' had not been a success. The high death rate must have been quite apparent since it was happening on the premises. Clearly floundering, the governors 'applied to several ladies and gentlewomen of this city for advice and assistance'.[45]

Seemingly on the advice of the 'ladies and gentlewomen' who 'for a time met frequently at the Work-house, and made several good regulations', from March 1736 the practice of putting infants out to wet nurses was resumed, but this time with a drastic change. To prevent 'frauds and impositions' each baby not only had a badge placed around its neck, but each one was also 'marked ... in the flesh of the arm'.[46] Later accounts describe how each baby was tattooed on the arm with a letter signifying the year, above an individual number. The brand was made 'with ink and gunpowder, by means of needles fixed in a handle for that purpose'.[47] First the numbers and letters were marked in the skin with a sharp implement, then a mixture of ink and gunpowder was rubbed into the wound to form an indelible tattoo. Girls were tattooed between the shoulder and the elbow, and boys between the elbow and wrist.[48] The number was then recorded in a register together with the child's name, and the name and dwelling place of the nurse. All this was on the advice of the 'several Ladies and Gentlewomen' whose input the governors had sought. This practice, the tattooing or 'branding' of infants was to continue for at least a hundred years.

But what was life like for the inmates of the Workhouse at this time? During this period the Workhouse was divided between the 'foundling side' and the 'foundation side'. The 'foundling side' dealt with all children up to 6 years of age, including the distribution of infants to wet nurses, while the 'foundation side' housed children over 6, as well as adult paupers, who continued to be admitted, though in smaller numbers, and the insane.

As we have seen, except during the experiment of 1734 to 1736, the vast majority of babies under 2 years old were distributed to wet nurses outside the Hospital within days of arrival. But a small number in this age group remained. These were either too sick to be distributed and were being nursed in the infirmary, or were waiting temporarily for a nurse to become available. Many of these were spoon-fed for as long as they survived.

However, the vast majority of the children in the foundling side were between 2 and 6 years of age. These children ate their meals together, not in the great hall but in the nursery, a separate building. Breakfast consisted of 'a quarter of a pound of bread and one pint of new-milk', while dinner, in the middle of the day, consisted of 'a quarter of a pound of bread and one pint of milk-porridge'.[49] For variety, supper was 'a quarter of a pound of bread with butter spread on it' and no milk. On Mondays and Wednesdays a pint of 'burgoo' ('oatmeal stirred up in cold water, seasoned with salt and enlivened with pepper')[50] was substituted for bread and milk at dinner and on Tuesdays and Saturdays three ounces of cheese was served. If these were indeed the rations served, then they must have represented a considerable improvement on the diet outside.

On Monday, 19 December 1737, the beginning of Christmas week, there were 154 children in the nursery. By Tuesday there were only 152 as 'Henry Chapman No. 214 and Edm[und] Onge No. 192 died this day'.[51] The following day 'Child, No. 178', was 'delivered to its parents', further depleting the numbers, while on Saturday, Christmas Eve, 'Anne Stone, No. 212, died this day'. More happily it is recorded that there was 'an extraordinary allowance of ten pounds of butter, for a pudding on Christmas-Day' for the children in the nursery.[52]

All 150-odd children were cared for by '12 nurses and Rose Findlater (a servant)'.[53] As we know, the term 'nurse' did not imply any professional experience, let alone training or qualification. It simply meant a woman who looked after dependents. It may be assumed that even the 2-year-olds quickly learned to feed themselves.

Meanwhile, in the great hall nearly 400 older children and adults were fed. Roughly half of these were 'young persons' – between the ages of 6 and 15 – and half were 'grown persons' ranging from 16 years old to the elderly.

The young were allowed a half-pint of beer twice a day instead of milk, more bread, and a '½ pound of beef' twice a week.[54] (Low-alcohol or 'small' beer was widely drunk by young and old, and considered healthier than water.) All meals, breakfast, dinner and supper were taken in the echoing great hall. Both the regulations and later eyewitness accounts refer to the seemingly rigid orderliness with which meals were conducted.

Early in the morning – at 6 or 7 a.m., depending on the time of year – the nurses and servants were to escort the older children in their charge to the hall, 'immediately after the toll of the second bell',[55] where they were to kneel on the stone floor for morning prayer, with each nurse kneeling at the end of a row (or form) 'to keep the children quiet and attentive'. After prayers, a roll was called, 'by the senior officer in the Hall', which might be the treasurer, register, or foundling clerk. Any absences were queried. If ill, the absentee was committed to the care of the surgeon. If 'slothful and idle, they may be corrected'.

Following this, breakfast – of plain brown bread and beer – was eaten. After breakfast the children were handed over to the care of either a schoolteacher or a 'task-master', who would supervise them at manual labour.

Dinner was held in the middle of the day and consisted of plain bread with either 'milk porridge', cheese or beef (a pound for 'grown persons' and a half pound for those younger) each served two days a week and all washed down with a pint or half pint of beer, depending on age. As before, the nurses and male servants supervised the children 'to keep them orderly and quiet at their meals'.[56]

Again, the children were escorted back to workshop or schoolroom by the nurses and servants, later returning to the hall for evening prayer and a supper of plain bread and beer. Following this, certainly in later years, the children were allowed play. But boys and girls were not allowed to play together 'promiscuously'. Rather, the boys played 'on one side of the house; and the girls on the other'.[57]

At night, the nurses slept in the wards with the children, having locked themselves and their charges in. At this time nurses were exclusively female. Male 'officers or servants' slept with the older boys and adults.

Sunday was the only day that allowed any variation. There was no work on Sundays and the children and their nurses did not have to be in the hall until 8 a.m. on those mornings, which probably meant rising at 7. Then, under the supervision of the schoolmasters and mistresses, they read 'the psalms, the lessons, the collect, epistle and gospel' of the day, in preparation for the morning service, which was open to members of the public. After dinner the children prepared for and attended the afternoon service, and the evening service, all in the great hall, after which 'the Chaplain shall catechise as many children as conveniently he can in one hour; and afterwards shall read some exposition of the said catechism, for half an hour, for the benefit of elder persons'.[58]

Transgressions resulted in harsh punishment. For example, as recorded in the governors' minutes of August 1732, one boy, William Mills, was ordered to be confined in the Bridewell.[59] This was the small prison outside the front wall of the Workhouse, which was used to house recalcitrant beggars and prostitutes. Bridewells were notorious sites of cruelty and depravity. In addition to his confinement, Mills was to be whipped on three successive days. He was then to be brought back to the Workhouse and put in the 'Dungeon' and 'tyed with a chain to a piece of logg'.[60] Another boy, Richard Taylor, was to receive the same punishment. However, two months later William Mills was found to be still in the Bridewell, the reason supposedly being that the chains and other necessary accoutrements had not been provided to allow his punishment to proceed to the next stage. Three other boys were similarly affected. An alternative punishment was to be 'whipt through the Workhouse yard', that is, in front of the other inmates. Wodsworth relates that religious instruction was a frequent source of punishment.[61]

Responsibility for distributing the provisions among the various branches of the Hospital, particularly the bread, drink and beef, lay with the butler. He was also required to account for these and kept a record of all provisions he received. In a later examination of the Workhouse, these books were scrutinised and it was found that the record indicated the butler had received considerably more provisions than he had dispensed.[62] When asked to account for this he cited two things: theft, and abuse of the system by the treasurer and register.

On 22 February 1735 it was discovered that two boys, John Casey and James Byrn, had found ways to rob the pantry and a cellar containing provisions. The boys were dealt with harshly. They were 'tried, convicted and transported'.[63] Transportation at that time was largely to the American colonies, after languishing in jail for an indefinite period waiting for a suitable ship. On arrival, the boys would be bound as indentured servants to colonists for seven years or more. There they would toil for little or no pay, could be beaten at will by their master, and had few rights.

But the incident is even more interesting for the light it throws on the inner secrets of the Workhouse at that time. The two were convicted on the evidence of two other boys, Patrick Ferrall and Daniel Murphy. However, sometime after the trial, these two themselves mysteriously disappeared, 'carried off to the West Indies'.[64] But it emerged that prior to their disappearance, the two boys had been imprisoned in the Bridewell, although not accused of any offence. Rather, they had been detained simply by way of a request by the foundling clerk, John Hodgson, to the keeper of the Bridewell, who owed him a favour. Later, Hodgson arranged for the two boys to be brought against their will to sign indenture papers at the Tholsel. Indenture was a legally binding contract, often entered into by the vulnerable, illiterate or desperate, signing over their labour for a set number of years, in exchange for a trifling sum, payable at the end of the term, which they were often cheated out of anyway. In the West Indies, although not 'chattel slaves', these indentured labourers suffered the same horrific working conditions as African slaves.

But the apparent reason for this appalling treatment is what throws light on the hidden world of the Workhouse. Later investigators alleged that George Grueber, assistant to his father, the treasurer, took the opportunity of the theft by Casey and Byrn to conceal a larger-scale misappropriation of provisions.[65] The discrepancies in the books were falsely put down entirely to the theft by the boys. In order to succeed in this fraud, witnesses had to be removed, including Murphy and Ferrall.

However, it was an announcement in the Dublin newspapers early in 1738 that alarmed the whole city and drew additional, unwelcome attention to the Workhouse.

Out-Matron Quayle

On Sunday last was discovered, in the hollow of the sandbank near Kilmainham
Bridge, in the passage to the Gallows, thirteen Foundling infants, viz. three
males and ten females, with the workhouse mark and number on their arms,
the males marked and numbered between the elbow and wrist, and the females
between the shoulder and elbow. They were all buried in one hole in the said
bank, several of them with marks of violence on them, as if murder'd, and most
of them fresh, and lately laid there …[1]

Dublin Gazette, 17 January 1738

The location of the find was along a lonely stretch of the River Camac,
between the old Kilmainham Jail and Gallows Hill (the location of the current
Kilmainham Jail). This was beyond where the city gave way to open fields and
hedgerows, yet not a quarter of a mile from the gates of the Workhouse. Here
the Camac, little more than a stream, divided in two, forming a small island
and sandbanks. Accounts differed as to how the find was made, with one paper
claiming that some boys playing in the sandpits had heard a baby's cry, while
another claimed the bodies were found by a child and its mother.[2]

The bodies were examined by Mr Stone, surgeon to the Workhouse, but his
findings were inconclusive. 'Marks of violence' appeared on some but others
were 'so mangled, that he could make no judgement of them; and as to the
rest, they might have been murdered, though no marks of violence appeared'.[3]
Stone was right to be cautious since even in modern times the interpretation
of infant post-mortems is difficult. Lividity, caused by the pooling of the blood
in the lowest part of the body could be mistaken, by the inexperienced, for
bruising, and fatal injuries could easily be missed.

Far more can be learned from the location and nature of the concealment.
As so often with the workhouse, there is a preponderance of females. Most of
the bodies were 'fresh' and therefore buried at the same time, or within a short

time of each other. They were buried close to the Workhouse, and yet on a route heading away from the city and the area where their nurses lived, hinting that they never reached the homes of the nurses to whom they were assigned, but died within a short time of leaving the Hospital. The only reasonable conclusion is that they were murdered.

Even by 1738 there seems to have been an extraordinary level of suspicion of the Workhouse among the public, for the newspaper reporting the discovery of the bodies also commented that 'this is a confirmation of what has been long talked of, that there was some extraordinary malpractice among the nurses of those innocent babes' and 'it is feared that several others have been buried in other places, unknown as yet, and that this barbarous and inhuman practice has been long carried on'.[4] In fact, over the following weeks, another eight bodies were found in the same area.[5]

A committee of the House of Lords was enquiring into the affairs of the Workhouse at the time the bodies were discovered, and 'being themselves alarmed, and finding the whole city alarmed … resolved to inquire into that matter'.[6] But before the Lords had finished their enquiries, there was another appalling find. Two more bodies were discovered, by a Patrick Connolly, who was duly summoned to give evidence before their Lordships. Connolly had had the foresight to make a record of the numbers on the infants' arms. The location of the find is not given, but he testified that he had found them 'both wrapped up in one cloth'. The Lords ordered the Workhouse's books be produced. However, on scrutinising these, they were puzzled to find that the two infants had been given out on different dates, and to nurses at different locations – one to be nursed at Ringsend, and the other at Castleknock, on opposite sides of the city. How then did their bodies end up dumped in the same location?

They summoned one of the Workhouse employees to appear before them. As 'out-matron to the foundlings', Elizabeth Quayle's main job was to find suitable nurses for the hundreds of foundlings arriving at the Workhouse gates. It had fallen to the out-matron to put into effect the good intentions of 'the Lords spiritual and temporal, and commons in Parliament assembled' in the 1729 legislation.

Quayle had started by employing nurses in the city of Dublin – poor women from the smoky lanes and courts of the crowded city.[7] As we have seen, in the first year wet nurses had to be found for no fewer than 259 children. Nothing of this kind had been undertaken on such a scale in Ireland (or Britain) before. Yet, in the second year the number had increased to 308 infants needing nurses. Numbers continued to climb after this – nurses had been found for 452 foundlings in 1732–33, and for 441 in 1733–34.

This was the context that caused the newspapers to voice their suspicions of the Workhouse and to claim that some nurses had given a series of false names at the Workhouse, allowing them to take up to eight infants each – that wages had been received 'for nursing four, six or eight children all at one time by the same individual woman, under different names'.[8] The fact that the women came from the poorer slums probably added to the suspicions. 'Several of the nurses liv'd in Thomas Court, and the alleys belonging to it,' one paper reported, and some of them 'were taken up the same night and yesterday and committed to Kilmainham gaol', it continued, with evident satisfaction.

Out-matron Quayle told their Lordships' committee that the 3*s* advance given to the nurses on receiving a child had been stopped in 1736 and, as if her job hadn't been difficult enough, that she had been ordered to employ 'country nurses' instead of those in the city. This practice was to be followed for the next one hundred years. The change was introduced following the failed experiment of 'hand-rearing' all the infants in the Workhouse from 1734 to 1736. As we have seen, the main concern of the governors had been that mothers were conspiring to abandon their children in order to later retrieve them and rear them at the expense of the institution. No doubt the governors believed country nurses and life in the country air would be healthier for the infants (a common belief at the time). But another significant effect of the change would be to remove the infants from all contact with parents and relatives (who would be predominantly Dublin-based) who could frustrate one of the main aims of the institution – the rearing of the children as Protestants.

But it seems little thought had been given by the governors as to how 'country nurses' might be procured in such large numbers. Quayle went about her task by using 'room-keepers' as intermediaries – country people staying in rented accommodation in the city. The room-keepers would put the word out in their home parishes. And when the out-matron 'had any children to put out, she gave them to such persons as they brought her in country dresses: When she had not children, at the time that the country women were brought to her, she afterwards sent the children (as they happened to come in) to the room-keepers, to be sent by them to the women in the country, some of whom live twenty miles from town.'[9]

Quite how, given the change in practice, Elizabeth Quayle was to fulfil the second part of her role – that of visiting the children at nurse to inspect their care – does not seem to have been thought about either. Given the huge demands of her role, she surely would have been limited to visiting city-based children only. In oral testimony Elizabeth did indeed testify that she visited approximately fifty children in the city to enquire about their welfare.[10] This represents a small fraction of the number with nurses.

The potential for abuse hardly needs to be stated. Even if she actually did set eyes on them, Quayle had nothing to judge potential nurses by, other than that they were in 'country dresses'. Even worse, she was handing infants directly to go-betweens who had an ulterior financial motive. In particular, Quayle named two intermediaries – Margaret Malkin and Ann Bryan – whom she accused of giving children to women that Quayle 'did not see or approve of' and of giving children to nurses 'that the Court of Assistants have ordered should not be employed' – including to nurses in the city. She further revealed to the committee that Malkin and Bryan were among two of eight women detained in Newgate jail accused of the murder of the infants found at Kilmainham.

Their Lordships were later to conclude that there was 'but too just cause to suspect that much greater numbers have, from time to time, been destroyed, by the savage cruelty of nurses, than are, or probably ever will be, discovered'.[11] But for now their enquiries had hit a brick wall, and, 'after two or three days spent in examining several persons, whom they summoned before them, received so little satisfaction, that they thought it to no purpose to go any further. Some of the persons suspected of this villainy are fled; the rest are in the hands of the law.'[12]

Instead their Lordships decided to focus more on the financial management – or mismanagement – of the Workhouse. And in this the hapless Gruebers, Nicholas and George, lay in the firing line.

The first indication of the Lords' dissatisfaction with the Gruebers comes almost at the beginning of their report when they referred to 'difficulties which they often [met] in obtaining due information'. The Gruebers were summoned before the bar of the House and there were ordered to lay before the House a statement of their accounts 'in the method appointed by their Lordships'. But they were described as 'either unable or unwilling to comply properly' with these orders. And even though, according to the Lords, they were granted sufficient time, 'yet they made several applications for more'.

And when 'at length' the accounts were produced they found them 'very defective and unsatisfactory, and calculated rather to deceive, than inform'. They found when they asked Nicholas a few questions that he 'was almost entirely unacquainted with his own business' but 'upon all occasions, referred to his son'.

Accordingly, George was again summoned before the bar 'and he, finding that the carelessness or art with which the paper was drawn up, could no longer be concealed' was forced to admit to several 'mistakes' in the evidence that he had given on oath and 'to beg a little time to rectify them'. The Gruebers were obliged to produce a second set of accounts, but the Lords, still unhappy, ordered a parliamentary clerk, William Hawker, to trawl through the books and produce independent accounts – a 'work of great intricacy and delicacy', they conceded.

Following this, the Lords accused the Gruebers of a form of conspiracy to defraud, by paying excessive prices for supplies such as malt. The accusation was that the Gruebers would procure the items from persons known to them at a higher than market price, then have part of the payment returned to them in the form of a 'kick-back'. However, for evidence of this the Lords relied on the testimony of one or two competitors of the actual suppliers, who naturally had a vested interest in criticising the prices of competitors. Their lordships suspected 'a combination between some of the persons who furnished [the goods] and the Treasurer or his Assistant'. But they were forced to admit that they could not 'make any discovery of this nature' and that the witnesses they examined on this issue, some of them on oath, 'utterly denied their having ever given or promised to give Mr Grueber any premium, present or poundage'.[13]

In fact, there was direct evidence from the actual suppliers (Francis Courtney, who supplied butter and cheese, and Anthony Allen, who supplied hops and groceries) that the reason for the higher prices was because of the bad debts of the Workhouse, which increased the risk of doing business with it. But the Lords wasted no time in blaming these bad debts on the Gruebers, too. They claimed that it was the 'want of care or skill or honesty' in the Gruebers that was the principal cause of the 'great debts' and 'excessive prices' paid for provisions.

Their Lordships even quibbled over the amount of beer (twenty-six barrels) produced from eleven barrels of malt, whereas 'in Mr Cook's time' (the Lords considered him a model treasurer) it would have been thirty-three, and in Mr Ormsby's, forty-four barrels. But the Workhouse brewer had already given evidence that the malt was of inferior quality – for which of course the Gruebers were also blamed.

One of the most serious accusations that the Lords' committee made against Nicholas Grueber was that he altered receipts he had given to some of the collectors of taxes on houses.[14] Two tax collectors, Jerome Smith and Best Pakenham, testified in sworn evidence before the bar of the House of Lords that Grueber had given them receipts for money and then afterwards altered the dates on these to a later date. The two men even produced examples of these altered receipts. However, the explanation they gave was that sometimes, if Grueber had received the money a little before the 'close of a quarter', he subsequently might change the date on the receipt to after the quarter 'that he might avoid bringing the money to account as early as he ought'. To an untrained observer this seems more like an effort to balance the books in a desperate situation than an attempt to defraud. Even the hostile Lords, while citing this practice as further evidence against Grueber, do not make any assertion that he benefited personally from it.

Another charge the Lords make is that of embezzlement. By reconciling the number of residents and their respective dietary allowances, with the amount of raw ingredients brought into the Workhouse, the Lords conclude that there is a 'most improvident consumption and embezzlement in the Workhouse'. By their calculations, over the course of nearly two years, the Lords found a discrepancy in spending on wheat of £29 1s 1d. However, this was out of an expenditure of nearly £1,000. In other words, by calculating the amount of bread distributed in all the various weights to each of the residents and staff of the Workhouse over the course of nearly two years and working backwards, attempting to estimate the amount of raw materials needed to produce that amount of bread they could find a discrepancy of only 2.9 per cent. This seems like an impressively low amount of wastage for such a long and complex production chain. Yet the Gruebers were castigated for this.

When the butler was confronted with discrepancies in his books (where he recorded the quantities of food received and distributed by him), he promptly blamed these on both theft and over-drawing of their allowances by the treasurer and register (but not, seemingly other officers or staff). However, the notion of these two men over-indulging themselves in the coarse bread and small beer of the poor seems somewhat ludicrous.

When the Lords happened upon the evidence of the transportation of Casey and Byrn and the disappearance of Murphy and Ferrall they lost no time in linking these to the Gruebers. George Grueber was again formally summoned to appear at the bar of the House and cross-examined by the Lords. An entry in the butler's books in Grueber's own handwriting ascribed all the losses to theft by the boys. The Lords found that 'he could neither deny what he had done, nor give a satisfactory account of it'. But 'upon a second examination, he said … that the Butler had made an affidavit, that all was stolen by the boys'.[15] However, the Lords did not believe Grueber. They interpreted his entry as evidence of dishonesty, when in fact it was perfectly consistent with his testimony. Effectively it boiled down to his word against the butler's (who remained unnamed throughout the report and free from any criticism, even though it was while in his custody that the provisions allegedly 'disappeared').

The report produced by the Lords heaped criticism on the Gruebers. William Hawker's trawl through the accounts had found a discrepancy of £108, out of a total balance of £20,731, for which the Gruebers were blamed. But this pales into insignificance compared to the arrears of over £5,000 on the house tax and nearly £4,000 on carriage tax that had accrued over the four years to December 1737. The Gruebers couldn't be blamed for this as the problem lay in the legislation underlying the collections, and the difficulty of collecting taxes from hostile householders and carriage and cart drivers in a teeming early eighteenth-century city. As the Lords themselves observed in relation to the tax on cart and carriage drivers, this was 'paid for the most part by people of a very low rank, so it must be levied with exactness and care'.[16] Instead, they accused the Gruebers of a 'confused and careless manner of collection' of the taxes in general.

The Lords were clear where the blame lay. 'The choice of the present Assistant,' they argued, 'the Lord's committees cannot but think to have been very unfortunate, as well as that of the Treasurer.' And so it was 'resolved by the Lords Spiritual and Temporal in Parliament assembled that Nicholas Grueber, not being qualified to execute the office of Steward [sic] of the Workhouse, ought not to be employed any more therein'. The same was found in relation to George Grueber, John Hodgson (the former foundling clerk, who had already been replaced) and Elizabeth Quayle, the out-matron. The other main recommendation was that the Workhouse accounts should be published annually in 'one or more of the public newspapers', including an account 'of what foundlings have been received' and 'what died' – a resolution that was quickly forgotten.

Quayle had survived the turmoil of the Foundling Hospital's early years, whereas Charles Sprainger had not. Now she was to be sacrificed along with the Gruebers. We shall see if this sacrifice brought stability to the Workhouse and foundling hospital.

But there was one figure that the Lord's do not seem to have been overly concerned with in their enquiry, and which is dealt with in less than a paragraph towards the end of the report. Of 4,025 children admitted from 25 March 1730, 1,728 had remained in the Workhouse nursery. Of these, 1,246 had died. Over the same period, 2,297 infants had been given to nurses outside the Hospital. Of these, only 307 had survived. In all, of the 4,025 children admitted, 3,236 had died.[17] The Lords spent more time on the £26 discrepancy in the supplies of wheat than on this figure.

But whether or not the removal of the Gruebers was justified, any benefit it brought was short-lived, for within a few years the Workhouse and foundling hospital was to be plunged into crisis again.

In 1740 Ireland was struck by an extreme cold spell during which temperatures plummeted and rivers froze. This was followed by drought and a famine so devastating that it's estimated as much as sixteen percent of the population died. The Workhouse was central to relief efforts in the city of Dublin. Financed by Archbishop Boulter and other leading government figures, in early 1741 the Governors began distributing meal tickets to the city poor, many of them out-of-work artisans.[18]

By March, nearly four and a half thousand meals were being distributed each day at the Workhouse to named ticket-holders.[19] As so often with large scale public charity, there was a political/religious context. Boulter wanted to discourage members of the rural poor majority from migrating to the city seeking alms.[20] These were treated with suspicion by those in power because of their religion and their supposed disloyalty towards the state.[21] Instead relief was to be channeled to the urban poor while the rural migrants – 'vagrant beggars' and 'idlers' were to be threatened with Bridewell and hard labour.[22] Boulter, who died the following year, was commemorated by a large portrait which hung in the Great Hall of the Foundling Hospital, in the establishment of which he had played such a leading role.

The Death of Emy French

On Thursday, 28 February 1745, the governors of the Workhouse and foundling hospital assembled in one of the grand upstairs chambers of the Tholsel, the old city hall in the heart of the city where they held their regular meetings.[1] They gathered at noon, when the tolling of the Tholsel's own great bell was succeeded by the bells of St Nicholas's church next door, the clamour drowning out the usual sounds from the narrow street below, where printing shops, booksellers and coffee houses predominated.[2]

The meeting had been called to examine allegations against the treasurer of the Workhouse, Joseph Pursell, by the seamstress Margaret Hayden. The governors' meetings were usually sparsely attended – the weekly Court of Assembly often struggling to meet the quorum of five. But today was different. Today, in anticipation of this extraordinary matter, no fewer than twenty-seven governors had climbed the stairs to the spacious formal room.[3]

When Margaret Hayden entered to be questioned, she was probably the only woman present. As seamstress to the Workhouse,[4] Hayden was a relatively lowly employee, earning a mere £4 per year – one tenth of the pay of the treasurer, about whose conduct she had complained. She had first been required to submit her complaint in a formal written 'petition' to the governors. Now she would have to endure the details of her account being read aloud to the room of merchants, clergymen, MPs and even peers who made up their number. Soon she would be required to recount all the details again, in person. Some ordinary business was attended to first before the meeting, chaired by Lord Lanesborough, turned to Hayden's petition.[5]

In the modest, even obsequious language required of her in her petition, Hayden relayed how, a few weeks before, on 9 January, (which according to her was a day of 'public fast and prayer' and a holiday), she had gone to the bedchamber in the Workhouse of the treasurer, Joseph Pursell. The officers' apartments were located in the eastern wing of Workhouse, adjacent to the great hall. She had gone there, Hayden had written in her petition, in order to return a cup and two spoons that had been borrowed the day before. Pursell was in bed when she entered the room but as she was leaving, she later wrote, Pursell left his bed and 'ran' at her. He took hold of her 'and said, she should not leave a bachelor's room so'. Hayden replied that she was a married woman 'and desired to be let go'. But instead of releasing her, Pursell struggled with her 'and threw [her] by force on the bed, and then and there in a most rude and violent manner assaulted your petitioner, and by force and rudeness had put his hand in your petitioner's bosom, and lifted up your petitioner's petticoats in a most rude and indecent manner'. Furthermore, Hayden alleged in her petition, 'by the rude and indecent behaviour, and by the expression of said Pursell when he was getting out of the bed, [she was] thoroughly convinced that said Pursell so assaulted your petitioner with intent to ravish her'.[6]

Whether Margaret Hayden's feelings were of determined anger, or of humiliation, as the details of her ordeal were read aloud to the room full of men, is not recorded. But we know from the minutes that she was 'at once afforded a full opportunity of personally stating to all the Governors assembled all the particulars of what had happened'.[7] This must have heaped mortification upon embarrassment. What's more, it's likely that Pursell himself was present. Normally, the most senior officers of the Workhouse, including the treasurer, would attend a board meeting. A later account of the meeting implies that Pursell was there, despite the extraordinary nature of the proceedings.[8]

Pursell, as we shall see, was a man of considerable energy and guile. As the principal resident officer he had unrivalled authority in the Workhouse – unrivalled except for the rather ineffectual oversight provided by the governors. According to Wodsworth, 'more than once he was trusted unwisely and too well'. His very presence at the meeting must have been a source of horror to Margaret Hayden. It's likely that Pursell would have known about the petition and its contents in advance. Whether it was he who insisted that Hayden herself attend in person to defend its contents – in an effort to intimidate her into withdrawing it – is unclear. On the other hand, the minutes recorded not a word from him in his defence.[9]

Was the questioning of Margaret Hayden carried out sympathetically, or with prurient titillation? We don't know. In any event the governors 'on enquiry' found in Hayden's favour, and then and there dismissed Pursell from his post.

Pursell, however, was not one to give up easily, despite his sacking. A further meeting was arranged for 12 March. On the day of the second meeting no fewer than sixty-six governors attended. According to one account, these were 'friends and admirers' of Pursell.[10] How he could have persuaded so many gentlemen, of significantly higher social status than himself, to attend remains unclear. Pursell presented this second meeting with a written statement that can only be described as abject. He lamented that he 'should have the misfortune in any wise to fall under your Lordships' and Honours' displeasure'.[11] The statement was a partial admission of guilt. Pursell acknowledged 'with much sorrow the indiscretion of his conduct, but assureth your Lordships and Honours, that his intentions were very far from being such as they have been represented by his accusers'. He continued that 'in other respects, he hopes his behaviour void of censure, and that he is resolved to give no occasion of offence or suspicion for the future, and therefore humbly prays that you would show some lenity to his first fault, and restore him to his employment, where he humbly hopes he shall hereafter behave so as to deserve the return of your Lordships' and Honours' favours'.

After 'a warm debate', the governors decided by a majority of votes that Pursell should be 'restored and reprimanded'.[12] And according to the minutes signed off by Lord Lanesborough, who was again in the chair, Pursell 'was reprimanded accordingly' and restored to his post. Margaret Hayden's humiliating ordeal had been in vain.

What's worse, as Wodsworth pointed out, it is likely that 'the undue leniency shown to the Treasurer led inferior officers to suppose that they could err likewise without punishment and must have deterred many poor girls from following the example the seamstress had set of complaining to the Governors when there was cause'. Wodsworth feared that from then on 'the female officers and nurses as well as the grown [foundling] girls … were left open to the solicitations and blandishments of the male officers'. Wodsworth was perhaps correct to be fearful, for some years later John Johnston, a staff member, was dismissed for 'abusing Charlotte Grey, a foundling'.[13]

We hear no more of Margaret Hayden; her name disappears from the records. She must have found working under Pursell's authority difficult after this, and it is possible she left the employment of the Workhouse. Pursell married a Catherine Davice in 1751.[14] But if there were hopes that this would curb his behaviour, the fate of Emy French some years later was to reveal otherwise.

Emy French was a blind woman who had been admitted to 'Bedlam' around 1751 after attempting to drown herself. Bedlam was the section of the Workhouse where the mentally ill and intellectually disabled were housed. It was located in the subterranean vaults below the long barrack-like building that formed the rear boundary of the Workhouse yard, parallel to, but furthest from the street. As previously mentioned, Sir William Fownes had 'six strong cells' installed there in 1708.[15] The basement cells were mostly underground and were described as 'nauseous', dirty and wet. There was no glazing in the windows of the corridors and probably no windows at all in the cells themselves. They were described as 'a very improper place to receive lunatics in, as all those who in any degree recover their senses lose the use of their limbs' due to the severe conditions.[16]

Confinement in Bedlam was used as a punishment for the sane. Such was the ignorance and fear of mental illness at the time that the thought of being confined with a 'lunatic' was a source of genuine terror to children and adults alike. The use of Bedlam as a punishment was long standing. For example, the porter had been confined there in 1729 for one night for 'getting drunk'.[17] But its use as punishment seemed to escalate under Pursell. Children were confined there for running away.

Emy French had been admitted on the application of an alderman Aldrich, but when he died it seems there was no one to look after her interests. Despite her blindness, French was considered very capable, and was always well turned out. Eventually she was allowed the freedom of the Bedlam yard and was sometimes entrusted with minding young children. However, she was described by several people as a 'passionate, turbulent woman' who angered easily and 'frequently cursed and swore greatly'.[18]

It was about the summer of 1755 that Pursell had a fateful encounter with her in the Bedlam yard. Mary Molloy, wife of the Bedlam keeper, and Thomas Brackan, Bedlam assistant, were also present in the yard at the time and it is from their later testimony that events can be reconstructed. Pursell accosted Emy French and accused her of throwing stones over the wall into his private garden, which adjoined the yard.[19] (See Rocque's map in plate section.). French denied the accusation, but when Pursell persisted, she in turn accused him of lying 'and abused him very grossly'. Pursell ordered her back down to her cell to be locked up, but French refused to go. Pursell then took hold of her, upon which Mary Molloy, perhaps sensing the danger the blind woman was in, pleaded with him, saying, 'Sir, don't put yourself into a passion with her, leave her to me, I will take her down and lock her up.' Instead of listening, Pursell dragged the blind woman to the top of the stone steps that led down to the cells and 'threw her down the stairs'. However, Brackan was already at the bottom of the steps, probably having gone ahead to open the cells. Fortunately, he was able to catch French as she fell, otherwise 'she must have been much hurt' or, as Brackan graphically put it later, 'either her brains would have been dashed out, or some of her limbs broken by the fall'. Pursell followed her down the steps and dragged her to the cell door but 'in the struggle she tore his ruffle' (the frilled cuff of his chemise). The witnesses heard the blind woman 'bawl out and say Pursell had kicked her in the belly' and that 'he had given her her last blow'. However, this didn't stop Pursell giving her two or three blows to the head with his hand as she entered the cell.

About half an hour later when Brackan went into the cell to check on French, she 'abused him' for having broken her fall, saying that if it had not been for him, 'her brains would have been dashed out', which she would have welcomed, having no regard for her own life, but that Pursell would have been hanged for his crime.

The evidence states that French never complained about the blows to her head, which had been witnessed, but continued to complain that she was 'tortured with the pain' in her abdomen, resulting from Pursell's alleged kick.[20] She suffered severe pain and grew very ill in Bedlam. Mary Molloy informed the old surgeon, Mr Stone, who had French brought to the infirmary. There, French continued to remonstrate with Molloy, alleging that she would 'rather stand by the head than the foot, she will rather stand by Mr Pursell than by me, a poor woman'.

French continued to accuse Pursell loudly, so much so that the infirmary nurses complained that 'we can get no rest from the cries of this woman'. French, in her turn, complained that she herself could 'have no rest in the Infirmary for these women (the nurses) who are cursing and using me ill, I will feign myself mad and go again into Bedlam where I shall have quiet-ness'. A short time later, French was indeed moved back to Bedlam. But she continued to complain of the pain in her abdomen over the following weeks, and some time before Michaelmas (the end of September) she was readmitted to the infirmary. Four days later she died, the victim, as far as the staff were concerned, of Pursell's violence.

Whether Emy French was indeed 'mad', and whether she died as a direct result of Pursell's violence is difficult to ascertain at this distance. We know she had attempted suicide prior to her admission to Bedlam. She was frequently described as 'turbulent' and also as a 'passionate woman, and much given to cursing and swearing'; that she was 'much addicted to cursing and swearing … very turbulent and uneasy on account of her being confined in Bedlam'. It was also reported that while in Bedlam she had attempted to strangle herself with a garter. Indeed, Mr Fitzgerald, the apprentice surgeon, had been shown the garter, but was unable to remember who had 'cut it from her neck'.[21]

What was clear, though, was that Pursell's grip on the Workhouse was unchallenged. Ably assisted by John Fauchey, the butler, and Mrs Whistler, the housekeeper – who happened to be Pursell's own sister – he imposed a rule of iron. The cat-o'-nine-tails was frequently used on children and adults alike. Victims were ordered to be stripped to the waist before receiving their 'stripes'. Although Thomas Eaton, the register, was second in command he seems to have taken a rather passive role and in Pursell's absence punishment was ordered by Fauchey, who was 'often seen … much in liquor' in the dining hall. Fauchey was reported to wait at the foot of the stairs, 'and if the children delayed but a few moments beyond the time they were to go to bed, he had them whipped very severely'. William Bennett, the writing master, reported that 'the usual time for correcting the children is after breakfast, that they are put into stocks, and stripped down to the waist to be chastised … some for making water in the bed received six, others for thieving received twenty stripes'. He confirmed that Fauchey punished children for not going to bed on time, reporting that 'children about seven or eight years of age, have got eight or nine lashes of a cat-o-nine tails on that account'. Mrs Whistler, who appears to have been equally formidable, is reported as saying, after a complaint had caused some unwelcome outside scrutiny, that as soon as 'the hurry was over … she would make both old and young tremble in their skins'.

The next account we have of life in the Workhouse and foundling hospital comes from the clerk of the foundlings, Stephen Fauchey (not to be confused with the butler, John Fauchey), who sent a report to the governors in 1756, seemingly on his own initiative.[22] This was unusual, since most interactions with the governors would have been through the treasurer and register, Fauchey's superiors. Perhaps this indicates some disenchantment in Fauchey with the treasurer. There are other indications that he held himself somewhat aloof from Pursell's regime.

However, Fauchey's initial concern was about indirect contact between the foundlings and their own parents, which was forbidden. This could happen, he claimed, because of 'improper' contact between the country-based wet nurses and the workhouse nurses and subsequently between the workhouse nurses and parents of foundlings. The nurses' task of washing and drying the children's clothes brought them out of the nursery and into other parts of the Hospital, where they could meet visiting tradesmen or other outsiders. Chillingly, another means of contact was via 'persons who come … to buy the children's clothes'. Only a substantial death rate could allow a regular trade in surplus children's clothing. (We later learn that the trade in the clothes and shoes of the dead children was carried on by the housekeeper and the butler).

By these means, Fauchey was concerned, parents could learn the whereabouts of their children at nurse in the countryside. The main objection to this was the perennial concern of the workhouse proponents – the fear that instead of being raised as Protestants, the children would come under the influence of their 'papist' parents, thereby undermining one of the main ostensible functions of the institution: increasing the Protestant population. Later Fauchey was to outline an even more formidable obstacle to this goal – his belief that the country nurses themselves were 'mostly, if not all papists'.[23] The other main concern was that parents could somehow arrange to end up nursing their own children at the expense of the state. This would effectively mean the state subsidising the rearing of Catholics – a troubling proposition.

Active persecution of Catholics was by now in abeyance since it was counterproductive and very costly. It merely stirred up resistance among the majority population, who were otherwise subdued and quiescent. Instead, the ascendancy contented itself with the continuation of severe civil, legal and commercial restrictions. As one historian put it, 'Catholicism was despised as a religion and feared as a subversive influence in the state, but so long as its adherents were deprived of wealth and power the ascendancy saw no reason for upsetting the status quo.'[24] Although the Catholic Archbishop of Armagh had had to go into hiding in 1741 to escape arrest, and the Bishop of Ferns had been arrested in 1751 on trumped-up charges, the execution or deportation of Catholic clerics had also ceased by now.[25] Catholic mass houses had been banned as late as 1744 but this was relaxed again in 1745.[26] However, the ruling elite would have been appalled by any situation in which the state was subsidising the rearing of Catholics. Hence the significance of Fauchey's concerns.

In fairness to Stephen Fauchey, he didn't solely dwell on the issue of religious influence. He also concerned himself with the physical welfare of the children. He pointed out the unsatisfactory nature of the nurseries. The nearby latrines were so inadequate and 'the stench occasioned by the lunatics' (who were confined in the basement), 'the filth of so many children and their nurses, and the closeness of the rooms, cause such bad air, that no person of delicacy cares to visit' the nurseries. And this was the cause of 'so many complaints of the foulness of that place'. Fauchey recommended moving the 'lunatics' to another location.

'Lunatics' – the mentally ill – and 'idiots' – the intellectually disabled – had continued to be admitted to the Workhouse and foundling hospital. For example, figures we have for the seven years up to June 1743 show that during that time fifty-six were admitted, of whom eighteen 'recovered', seventeen died, three 'ran away' and eighteen remained in the Workhouse.[27] Now Fauchey was recommending moving them to another location within the site. He hoped by improving the conditions of the infants 'to induce persons of distinction to visit them, and probably promote [this] useful charity'.

In his report, Fauchey apologises for not raising these issues before (he had been in his post since 1748) but explains that constraints on the Workhouse's budget, and 'the constant hurry of business at the general meetings prevented him, so that the decent provision which might have been expected for these poor infants hath escaped the notice of this honourable Board'. This seems to echo Jonathan Swift's criticism of the Board in 1737:
'I have found the Court of Assistants usually taken up in little wrangles about coachmen, or adjusting accounts of meal and small beer; which however necessary, might sometimes have given place to matters of much greater moment.'[28]

Fauchey finishes by earnestly appealing to the governors to take action, which would 'undoubtedly save the lives of many of [the children], and add many Protestant members to society'.

However, little or nothing happened in response to Fauchey's report. A committee was formed and it reported back to the General Board of Governors with a few recommendations. These were promptly referred to the Court of Assistants with the direction to have plans drawn up to address some of the shortcomings. And there the matter seems to have come to a dead stop: 'nothing being done by the said Court of Assistants … said intended enquiry dropped, and nothing has been … done for the improvement or benefit of the … foundlings; by which means great clamours have been raised against the Governors of the Workhouse, touching their neglect and inattention, as to the administration … of the said House'.[29]

Seemingly moved by the plight of the infants, Reverend Tisdall, vicar of St James's parish, within which the Workhouse lay, and – like most of the Protestant clergy of Dublin – one of the governors, took it upon himself to carry out his own enquiry.[30]

Mr Adderley's Complaint

Reverend Tisdall, who set about his work in early 1757, was a compassion-ate and meticulous observer. He started his report by referring to the 'many clamours raised' about the care provided to the 'sick, sore, and weak' at the Workhouse, noting that it had changed from its original purpose to that of a 'foundling hospital' whose child inmates should be considered 'children of the public'.[1] And since the children were 'admitted in very great numbers, and most of them … in a very… diseased state, it seems necessary to consider this foundation more as an hospital for the sick, than a workhouse for the poor'.

He pointed out some obvious failings. The wages of the wet nurses within the Hospital (who would feed newly arrived infants, while they awaited placement with 'country' nurses, or were perhaps too ill to be accepted by country nurses) were far too low. And yet the job was arduous, with, incredibly, each woman often having to feed three or four infants – and sometimes five. These conditions meant that the few women who offered themselves for employment were 'but the lowest, often the most abandoned of the people', according to Tisdall.

On the other hand, the wages paid to the country nurses, who took infants from the Hospital to raise at home, were so 'extremely small' (40s a year), and there was so 'little inspection into their conduct' that it was 'very probable that many children perish by the neglect and ill [treatment] of those very poor people' who were the only ones tempted to apply.[2] Also, he noted that no pro-vision was made for 'clouts' or rags to be used as nappies 'to keep the children dry and clean' and how it was not unusual in the Workhouse to see a healthy child, a 'diseased' one and a dead or dying child sharing the same cradle. Tisdall echoed Fauchey's complaints about the 'stench' from the latrines, which were unsuitably located and 'not sufficiently attended to'.

Tisdall pointed out how the same price was being paid for the children's shoes and stockings as thirty years previously. As a consequence, due to infla-tion, their quality had dropped drastically, so that they wore out and the children were 'half the year without either'. Tisdall commented on the prevalence of 'pains and disorders' in the children's limbs resulting in 'often the total loss of them'.

The location of the nurseries at this time was almost certainly in the long, barrack-like building forming the rear boundary to the main yard. This plain two-storey building is designated 'Bedlam' on John Rocque's map drawn in 1756 and, as we have seen, it was in the basement cells that the mentally ill and intellectually disabled were detained, well away from the front entrance where their cries might be heard on the street.[3] One advantage this building should have had, on the upper floors at least, was a magnificent uninterrupted view southwards over meadows to the Dublin mountains.[4] But Tisdall found that the southern windows of the nurseries were bricked up 'to save repairing'. Tisdall wasn't so much concerned about the view as about the ventilation of the rooms. At the time 'bad' or stale air was considered as the root cause of many illnesses, and freely circulating fresh air as essential for restoring health in the sick. He also noted the 'delay in enclosing the south ground' – the extensive area of land south of the Hospital and directly behind the nurseries that, if enclosed, could have been used for 'airing the nurses and children'.

Tisdall also pointed out that the Workhouse had as many surgical and medical patients as any true hospital in the city. These cases, he argued, should not be left to 'the precarious attendance of a voluntary physician without an attending apothecary, whom the board have no right to call upon, or punish for neglects by suspension or otherwise'. He suggested that the physician and surgeon should be given a written set of instructions, based on those used at the Royal Hospital. Ever thorough, he supplied a copy of these to the register himself. He also proposed that written instructions be prepared for the senior staff, in order to clearly delineate responsibilities and lines of authority, and to prevent the arbitrary exercise of power – a hint that he had discerned the nature of Pursell's rule over the Workhouse.

Tisdall highlighted the appalling attendance of the governors at the Court of Assistants, where six weeks or two months could elapse without the quorum of five members being reached. (Compare this to the twenty-seven who appeared to watch Margaret Hayden being questioned about her complaint and the sixty-six that Pursell mustered in response). This would have significantly hampered the business of the Workhouse. Also, since the governors were charged with policing the carriage and sedan chair business, this caused considerable inconvenience and expense to complainants and offenders. Prosecutions were often dropped because of a failure by 'gentlemen to attend as they had promised to do on their election'.

Tisdall carried out his enquiry on his own initiative, and submitted his report to the Board of Governors in June 1757, whereupon they formed yet another committee, which, at least, this time, included Tisdall himself among its members. This committee, after an initial assessment, came to the extra-ordinary conclusion that there were so many problems within the Workhouse that required correction that they would confine themselves entirely to the welfare of the foundlings and 'would interfere no farther with the foundation side'. Nevertheless, this committee did make a significant number of recom-mendations addressing many of Tisdall's concerns. And, as a sign of growing suspicions about Pursell, they appended to their report documents from thir-teen years earlier outlining Margaret Hayden's complaint, the effective finding of sexual assault against him, his dismissal and his reinstatement.

However, since it is clear from Tisdall's initial report that, with honourable exceptions, such as Tisdall himself, the governors carried out their functions in a desultory manner – failing to attend meetings in sufficient numbers even to fulfil their statutory functions, never mind to ensure the welfare of the poor in their care and curb the excesses of Pursell – it is likely that not much would have come of their recommendations. But things were worse even than Reverend Tisdall had imagined.

The appointment of two physicians was one of the few positive develop-ments in 1757. The old surgeon, Mr Stone, had died in November 1756.[5] Dr Edmund Blackall and Dr Thomas Knox were appointed the following May, before Tisdall's report was completed, but probably in response to his advice.[6] The appointment of a physician to the Workhouse, instead of a surgeon, was a new development. Physicians were university educated, whereas in that era most surgeons had simply completed an apprenticeship. Physicians were better paid and of significantly higher social status.

Dr Blackall was later to describe the conditions of the infants on their arrival at the Workhouse. They were mostly in 'a bad state of health … disorders mostly venereal, [they] frequently don't feed for three days [before arrival]'.[7] He described how he had seen twenty children assigned to five wet nurses, and believed that 'many of them are therefore starved'. In the circumstances he believed feeding 'by the spoon' would be more effective (notwithstanding the high mortality associated with that practice). He described how there were only two nurses in the infirmary – one for female patients and one for males. The nurse looking after the females had thirty patients under her care. She would have spent all day with her charges, perhaps with occasional short breaks, and slept in the same room or an adjoining room, so that her duties would have been more or less twenty-four hours a day six and a half or seven days a week.

Dr Blackall described how he found the infirmary 'extremely dirty and offensive', with up to four children to a bed, and how his directions as to diet (one of the most important aspects of treatment for an eighteenth-century physician) were not followed and that he had 'found a child in a fever drinking small beer'. Small, or weak, beer was considered healthier than water to drink at the time, even for children, since it was less likely to carry potentially fatal toxins. Dr Blackall's concerns would not have been with the alcohol content, but that in the prevailing medical theory of the time, beer would be considered a 'stimulating' drink and so likely to exacerbate fever. He had brought his concerns regarding the diet of the sick children to John Fauchey, the butler, and to Mrs Whistler, but in a show of apparent contempt or indifference to Blackall's status as a physician, they had been tardy in addressing the problem. He reported that 'where the children lie, the windows are much broken and shattered, and the children thereby exposed to cold and wet'. The children were poorly clothed often without shoes and stockings. The great hall was very cold, and in wet weather very damp. The children's hands and feet were 'much swelled and disordered with cold and sores, many of them not fit to be employed at work on that account'. But it was Blackall's encounter with Bedlam, and subsequent confrontation with Pursell, which was to have major repercussions for the Workhouse.

Blackall recalled visiting Bedlam in August 1757 and seeing there, in the semi-darkness of the underground cells, a girl of about 15 years of age. Like Emy French – who, however, was older, and who had died two years previously – this girl was also blind. Blindness was common at the time for a variety of reasons, not least the transmission of trachoma, a parasitic infection, spread where people lived in close proximity. On enquiring how long the girl had been 'out of her senses' – or mentally ill – Blackall had been informed that she wasn't, but had been placed there for punishment 'for some misdemeanour'. Blackall ordered her release, but the Bedlam keeper refused, in the absence of Pursell's orders. Blackall then met with Pursell and demanded the girl's release. Pursell reportedly ignored his demand and the girl remained in Bedlam a further three weeks. In an apparent escalation of the dispute, Pursell, during that time, 'sent for' the physician to attend the girl in Bedlam. Blackall refused, citing the appalling conditions in the cellars. Eventually the girl was released, after Pursell had sufficiently demonstrated his authority, it seems. But Blackall was not to forget the encounter. Pursell's apparent contempt for the authority of the physician probably arose from his having successfully manipulated the Workhouse governors for years, and even having survived the finding of sexual assault against him. To Pursell, the failure of the governors to control him could be seen as a sign of tacit approval of his conduct.

But storm clouds were gathering for Pursell, and for the Board of Governors. Early in 1757 yet another committee had been established by the governors, this time to look into a complaint that the children on the 'foundation' side were being cheated of their daily bread allowances. The complaint focused on the spinning school, whose master, Alexander Lyon, was interviewed by the committee in the Workhouse. Lyon reported that he had noticed a falling off in the productivity of his young workers in 1755 and, 'upon his attempting to correct them for what he thought proceeded from idleness, they in excuse said, they were not able to do the work ... for want of a sufficient allowance of bread'.[8] Lyon had asked the children to bring him the pieces of bread they were given at their meals so that he could verify their complaints. He weighed the pieces and found that they were indeed less than the weight set down in the Workhouse regulations. However, Lyon felt unable to raise the matter with the Workhouse management in case the children 'should be ill-treated on that account'. But he did acquaint his supervisor. Further investigation was thwarted by the staff cutting the bread into pieces before serving, thus preventing the weighing of whole portions.

The governors took a sceptical approach to the complaint. Firstly they enquired whether Lyon had weighed two servings of the same child in the same day – implying that a deficiency in one serving would be likely to be compensated for in the next. They went further and, after interviewing him, actually placed sample portions of bread on the table in front of Lyon and asked him if the samples he had weighed appeared larger or smaller – sometimes larger, sometimes smaller was his reply.

Isabella Craig, the spinning mistress who supervised the female children in the spinning school, was also questioned by the governors. She had worked there for four years and 'she had observed from the beginning a deficiency in the children's labour, occasioned by their having too small an allowance for their support'. She too had weighed the bread and found the portions wanting. When she reported her concerns to more senior staff she was told bluntly that it was useless to concern herself with the welfare 'of persons who were sold for slaves' and she was threatened with confinement in either Bridewell or Bedlam should she pursue these matters. 'Therefore she mentioned them no further', although the children continued to be short-rationed, and the bread was 'cut in the Hall, of late, to prevent her weighing it'.

In general, the governors were dismissive of the complaint and, based on the questioning outlined above, seem to have taken considerable pains to undermine it. They interviewed 'several' children. Tellingly, they found three to be sickly in appearance but they did not feel that they had been weakened by lack of food. Regarding the subdividing of the children's portions, they reported that some children had told them that this was to prevent their bartering it 'for china taws and other play things'.

The spinning school was run on a contract basis, whereby the Workhouse supplied labour and premises on the Workhouse site in return for an annual fee. The contractor then hoped to make a profit by selling on the textiles produced. The head contractor in this case was Thomas Adderley. The spinning school was, effectively, one of his businesses. Adderley was a dynamic and innovative industrialist and a rich landowner. He owned, among other holdings, most of the village of Innishannon, County Cork, and had already established a linen manufactory there. In addition to being very wealthy, Adderley had connections through marriage with one of the most important noble families in the country (he was the stepfather of Viscount Charlemont). He was also an MP and an active politician. Adderley had either made the complaint himself, or at the very least he seemed supportive of those making the complaint, so that eventually the issue became known as 'Mr Adderley's complaint'.

The committee examining Adderley's complaint had none of the interest in the children's welfare shown by Reverend Tisdall. Rather, all its energy was directed at forensically cross-examining the complainants in a quasi-judicial manner. Relations between the committee of governors and Adderley appear to have turned frosty. The committee was adjourned when Adderley had to leave at short notice to conduct business in England. Several further hearings were scheduled but abandoned, before the committee finally lapsed.[9] But if the governors felt they had seen off Adderley's challenge, they were mistaken.

9

'Up Many Stairs to the Garrets'

On St Stephen's night in 1757 the governors gathered in the large, grandly decorated, but seldom used boardroom in the east wing of the Workhouse.[1] The 25th of December was, inconveniently, a 'quarter day' – one of the four days of the year on which a general board meeting had to be held on the following Monday – which this year was St Stephen's Day. Away from their more usual meeting place of the Tholsel, in the centre of the city, the governors were, for once, more accessible to the Workhouse inmates. Taking advantage of this, John Bishop, along with three other boys (all are referred to as 'boys' in subsequent reports, despite Bishop, at least, being in his twenties) approached the door of the meeting room.[2]

Bishop had arrived at the Workhouse as a foundling child. As we have seen, foundlings were admitted briefly to the Workhouse, before being dispatched with country nurses. Then at about 6 years of age they were returned or 'drafted' back to the Workhouse. When he was about 10 years old, Bishop had developed a disorder of his knee, which was worsened, he believed, by the atrocious conditions in the Workhouse, to the extent that 'his leg was obliged to be cut off'. Another time, he recalled, he was put in the stocks on Pursell's orders (for weighing his bread) and given twenty lashes. These were generally given by the cat-o'-nine-tails, on the bare back, in public after the recipient had been stripped to the waist. It was probably because of his disability that Bishop, as he grew older, was allowed to stay on in the Workhouse, where he worked as an assistant to the tailor from the age of 13 (even though he was never formally apprenticed).

At the door of the boardroom the boys met a man they later identified as 'Mr Cobbe' – probably Reverend Dr Cobbe, one of the governors – coming from the meeting.[3] One of their number, James Doran, showed Cobbe a piece of meat and bone 'full of maggots', which he claimed was part of the meat the residents were to be served the next day. Cobbe returned to the boardroom, but what effect their complaint had on the board members, if any, the boys never heard. The following day, however, Pursell confronted Bishop about the affair, demanding to know where he had got the meat. Bishop, it appears, promptly identified his accomplices. The day after that, in the great hall at mealtime Bishop, Doran and the two others were 'called out' by Pursell. He demanded to know what fault they had found with the beef. Doran defiantly replied that it was 'full of maggots', whereupon Pursell 'ordered all of them to the stocks, where they were obliged to strip, and by Mr Pursell's orders, each received twenty lashes'.

If the governors attending the board meeting on 26 December had not deigned to hear the complaints of the boys about the rotten beef, it may have been partly due to a pressing matter to which they had to attend. For the 'clamours' that the Reverend Tisdall had referred to in his report earlier that year, concerning standards in the Workhouse, were growing to a pitch that could not be ignored. The concerns raised in the various reports, the arrival of influential outsiders such as Dr Blackall in the Workhouse, and Pursell's contemptuous treatment of them, combined to increase the pressure on the governors for something to be done.

As we have seen, Thomas Adderley was the merchant, linen manufacturer and MP whose complaint had been subject to such forensic analysis earlier that year by a committee of the governors, and which had subsequently languished, unanswered. The committee itself lapsed. But while the proceedings seemed to have petered out in mutual coolness and polite disdain,[4] it appears that, privately, Adderley was incensed. A supporter of Adderley's was later to describe the governors as 'setting themselves up as judicial inquisitors' and derided them for failing to make 'the long and disagreeable journey [from the boardroom] through much filth, and up many stairs to the garrets' in order to see for themselves the conditions under which the inmates lived.[5]

Then in December 1757, just four days prior to the St Stephen's Day meeting, in the House of Commons, it had been announced that an enquiry was to be held into the Workhouse. Ominously for those involved, the committee's sweeping terms of reference were to enquire into 'the conduct of the officers and servants of the said house for ten years last past'. This was to be far broader than any previous enquiry. Most worryingly of all, the committee was to be chaired by none other than Thomas Adderley himself.

This was the development that the governors had to discuss at their St Stephen's night meeting, the meeting that was almost interrupted by John Bishop and his friends. Pursell was almost certainly present, since it was his normal role to attend and since we know he was present in the Workhouse the next day to confront Bishop. We have seen how expertly Pursell was able to influence the governors. In many ways he was the 'permanent government' of the Workhouse – the experienced technocrat permanently on site, as opposed to the gentlemen volunteers who met infrequently and relied entirely on his briefings. Indeed, the butler Fauchey, Pursell's accomplice, is reported as telling one of the nursing staff that of 'one hundred and fifty' votes on the Board of Governors 'Pursell had one hundred'.[6]

Pursell, therefore, was no doubt central to the board's response to this ominous development. Its answer was to revive the committee enquiring into Adderley's original complaint about the Workhouse, but this time to alter the terms of reference 'to enquire how far the said Mr Adderley has complied with his contract' with the governors. Effectively the governors were turning the tables, and enquiring into Adderley himself. Aggressive, and somewhat crude, this strategy certainly bears Pursell's hallmarks.

The very next day, the same day he confronted Bishop, Pursell proceeded to the Tholsel to meet the governors again, in their more normal setting, this time bearing a copy of Adderley's contract, along with his accounts. The committee concluded, and it can only have been with heavy reliance on Pursell's evidence as treasurer, that Adderley had failed to pay any 'rent' for the previous three years, and was in debt to the tune of over £160 – information it would subsequently try to use against him.

Meanwhile, the House of Commons had begun its enquiry. This was unlike nearly every other enquiry into the Workhouse up to then, in that it relied almost exclusively on direct interviews with staff and inmates, and eschewed the usual reliance on tables of figures and accounts. Instead we learn about day-to-day life in the institution.

The first to be interviewed was the Reverend Mr Hill, chaplain to the Workhouse since 1737. Despite his twenty-one years' experience in the Workhouse, Reverend Hill claimed to know very little of the 'foundling side', 'as it was not his duty to attend there' – although there was no other chaplain.

One of the chaplain's roles was to officiate at burials. Reverend Hill took a rather unusual approach to the burial service. While the grave diggers proceeded to the burial site, the reverend remained some distance away at the gate of the burial ground and conducted the ceremony from there, 'lest there should be any infection' (to himself). He reported that up to twelve bodies were buried at any one time and that the burial ground was 'so full of dead bodies that in digging a grave, [other] bodies are frequently thrown up'. A branch of the Dodder that formed the main water supply to the city of Dublin – the so-called 'pipes' – ran along the site, in a raised conduit, which sometimes overflowed its banks.[7] Reverend Hill reported that 'the burying place is at times so overflown with water, as to prevent burying, and frequently the dead bodies are left bare on the ground on account of the water washing away the earth'.

Burials were conducted approximately three times weekly, with the bodies stockpiled between burial days. The 'dead room' or 'dead hole' was 'within a step or two of the infirmary door'. He did not know whether the 'ill smell from the dead bodies' placed there affected the sick in the infirmary, although others testified that they did 'not know whether the stench [they] often perceived on going into the infirmary came from the dead hole or the infirmary'.

Reverend Hill conducted the twice-daily prayer ceremonies in the great hall, the morning service starting at 7 a.m. in the winter and even earlier in the summer. These were attended by all the children aged over 6 and the adults. In the winter, he reported, the great hall was extremely cold and 'very damp and wet'. It seems the impressively large fireplaces at either end of the hall were for appearances only, as 'no fire is kept in the Hall but of Christmas holy days and sometimes of a Sunday' (when wealthy sight-seers – potential donors – might be visiting). Since many of the children were often barefoot, they were exposed to the cold, wet floor, so that he allowed them to sit instead of kneeling. It was after morning prayers that punishments were carried out by Pursell. As we have seen, this often involved public whipping with the cat-o'-nine-tails and children who ran away were confined with the 'lunatics' in bedlam in order to terrorise them.

Although Reverend Hill criticised the quality of the milk coming into the Workhouse, this did not stop him partaking in one of the most notable acts of meanness carried out by the senior Workhouse staff. For Hill revealed that the 'milk is frequently skimmed … before the children get it' and that he himself consumed the cream (along presumably, with the other officers).[8] He does not seem to have made any connection between this and his role in burying children in large numbers. The 75-year-old inmate Daniel Palmer was later to testify that what reached the inmates was 'no better than water coloured with milk'.[9]

The only inmate of the Workhouse that we know Hill to have taken an active interest in was an adult woman, a Mrs Cuttle, who was an inmate of Bedlam. Something about the vulnerability of a woman detained in such circumstances perhaps excited his interest. Whether he visited her in her cell or met her elsewhere, he formed the opinion that she was detained 'while in her senses' – i.e. while not mentally ill. As his single act of protest about matters in the Workhouse, Hill made this 'known to a gentleman' (probably a governor) and Mrs Cuttle was released. Ironically, however, as it turned out, Mrs Cuttle did appear to suffer from mental illness, even by Hill's own account, and sometime later she was readmitted – this time 'out of her senses' and was still confined at the time of the enquiry.

The other issue on which Reverend Hill did get exercised was his own salary. This he complained was only £30 per year, with 6*d* a day for diet. Repeating this figure, he insisted that this was 'too little to support him'. Admittedly this is low for a clergyman; however, the chaplain also received free accommodation, and the 1737 accounts show that he received an additional £13 annually in allowances for such items as candles, soap and coals.[10]

Hill concluded his evidence with a metaphoric shrug of indifference. If a child could survive the Workhouse, he declared, it could survive anywhere.

As the parliamentary committee chaired by Adderley continued its enquiry, Bridget Robinson was called to be questioned. She had worked for three years as a nurse on the 'foundation side', before being dismissed the previous July. Ostensibly she had been sacked because 'she gave out the milk at dinner before the psalms were ended' – even though, she said, she had seen the other nurses do the same. The real reason for her dismissal, she believed, was that 'it was thought by the heads of the house that she spoke too freely about the affairs of the house, and concerning the children not getting sufficient diet'. At one time, of twenty-nine children in Bridget Robinson's care, thirteen were sick. Forthright and unrepentant, Robinson – whose pay was one thirtieth that of Hill's – had frequently bought milk and 'sowings and turnips' out of her own money for the children who were sick, when their allowance of milk was not sufficient, she said. And when sick children were placed on a milk diet, the enterprising Robinson had somehow ensured that she continued to obtain their allowance of meat and bread, which she then sold in order to buy them extra milk.

But she wasn't the only one to suffer dismissal, or the threat of dismissal, which were used to maintain compliance amongst the staff. A similar fate was suffered by Eleanor Sutherland, who had been let go by the housekeeper, Mrs Whistler – Pursell's sister – in order to give the job to another woman, who, it turned out, only lasted six weeks. Also, Mary Molloy, the wife of the Bedlam keeper, reported being afraid to complain to Pursell about the badness of the food, for fear he 'would turn her out of the house'.

Isabella Craig, mistress in the spinning school, had already given evidence to the governors' enquiry into Adderley's complaint early the year before.

Now she gave further details about conditions in the Workhouse. Like all the staff, she lived in fear of Pursell – specifically, that he would imprison her in Bedlam if she were to pursue any complaint. She complained of the badness of the meal from which the children's stirabout[11] was made, and how it frequently contained 'clocks' – black beetles – and 'crickets' – possibly cockroaches. Many of the witnesses were to echo her testimony about 'clocks and crickets' in the meals. Other evidence blamed the bad colour, bad taste and dirt of the stirabout on the lack of cleaning of the cooking vessels. It was also reported to be excessively thin, so that if allowed to stand for even a short time 'a great deal of water settled upon the top' so that the children could drink it without even using a spoon – but 'on Board days (when the governors met) it has been good and thick'. Earwigs were also seen in it and one nurse, Eleanor Newman, claimed that sand was sometimes mixed into it. Cabbages were sometimes 'rotten and jellied', but still served. Tainted and foul-smelling beef was allegedly supplied by the butcher, who was Pursell's nephew.[12] There were frequent complaints of maggots in the beef and in the broth.

The produce of the walled workhouse garden could have provided some fresh produce for the children. A gardener and the seeds for the garden were paid for by the governors. But it is uncertain how much the children received. The garden was 'under the care and command of Mr Pursell', according to Reverend Hill. In his first appearance before the enquiry, Hill testified that some, at least, of the produce of the garden was 'sent out' of the Workhouse, and therefore diverted from the children's use. However, on his second appearance, this time 'on behalf of Mr Pursell', a more cautious Hill clarified that 'he never saw any of the garden stuff sent out' apart from 'a nosegay or some small present of that kind'.

Regarding the children's clothing, Isabella Craig revealed that the girls wore a single serge petticoat only, without a lining, made out of their worn-out outer dress. But many of the petticoats were not large enough and so did not close properly in front, leaving 'their shifts exposed and bare'. Their clothes were so infested that after being with the children 'she ha[d] often stripped herself, in order to sweep … the vermin off her clothes'.

The nurses were supplied with an allowance of cloth to make their own clothes. Eleanor Sutherland, a nurse on the foundation side, described receiving, besides her 20s a year wages, 'a cloth serge gown, seven yards of three quarters and a half wide [cloth] for shifts, three yards and half quarter of chequer to make aprons, one yard and a quarter and a half quarter of linen to make handkerchiefs and nightcaps, two pair of yarn stockings, and two pair of shoes'.

For those clothes not made by the children themselves or their supervisors, the tailor was paid 2*d* for making a coat, and 1*d* for making a waistcoat.

Isabella Craig also noted how many of the children were 'for a great part of the winter, without shoes and stockings'. We have already seen how shoes were supplied twice a year. 'Shoeing time' was in March and September, but the shoes supplied by George Brindle, the shoemaker, were said to be of such poor quality that they often wore out long before their replacement was due.

David Melvill, Isabella Craig's boss, who supervised the spinning school but was not employed directly by the Workhouse, reported that in winter time he had often seen the girls come to spin without shoes and stockings, and that they had continued like this until 'shoeing time' the following March, that their hands and feet were extremely swelled with cold and that he had seen two children's toes 'mortifying … he thinks with ulcers'. While the clothes of dead children were given to Mrs Whistler, the housekeeper, for her to sell for her own gain, the shoes and stockings went to the butler, Fauchey, for a similar purpose.

Many witnesses testified about the effect of cold and lack of footwear on the children's feet and limbs. Their ability to work was affected by 'their fingers and feet being much swelled with the cold and afflicted with sores'. Dr Blackall testified that the 'childrens hands and feet [were] much swelled and disordered with cold and sores, many of them not fit to be employed at work on that account'.[13] Eleanor Sutherland reported that 'their feet were so swelled, and so sore from the cold, that they could scarcely walk'. Also they 'were sadly overrun with itch'. Isabella Craig testified that 'many of the children's hands were so much swelled, and so thick with itch sores and scabs, that they were not able to draw the thread'. Mary Molloy, wife to the Bedlam keeper, reported that Bedlam was so 'extremely cold and wet' that 'persons have lost the use of their limbs by being confined in it'. Even the Reverend Hill had noticed the children's 'fingers and feet being much swelled with the cold'.

Mr Fitzgerald, the surgeon who had attended the Workhouse as an apprentice some years previously but was no longer employed there, gave a more nuanced view. He had 'never [seen] a mortified [gangrenous] toe with any of the children, during the time he was in the Workhouse' but he had seen 'some of them with ulcers and scrophulous [tubercular] humours in their toes' and while these 'proceeded mostly from nature' he believed 'cold in a great measure … increased them'.

Regarding the condition of the workhouse buildings themselves, Isabella Craig reported that 'the windows and roof of the children's bedrooms were so broke, that they were open to wind and rain' and also that the room in which they did their spinning was 'extremely cold, that it was open to the top, and in many places the wind and rain came in [and] that only a bushel of coals a week … was allowed for the fire'. The physician Dr Blackall had also commented that 'where the children lie, the windows are much broken and shattered, and the children [are] thereby exposed to cold and wet'.

On the other hand, the glazier Richard Eaton, one of the witnesses that Pursell had called on his own behalf, testified that 'Mr Pursell sent often to him, to mend the windows … and he generally obeyed immediately' and also that 'the glazing work of the house is in very good order'. He reported that repairs totalling 50s had been made since the previous May. He believed the children themselves were responsible for breaking the glass. Although he had known the Workhouse sixteen or seventeen years, he had never, he said, known it in 'so good order'. Nevertheless, this assertion was somewhat undermined by a report in the newspaper *Pue's Occurrences* for Saturday, 26 November 1757, which reported that 'two floors in the Foundling part of the Workhouse gave way, by which two of the foundlings were hurt'.[14]

Towards the end of her testimony, Isabella Craig gave evidence about the condition of the foundlings who were being nursed in the 'country'. About two or three weeks previously, Craig revealed, she had been visiting County Wicklow, and had seen two foundling children 'at Kate Floyd's house'. One was about 3 or 4 years old and the other about 6 months old. But she believed the 'wet nurse', Kate Floyd, was between 50 and 60 years of age, 'that she had not any milk in her breast [and] had no cow to support those children with milk'. Isabella believed that Floyd must either beg for the milk to feed the children, or pay for it some other way (which, it was implied would have been very difficult, if not impossible for a poor country woman), and that the children looked as if they were starved.

At any one time during this period there were approximately 2,000 children with wet nurses in rural areas, vastly outnumbering those being cared for in the Workhouse.[15] Yet apart from this brief glimpse, we have virtually no information about their care.

10

Pursell Under Fire

The parliamentary enquiry chaired by Thomas Adderley continued into the early months of 1758. As it did so, further details of conditions in the Workhouse and foundling hospital continued to emerge.

When the children in the Workhouse became ill, conditions could be terrifying. We have already seen how the bodies of the dead were stored so near the infirmary that it couldn't be determined which location the foul smell came from. Dr Knox, the second physician attached to the Workhouse at the time, who had begun attending in May 1757, the same month as Dr Blackall, commented on the large numbers of sick inmates, how there was no apothecary and how his directions were not obeyed.[1] He instanced how 'physic ordered for one recovering out of the measles, had been given to a child in a flux' (i.e. with diarrhoea). He had found sick and well children lying in the same bed because of a lack of beds, partly due to the fact that the infirmaries were 'crowded with superannuated people' rather than the sick. Indeed, the carpenter James Tynan had reported calling to the nursery early one morning and finding the nurses in bed and five dead children in different beds 'which he believe[d] the nurses knew nothing of till he told them, and that the nurses got up and put the dead into one bed'.

Knox's efforts to ensure that the infirmaries were kept clean and well ventilated were further hampered by the fact that the beds were chained together. The children lay on straw, without sheets, which encouraged infestations. 'The green nursery was too narrow, and so near the slates, that the heat in summer and cold in winter, must be intolerable', and although this had subsequently been improved, children on the foundation side still slept in 'the garret' with the same results. Moreover, they were 'crowded into little rooms, six or eight of them sometimes in a bed … and three or four beds in a room with the bucket in the middle' for use as a toilet. He reported that he believed six or more infants were being fed by one suckling nurse, but he believed the situation had recently improved (presumably in response to Tisdall's report). However, there were currently only two elderly nurses caring for sixty children under the age of 8 years old in the infirmary – the majority of them sick with fevers and diarrhoeal illnesses.

Dr Knox described one child he visited in the green nursery. The child was in a fever, but Knox thought it was likely to do well (the gender of the child is not given). However, when he visited the child a few days later he was surprised to find it in a 'languid, dying condition'. He enquired of the nurse whether it had had 'a flux' – diarrhoea – since he had last visited 'for it sometimes happened upon the going off of a fever a lax ensued'. He was told it had not. But when he stripped off the bed clothes, he found the child was 'lying in its dirt and filth, which occasioned a mortification in the backside of the child which eat into the body, of which the child died that night or the next morning'.

Not all the inmates of the Workhouse were cowed by Pursell and the senior officers. Seventy-five-year-old Daniel Palmer was proud of his profession as a cobbler, and was dismissive of the support he received from the Workhouse, seeing it not as charity, but as barely sufficient compensation for the work he performed. Indeed he claimed to have been 'wronged of two coats and two pair of breeches'. He was scathing about the food he received and it was he who described the buttermilk as 'water coloured with milk'. He made clear that had he been spending his own money he would have ensured he got better-quality provisions. Palmer also helped out burying the dead, reporting that up to thirty-five children had been buried in one interment, and claiming that all the small bodies had been placed in a single coffin used to convey them to the graveside. He also reported being confined in Bedlam on one occasion with six others for failing to attend a burial and on another occasion by Pursell himself for 'having some words with the housekeeper', Mrs Whistler. Palmer's assertiveness was no doubt helped by the fact that he had only been resident there five years and nine months, and thus was a relative outsider.

Another man confined in Bedlam for punishment was George Forfar, who was at least 54 years of age and a veteran of the Workhouse. On the first occasion, Forfar, who seems to have been something of a favourite, had been sent across the city to a Ms Payne's in Duke Street to fetch clothes belonging to Pursell's daughter. However, on the journey back from Duke St to James's St. Forfar managed to become intoxicated. And although he brought the bundle 'very tightly bound up' to Mrs Whistler on his return, some items were found to be missing, either due to carelessness on Forfar's part or theft. Pursell confined Forfar to Bedlam for eight days, where he was given the choice of either walking the length of the corridor the whole night, or sharing a cell with a 'madman'. But the Bedlam keeper advised him that the man was 'quiet' as he was 'on the mending hand'. So Forfar chose the cell, where the man treated him in a friendly manner, even offering Forfar his coat for warmth.

Despite his unreliability, occasioned by his fondness for alcohol, Forfar seems to have been liked by the senior staff and was employed frequently by Eaton, the register, to run errands. His second incarceration in Bedlam occurred as a result of his 'leaving the Board books in town' when drunk. These were probably the minute books of the Board of Governors, brought to the Tholsel for board meetings so that the register could record the minutes, before they were returned to the Workhouse. This time Pursell privately gave instruction to the Bedlam keeper that Forfar was to be allowed back to his own room every night, but that he was not to give any hint that Pursell knew anything of the arrangement. This is a rare instance of kindness by Pursell.

Not all who received punishment in Bedlam were entirely innocent – or entirely sane. Robert Wilson, also aged about 54, and resident of the Workhouse for more than thirty years, was well able to nurse a grievance. Elsewhere, he was described as 'quarrelsome'. Like Palmer, he lost no time in telling the committee of MPs he had 'been wronged of a suit of clothes'. He recalled, almost to the very day, being incarcerated in Bedlam in 1749 – 'for hurting a man with a knife' as he put it. Another witness described how he had stabbed a man with a pair of scissors. He was confined until the following Christmas. But after his release 'upon frequently complaining of some things he was robbed of', was confined again the following March (again he remembered the exact date). Later he was 'removed into the vagabond house [i.e. Bridewell] to make room for a lunatic' and remained in custody until 1753. He was 'whipped twice in the Hall … for complaining that his things were stolen … [and] is now confined to the walls of the house'. It is a measure of the stigma attached to mental illness at the time that it was considered far more traumatic for a violent offender to be incarcerated with the mentally ill than vice versa. However, judging by Wilson's preoccupation with the alleged slights against him it is possible he was not entirely sane himself. Indeed, Anthony Molloy, the Bedlam keeper, and William Bennett, the writing master, both reported that Wilson had been deemed 'a lunatick'.

It emerged during the enquiry that a serious outbreak of disorder had occurred in 1753 – involving what were referred to as 'Mr Ewing's hackling boys'. As we have seen, contractors could pay the Workhouse 'rent' for the labour of inmates and also for space to carry on their activities within the Workhouse walls. The main activities involved the manufacture of textiles, principally linen. The production of linen was a complex process involving many laborious stages. Hackling was the method of separating the flax stem into separate fibres by dragging bunches of the stems through what looked like an upturned hairbrush whose bristles had been replaced with sharp iron spikes. This was the hackle. The process was repeated with progressively finer hackles until the individual fibres were ready for the next stage.

Mr Ewing supervised the hacklers, who all seem to have been older boys – which is curious, since hackling is neither the most physically demanding, nor the most skilful stage of linen manufacture. Perhaps because the contractors were paying the Workhouse, they could have their pick of the fittest and healthiest workers.

It is clear that Ewing took an interest in the welfare of his workers. Evidence was given that 'Mr Ewing's boys' were better dressed than the others 'because Mr Ewing had made an addition to their clothing'. Also, some of them were better fed than the general workhouse resident because Ewing was in the habit of paying 'premiums' to those who worked well, which they frequently spent on extra food. (We have already seen evidence of an internal economy among both inmates and staff, with children accused of exchanging food rations for china 'taws' and Bridget Robinson selling children's surplus allowances).

It's also clear that Ewing had had disdain for the care provided by the old surgeon, Mr Stone, and his apprentices 'and therefore when they were ill and required care, he made use of his own apothecary, and paid him out of his pocket'. As a result of all this the hackling boys seem to have developed something of an *esprit de corps*. They frequently defied Pursell's discipline and went missing, hiding in the sewers. Stolen goods were also concealed by the boys in the sewers and on one occasion a case of pistols, 'slugs' and a soldier's hanger (a type of sword) were found by staff.

John Allen, one of the hackling boys, was later to give evidence about the 1753 affair. It began one night when some of Ewing's boys broke through a wall in their dormitory into a children's room that adjoined theirs. Allen claimed it was to get water, since 'their work made them very thirsty, and it often happened that one room had water and the other had none'.

When he found out, Pursell had the ten or twelve boys locked up in one of the dormitories, to await punishment. The next morning he sent Fauchey, the butler, and Bennett, the schoolmaster, to escort two or three of the ringleaders to the great hall. But instead of the ringleaders coming peacefully, all ten or twelve boys rushed the door as soon as it was opened and dashed down to the hall. Allen was the first to appear. Pursell is reported to have said, 'Young man, you look as if you was angry.' Allen replied that he thought he had reason 'as he was about to receive punishment for so small a crime'. Pursell then ordered him 'to go to the stocks'. By now Fauchey and Bennett had arrived in the hall. Allen dodged around the tables in the hall to evade capture. Pursell ordered Fauchey and Bennett to seize hold of him. Meanwhile, to enlist whatever male help she could, Mrs Whistler, the housekeeper, had rushed to rouse the apprentice surgeon, Fitzgerald. Fitzgerald arrived in the hall to see Pursell himself grappling with Allen, assisted by the butler, the schoolmaster and the Reverend Mr Hill, all attempting to manhandle him to the stocks. Allen cried out for help to the other boys. One of them, Cullen, grabbed a horsewhip that Pursell was holding and broke it. Fauchey threatened to fetch pistols and this seems to have had the desired effect. The boys offered no further resistance and were escorted to Bedlam for punishment.

Calm having been restored, an hour or two later Pursell ordered the blacksmith to bring a heavy pair of 'bolts', and if necessary to get them from Kilmainham Gaol, which was nearby.[2] The 'bolts', which Allen believed weighed 'upwards of eighteen pounds', were put in place on his legs that day. The next morning, he was brought to the stocks, where he received sixty lashes of a cat-o'-nine-tails on his bare back. He was then ordered to parade around the hall, still wearing the 'bolts' and 'naked' (at least from the waist up) to demonstrate the punishment he had received, and from there back to Bedlam. Two days later he received another sixty lashes and again was ordered to parade around the hall, before the long and painful journey back to Bedlam. The procedure was repeated two days later again, this time with only 'forty stripes'. After a few days he was brought to the hall and the bolts were removed and replaced by a log of wood chained to one leg. Three other boys were punished in the same way. (Unlike John Bishop, Allen – who clearly possessed some leadership qualities – is careful never to implicate the others, or even to name them in his evidence).

As it happened this was a 'Board-day' on which the governors were due to meet in the Tholsel, and word came that Pursell wanted the culprits to appear before the governors. It's likely that Pursell wanted the boys confined in the Bridewell prison or some other more severe punishment, which would require the authorisation of the governors. Pursell ordered that the chains be taken off before the trip by coach to the Tholsel, worried perhaps that too severe a treatment might sway the sympathies of some governors. But the boys refused to have the chains removed, preferring to have the governors witness the nature of their punishment. They were escorted to the Tholsel by Fauchey and Bennett, the schoolmaster, who brought them to the door of the chamber where the meeting was held. Fauchey knocked and Pursell came to the door.

On seeing the boys still in chains he demanded had he not asked them to be removed. Fauchey explained the situation. It seems that on consideration Pursell believed either that the boys' defiant mood or the drama of seeing them confined in chains would upset his plans for the meeting. Shrewdly, he ordered the boys into another room to wait until they were summoned. This was a ruse to prevent an outright confrontation. He now had no intention of calling the boys in but feared that telling them so might provoke trouble. The boys were never called. After the meeting they were returned to the Workhouse in the coach. Although the boys had failed in their attempt to be seen by the governors in chains, they had managed to stymie Pursell's attempt to inflict more severe punishment, which would have required their appearance before the board.

✳ ✳ ✳

All told, the House of Commons enquiry of 1757/8 interviewed an initial sixteen witnesses. But true to form, Pursell fought back strongly. No fewer than twenty-four further witnesses were called 'on his behalf'. Many of these had already been interviewed, and they appear to have been cross-examined on their testimony. William Hawker, for example, a senior member of staff responsible for supervising the tax collectors, testified that 'the affairs of the house were never so well conducted' as they were by Pursell, and that the accounts were better managed than in the time of former treasurers.[3] Thomas Eaton, the unassuming register, reported that Mr Pursell had 'behaved himself very honestly and faithfully' and in his behaviour had 'been regular since he married'. Elinor Jennings, the 'mantua-maker', or dressmaker who had been in the Workhouse throughout the terms of five treasurers, believed 'the food is the same in general as it has formerly been ... and the bread rather better'. She did not think the way the children were corrected was very severe – adding that she had had several things of her own stolen by the female inmates. William Waters, a Kilkenny merchant who supplied the Workhouse, testified about Pursell's probity, and also about the quality of care in Bedlam. He reported that he 'saw one Dowdall, who had been an excise man, and had run mad in Kilkenny, and was sent from thence to the Workhouse, that he appeared to him to have recovered his reason'. Dowdall had informed Waters 'that he was restored to his senses in the poor-house, that Mr Pursell had treated him extremely well, and much better than his friends at Kilkenny had, and desired

[I] would acquaint them of it'. Waters had been 'once in the Hall and saw the children at dinner, and thought the meat and broth very savoury and good, and the children sat regular and in good order at their dinner'.

However, most of the witnesses examined 'on behalf of Mr Pursell' confirmed the earlier negative testimony about conditions in the Workhouse, while also making somewhat unconvincing and vague statements about Pursell's efficiency or lack of severity. Certainly their evidence, as recorded, did little to help Pursell. Allowance must be made, however, for the possibility that the parliamentary clerks were partial in their recording of the evidence.

And what about the testimony of Pursell himself? He was finally, called to give evidence as the last witness. However, after many pages of evidence[4] Pursell's testimony is afforded a single brief paragraph, in which he confirms that the 'whole management of the house is under his care... that many of the children have been without shoes and stockings, for a month and longer, in the winter season ... says he has been absent from the house five or six days at a time, has been in Limerick for five weeks at a time, and by permission of the Governors has been absent in England for eight weeks'. It is difficult to believe that Pursell as we have come to know him would not have had more to say. As mentioned, it is possible that the account does not give a fair reflection of what was said, or possibly Pursell was not given a chance to defend himself fully. Alternatively, Pursell may have been advised to say as little as possible and to rely on the efforts going on outside parliament to undermine the enquiry.

The parliamentary committee had begun its enquiry in December 1757. Almost simultaneously, the governors were undertaking their counter-enquiry into Adderley.[5] They reconvened several times, each time inviting Adderley to submit evidence to substantiate the complaint he, or others associated with him, had made earlier the same year in relation to the spinning school. On each occasion, Adderley either ignored them or declined to appear before them. On 13 January, poor Thomas Eaton was ordered to wait on Adderley in person to inform him of his last chance to make a submission, which Eaton duly did. The restrained language of the official report stated that 'Mr Adderley's answer was that he would not proceed any further', but one can imagine Adderley's response as being a good deal more emphatic. On 23 February, just as the parliamentary committee was finalising its report, a meeting of the Board of Governors found that Adderley's complaint was not substantiated, and furthermore, that he had breached his contract with the Workhouse.

Two days later, Adderley's damning report on the Workhouse, which consisted simply of the witness statements, was read to parliament. Within four days the governors had convened another general meeting, the second in less than a week (when there were normally just four a year). This time they took the extraordinary step of ordering their own report – with its criticisms of Adderley – to be printed, with no fewer than 1,000 copies to be distributed among the public.[6]

Within three days the luckless register, Thomas Eaton, was ordered by parliament to appear not just before the Committee, but in the Commons chamber itself. He was to be questioned before the whole House. He was ordered to bring with him the account books of the Workhouse. Eaton was duly 'called in, and at the Bar examined relative to entries in the said books, and he, by order of the House, read several of the said entries, and then was ordered to withdraw'. Following this the House summoned Pursell to appear before it and set a date for his questioning.[7] But just three days before Pursell was to appear, the Lord Lieutenant ordered parliament to adjourn for a week. There is no record that any new date was set or that Pursell ever appeared to be interrogated by the House.

Five weeks later the House again debated the report, this time outlining its findings and recommendations.[8] Although parliament made seventeen 'resolutions', fourteen of these were effectively 'findings', while only three were actual recommendations. The first recommendation was to consider the ending of the practice of rearing by country nurses, and instead retaining the infants in the Workhouse to be fed by spoon.

Unexpectedly, despite the horrors described by the witnesses, the MPs were actually recommending more children spend more time in the Workhouse and from an earlier age. During many hours of testimony about the appalling nature of the care in the Workhouse, there had been only two brief references to the care by country nurses. The first was Isabel Craig's brief description of her encounter with the two foundlings in Wicklow.[9] The second was foundling clerk Stephen Fauchey's comment that he believed that 'the nurses are mostly, if not all papists'.[10] A clue to the thinking of the MPs is the fact that they single out Fauchey for positive mention – the only one of all the staff and all the witnesses to receive such a mention.

The MPs made no explicit reference to the sectarian motivation but commented that the proposed arrangement 'might under proper regulations, be a

great means of avoiding most of the said mischiefs and inconveniencies, and
preserve the lives of numbers of infants, and may be done at a cheaper rate than
the present', although no evidence, apart from Dr Blackall's passing reference,
had been presented to support any of these assertions. However, time and
time again, the Workhouse was represented in parliament as 'protecting the
Protestant interest' on the understanding that the majority of those admitted
were the children of Catholics, and would emerge as Protestants (whatever
about the accuracy of both assumptions).

The shortage of wet nurses in the Hospital itself was also commented upon by
the MPs, who concluded in their report that this encouraged the 'infecting' of
nurses by diseased children, with consequent spread to all the children. It noted
the inadequate food, the inadequate clothing and the appalling physical conditions in the buildings – but made no specific recommendations to remedy these.
It noted the many deficiencies in the management of the sick in the infirmary
and 'the great danger of breeding a general infectious contagion throughout this
city' due to the 'great stenches and noxious vapours' arising there.

The parliamentary committee chaired by Adderley carefully made no
findings against the governors – many of whom were themselves members
of the House of Commons or the House of Lords. After all, those in the
upper echelons of society formed a relatively small interlinked group. Lord
Lanesborough was a member of the House of Lords, of course, and three of his
brothers were MPs. In fact, the enquiry went so far as to praise the governors'
report of August 1757. They also recommend that 'establishing and supporting
a well-regulated [separate] foundling hospital in the city of Dublin would be
an excellent charity, highly beneficial to the public, and greatly promote the
Protestant interest of this Kingdom'.

They made damning comments about Mr Ewing, supervisor of the hackling boys, and his contract with the Workhouse. This is ironic since Ewing
was one of the few people to materially improve the lives of some of the
inmates. On the other hand, they had no criticism to make, at all, of the
chaplain, Reverend Hill.

Most of the 'resolutions' of the MPs' committee are findings to the effect
that conditions in the Workhouse were just as the numerous witnesses had
described them. When it came to Pursell and his associates, the committee
pulled no punches, however. It referred to the 'mismanagements, frauds and
abuses of Joseph Pursell, Treasurer of said Workhouse, John Fauchey, Butler of
the same, and Mary Whistler, Housekeeper of said Workhouse, and sister to
said Pursell; and that it will be extremely difficult, if not impossible, to remedy
said mismanagements, and bring the house under due regulations, if the said

Pursell, Fauchey, and Whistler be permitted to continue in their respective offices in said Workhouse'.

The resolutions were put to a vote of the House, which found unanimously that Pursell, Whistler and Fauchey 'be removed from their several services in the Workhouse, and rendered utterly disqualified to serve longer there'.

But that was not all that Pursell had to contend with. Two weeks later in the House of Commons, the Chancellor of the Exchequer reported from the Committee of Privileges and Elections. The Houses of Parliament guarded their status jealously and sometimes aggressively. Joseph Pursell had been accused of a breach of privilege against one of the members of the House – none other than Thomas Adderley. The committee had held a hearing to consider the complaint and was now reporting its findings. It found that Pursell had committed a breach of privilege 'by publishing and dispersing a libel against Thomas Adderley, Esq, a member of this House'. The committee ordered 'that the said Joseph Pursell, for his said breach of privilege, [be] taken into the custody of the Serjeant at Arms attending this House'.[11]

It is not certain what the libel 'published and dispersed' by Pursell was, but it was most likely the report printed by the governors that alleged Adderley had broken his contract with the Workhouse. But in any event, Pursell had already disappeared. Within weeks, in May 1758, Lord Lanesborough – who had reinstated Pursell all those years ago – chaired a meeting at which it was recorded that 'Joseph Pursell, Treasurer, hath been charged with many instances of misbehaviour, and hath withdrawn himself, and having been this day called and not attending. Resolved unanimously that he shall be, and he is hereby dismissed.'[12]

The governors later calculated that Pursell had disappeared with £1,200 of the Workhouse's funds – equivalent to thirty years' salary. Later that year the following announcement appeared in the Dublin papers:

Whereas Joseph Pursell, late Treasurer of the Workhouse, hath absconded, and not settled his accounts with the Governors of the said House and is greatly indebted to them. The said Governors do hereby offer a reward of ONE HUNDRED POUNDS to be paid by their Treasurer to any person or persons, who shall, in six months from the date hereof, apprehend and lodge in any of His Majesty's gaols in this Kingdom, the said Joseph Pursell.[13]

A New Broom

On Friday, 4 April 1760, a procession of about 200 boys and girls emerged from the gates of the Foundling Hospital on James's Street.[1] Some of the children may have shuddered as they passed the shabby Bridewell on their right. Built up against the Hospital wall, this was where vagrants and abandoned women were locked in windowless cells – and where errant hospital children had been known to be sent for punishment.[2] They may have heard tales from the children who helped deliver meals to the prisoners, prepared in the Hospital kitchen.

They were familiar with the accents of Dublin – from some of the officers and servants of the Hospital – and its smells, which sometimes came wafting over the high walls. But for most, this was their first sight of the city and their first exposure to the outside world since they had been 'drafted' back to the Hospital at the age of 6. Whatever their parentage and place of birth, these were all country children, reared for their first six years by nurses in the rural parishes of Wicklow and Kildare, and then within the walled environs of the Hospital.

Heading east into the city, the streets soon narrowed and closed in on them. People would have stopped and stared – such a procession was a novelty. Perhaps the children wished that a long-lost parent would hasten forward and draw them from the column, but more likely they longed for a sight of their country nurse, the only mother they had ever known.

At the junction of High Street and Skinner Row, narrow Christchurch Lane fell steeply to their left. On the right they passed the Tholsel, with its arcaded ground floor and its upper floor chambers where the governors made decisions about their lives. Then they wheeled sharply into Werburgh Street and soon arrived at their destination, the church of the same name.

In some ways, the interior resembled the great dining hall, although on a smaller scale, with rows of wooden pews and a pulpit. If some of their stomachs grumbled in anticipation of being fed, today they would be denied even the sustenance of the communion bread, for it was Good Friday. Besides, there were no great tables between the benches, as there were in the Hospital, and when they kneeled, all the children faced the pulpit, not each other across the tables as they did in the great hall.

St Werburgh's church had been chosen for a reason – it was the parish church of Dublin Castle, where the Viceroy and his court attended services. The procession of the children and their presence at that Good Friday service was part of a carefully devised strategy to bring the plight of the Foundling Hospital children to the eyes and minds of the wealthy and powerful. The Good Friday procession was only a herald of what was to come. Reporting of it in the newspapers was accompanied by the announcement that three weeks hence, on Sunday, 27 April, in selected churches throughout the city, a series of charity sermons was to be held for the benefit of the Hospital. And a general collection was to be held 'throughout all the churches in Dublin for the support of the orphans in the Foundling Hospital' on the same day.[3]

The driving force behind this series of co-ordinated events was Lady Arbella Denny, whose name was to be associated with the Foundling Hospital for the next two decades and more. Denny had been born in 1707 to land-owning Anglo-Irish gentry, the Fitzmaurices, in County Kerry. From an early age she combined an interest in the welfare of the poor with an interest in practical science, which she combined in the running of a small apothecary shop for the poor. In 1727 she married a Colonel Arthur Denny. An anecdote told later by her nephew (who served as a prime minister of Britain) gives some insight into her character. Her husband was described as 'a very good sort of man, uninformed and ignorant' but essentially amiable. His brother Sir Thomas Denny, on the other hand, was 'a coward, a savage, and a fool who set himself to make her life unhappy'.[4] He succeeded in this to the extent that she at times felt suicidal. In her apothecary shop surrounded by shelves of potions and decoctions she contemplated overdosing on laudanum. As a precaution she placed it on the highest shelf 'that the motion of going up the step ladder to get at it might make her change so desperate a resolution'.[5] Rather than reveal the ill-treatment to her husband, and cause an irretrievable rift between the brothers, she resolved on her own strategy. She secretly learned to fire a pistol, and practised until she became a good shot. One day, the story went, she invited her brother-in-law to a remote spot, where she demonstrated her shooting proficiency. At the same time she intimated that if his behaviour towards her continued she would not hesitate to use her skill 'by coming behind him, or by the surest means she could invent', regardless of the consequences to herself. The approach, reportedly, was successful and she had no further trouble from

Sir Thomas. Denny's husband died suddenly in 1742, and sometime after this she moved to Dublin. Childless, comfortably off, and seemingly determined to remain single, she travelled widely abroad before returning to the city.

Denny retained an unusual and advanced knowledge of science and technology for a woman of her time. She was particularly interested in textiles, which was the most important manufacturing industry in Ireland at the time. She combined this with a deep piety and commitment to the Protestant faith, which pervaded her work and correspondence.[6] On her return to Dublin she is said to have begun the breeding of silkworms, in the grounds of the seaside villa overlooking Dublin Bay that she purchased and developed. She was the first female member of the [Royal] Dublin Society, the prestigious organisation aimed at encouraging scientific and technological developments in agriculture and manufacturing.

Precisely how Denny's involvement with the Foundling Hospital began is not recorded, but it commenced shortly after the scandal generated by Thomas Adderley's investigation and Pursell's dramatic departure.[7] She must have been well acquainted with Adderley, since they were both interested in textile manufacturing (Adderley also bred silkworms in his County Cork enterprise). They were both acquaintances of the famous diarist and socialite Mrs Delaney. Denny and Delaney visited each other and Adderley was a frequent visitor to the Delaney household, and even lived in their house for a period while they were abroad.[8] In any event, they were both part of a relatively small social elite in the capital at that time.

The children's procession of Good Friday 1760 appears to have been a success, for the promised co-ordinated charity sermons were delivered across the churches of Dublin three weeks later, as planned.[9] The printed text of one of them survives – delivered by the Reverend William Henry, in St Michael's church, in the shadow of Christ Church Cathedral.[10] It lavished praise on Lady Arbella as 'Protectress of the orphans' (even though she had been involved with the Foundling Hospital for no more than a year and a half at that time).[11] To evoke compassion for the foundlings, Reverend Henry reminded the congregation of the fate of Moses – who, after all, was abandoned in a basket – and his importance in divine plans. He recalled the appalling state of affairs that existed in the past when infants were carried from one Dublin parish to another until their misery was ended 'by being devoured by dogs or swine, or trodden to death'. Many thousands had been saved since then, and of these 'several' had become very useful members of society.

Interestingly, Henry pointed out that many of the foundlings were the children of soldiers and seamen 'commanded abroad' (or, in the case of sailors, kidnapped by the Royal Navy and forced to serve in ships with no provision whatsoever made for their families, who were often left destitute.) This was in the middle of the Seven Years War, yet another chapter in the conflict between Britain and France. A large part of the British Army was stationed in Ireland, leading to frequent troop movements in and out of the country, with the inevitable trail of abandoned families left in their wake.[12]

In his sermon, Reverend Henry raised the worrying prospect of the 'orphans' being abandoned to their fate, if left unsupported by charity. For despite its previous generosity, parliament had chosen to award no grant this session. He mentioned more frequent murders of infants being reported of late. He may have had in mind newspaper reports the previous year of an unmarried servant in Cuffe Street who had taken to her bed, apparently ill. Although she had returned to her duties the following morning, she 'from her appearance was fully suspected of having been delivered of a child. After searching her room, they broke open her box and found a newborn infant dead.'[13] Or the case of another unmarried servant, Mary McGrane in Templeogue, who was committed to Newgate prison the same year for 'choking' her newborn child.[14] Or perhaps the case in May of the same year when 'a carman who agreed to transport "a large box"' from Dublin to Kilkenny for a 'well-dressed gentlewoman' was horrified to discover on opening the box, when nobody turned up at the appointed place to collect it, that it contained 'the body of a dead female infant and paving stones'.[15]

Citing examples of famous foundlings from history in his sermon, Reverend Henry went on to say that 'there have not been wanting in this city, instances of foundlings who have excelled in virtue, learning, and every amiable quality; and have amply rewarded the care their country took of them; by continually doing good while living, and at their death bequeathing very large sums to such charitable uses'. The printed version of the sermon indicates that he was referring to the late Reverend Mr Worrall, a friend of Swift's, who, it was claimed, was a foundling and who, on his death, left £200 to the Foundling Hospital.[16]

Even if these foundlings were the children of prostitutes and vagabonds, he went on, they were still deserving of charity. In fact, that may have made them more deserving. But even good parents may 'fall into distress'. Parents of large young families were particularly vulnerable and may not have been able to support them even with their 'utmost industry', leading them to be forced 'to convey them into the Foundling Hospital'. The distress this may have caused to the parents was evidenced by the joy apparent in some parents, who having come into better circumstances, had applied for and received their child back again. (Between 1751 and 1773, 605 children were thus returned – about one in thirty – but only to Protestant parents.)[17]

Reverend Henry then turned to the reports of mismanagement and high mortality in the Hospital. As contributors to the high death rate, he pointed to the inherent fragility of all children, the especially vulnerable health of these children, given their origins, and the rigours of the journey to the Hospital. He implicitly referred to the parliamentary enquiry of 1758 and assured his congregation that improvements had been put in place over the previous two years. All possible care was now taken of the funds and 'in watching over the health and safety of these tender infants. 'What's more, 'everyone who pleases to visit the Hospital, may be fully satisfied by seeing this with his own eyes'.

He ascribed the improvements to 'a lady of very high rank' (Denny is only named explicitly in the dedication at the front of the printed edition) 'who hath condescended to attend constantly to this business, to look into the minutest branches of the children's management ... to suggest many prudent regulations and improvements'.

Reverend Henry then made the following plea, probably at Denny's request: 'Infants are the more immediate care of women. Men are strangers to their wants. This great city abounds with Gentlewomen ... it would perfect their amiable characters if such ladies formed themselves into small societies, and engaged to take it in their turns to make frequent unexpected visits to the Foundling Nursery, so that some of them might see the children, and observe, and report their condition every day.' He ended the sermon by quoting the Bible verse with which this book opens: 'In as much as ye have done this to one of the least of these my brethren, ye have done it unto me.'

However, it is worth reminding ourselves that this call to charity was exclusively for the benefit of children who were to be reared in the Protestant faith. Catholic children, the vast majority of those in the country, were still forbidden by law even from obtaining the most basic education.

There was, though, a broad range of charities active in the city, many of which were blind to religious denomination and actively supported by the Anglican community. These more enlightened and less coercive charities were often more attractive to donors. Examples included the impressive number of charitable infirmaries, and the Lying-In Hospital, one of the first of its kind in the world.

It is unclear how Denny organised a co-ordinated collection throughout all the churches of Dublin. She had, of course, the apparent advantage that 'the minister of each and every parish in the city and suburbs of Dublin' as well as the Archbishop himself, were automatically members of the Board of Governors.[18] No doubt Reverend Tisdall would have been of significant support, if she chose to enlist it. On the other hand, we know of the appalling attendance record of most governors, including the clergy. Most of the governors' minutes do not survive, but a rare survival is the minutes of a meeting on 24 July 1764.[19] There were nine governors present out of fifteen on the Court of Assistants, and only one of these was a clergyman – a Reverend Dr Mann.

Another advantage that Denny had was her connection to the Earl of Shelburne. Denny's brother, John Fitzmaurice, had come into the Shelburne title, and was now the earl. (Later her nephew would assume the title.) This connection is frequently referred to when Denny is mentioned and seems to have carried significant weight. In any event, Denny was adept at maximising whatever leverage she had.

All we know is that the Denny's campaign of procession followed by co-ordinated sermons was a success, and on that Sunday alone £711 3s was raised.[20] Contributions were even made by dissenting congregations.[21] And, regarding tardy contributors, the *Dublin Courier* announced 'it is hoped those who have not yet contributed … will send their benefactions to the ministers and churchwardens of this city for that useful purpose'.[22] (Perhaps this was heeded – by the end of the year the amount had grown to £888 1s 4d.)[23] But if the clergy were hoping to bathe in a warm glow of thanks for their sermonising, there was a mild sting in the tail. The paper went on to say, 'It is wished by many good people, that the clergy of Dublin would take their turn to visit this Workhouse, once a week, which would not be above three times in a year to each.'[24]

In the Hospital itself efforts were being made to deal with Pursell's departure. Pursell had absconded by May 1758 and along with him had disappeared 'the Ledger with several books of accounts in which were entered the Treasurer's receipts and payments', so that the actual state of the accounts could not be ascertained.[25] 'But from a weekly abstract which said Pursell's son sent to the Governors, a balance of £1,703 4s 11 3/4d appeared to be due to the

Workhouse from said Treasurer at the time he so absconded.'[26] As can be seen, the losses ascribed to Pursell's alleged embezzlement had grown. This was an astonishing amount – roughly forty-two years' salary.

Before he fled, Pursell left 'cash and sureties' to the value of £500 with his legal agent, one John Humphries. This was to be used as a settlement in case Pursell's family or guarantors were pursued for the monies owed. Pursell also had an interest in leases on two houses in Capel St to the value of £24 per annum. These assets were handed over to the Foundling Hospital, reducing Pursell's debt to roughly £1,200. This amount lingered on in the accounts until 1773, when it was finally written off.[27]

Parliament carried out a further enquiry into the funding of the Foundling Hospital in 1760.[28] A new treasurer, Henry Hardy, had been appointed shortly after Pursell's disappearance. Ominously, this enquiry, again headed by Thomas Adderley, found that the new treasurer had 'frequently applied to the Governors to have his account audited, but without any effect, whereby the whole account of his receipts and disbursements … remain still unsettled'. It seems that despite the publicity occasioned by the scandals, and despite Denny's high-profile involvement, old habits died hard. On the other hand, the governors might have felt unable to sign off on the accounts because of the crucial missing account books.

On this occasion the only recommendation of the parliamentary committee was that William Hawker, the chief collector of taxes on houses, should have his commission reduced, since he had managed to earn £124 in 1758, a large sum for a person of his rank, and three times that of the treasurer to whom he reported (notwithstanding the 'very great abuse' the collectors had to endure from the householders who paid with 'great reluctance', and that the collection took not less than eight or nine months every year).

Another unresolved matter was that of the physicians' salaries. The elderly Dr Knox had died in August 1758 without ever getting paid for his work.[29] The issue of the doctors' pay had first been raised in parliament in April 1758, presumably at the behest of the doctors themselves, when it had been found that they had 'never received any recompense' for their labour.[30] It was recommended that they should each be paid £80 per annum. Knox's successor, Dr Clement Archer, along with Dr Edmund Blackall, petitioned parliament again in November 1759, still having been paid nothing. But their petition got nowhere.[31] In October 1761, the physicians once more petitioned parliament.[32] Despite evidence that the death rate had decreased since the physicians had been attending the Foundling Hospital, the petition backfired. The parliamentary committee appointed to respond to the various petitions regarding

the Foundling Hospital did a little research. They found that the governors
had passed a resolution back in 1757 stating that the physicians were to attend
'without fee or reward'.[33] This appeared to be a definitive end to the question,
but in 1763 the physicians again petitioned parliament, citing the significant
reduction in the death rate as well as the parliamentary recommendation of
1758 to pay them £80.[34] This time parliament again found in their favour, and
that they were owed £720 between them. Difficulties in payment continued,
however, for another enquiry in 1771 found the physicians had not been paid
since 1769.[35]

Early on, Denny addressed the feeding of the infants in the nursery. These were
babies recently admitted and awaiting country nurses, or else considered too
ill to be placed out. Wet nurses or 'milch nurses' were difficult to find, so that
recourse was made to feeding by the spoon. As we have seen, spoon feeding of
infants was fraught with danger. (Although the 1758 committee had recommended it as safer and cheaper, and it reduced the chances of having to rely on
Catholic nurses). One extraordinary innovation introduced by Denny was to
have a special longcase or 'grandfather' clock installed in the nursery.[36] On the
clock was inscribed the following: 'That as children reared by the spoon must
have but a small quantity of food at a time, it must be offered frequently, for
which purpose this clock strikes every twenty minutes, at which notice all the
infants that are not asleep must be discretely fed.'[37]

In addition her younger cousin, Miss Catherine Fitzmaurice, with whom
Denny lived for much of her life, invented a 'most useful Bottle, resembling
a human breast' which apparently proved so successful that the governors
rewarded Miss Fitzmaurice with the presentation of 'a gold box, with proper
emblems and inscription'.[38]

It is not clear exactly by what method Denny exercised her undeni-
able influence over the Foundling Hospital. She was not a member of the
Board of Governors. She seems to have addressed meetings of the governors
occasionally, but not frequently. It was stated that the 'Officers and Servants'
were ordered to observe her instructions.[39] No such order appears in the
'Rules' of 1758 or 1774. However, an extract from the governors' minutes of
3 October 1774 reveals the following: 'Ordered: that the officers and servants
be ordered to obey the directions they may receive hereafter from the Right

Honourable Lady Arabella [sic] Denny as they formerly did under the late Corporation, so far as shall be consistent with the bye-laws and regulations of this Corporation.'[40]

It appears she suggested to the governors that 'a number of influential ladies' should visit the Foundling Hospital regularly, and this happened initially, but for whatever reason 'it was Lady Denny alone who persevered'.[41]

As well as her work outside the Hospital to raise its profile, she became deeply involved in its day-to-day operations. She was involved in the selection of the nurses to work there, and 'encouraged them to carry out their duties efficiently and kindly'.[42] One innovation was the offering of monetary rewards – 'premiums' – to nurses both in the Hospital and in the country parishes to care for sick and weakly infants. The premium was awarded when the children were found to be well cared for.[43]

By 1764 parliament was lavishing praise on Denny for her 'particular and constant attention ... to every article relative to the management of the said children' and that it was being 'conducted in the most exact and proper manner'. And 'that by the extraordinary care of the nurses in the Workhouse, excited by premiums given by the right honourable Lady Arbella Denny for retrieving such of the infants as are sent thither weak and sickly, many of their lives have been saved'.[44]

The two physicians, Archer and Blackall, in the ongoing saga over their sala-ries, had earlier submitted mortality figures for the infants. In the years 1756 and 1757, they reported, 1,748 children had been admitted, of whom 920 died (a 52 per cent mortality rate), whereas from 1757, when they had started, to March 1761, 3,503 had been admitted, of whom 1,285 had died (a 36 per cent mortality rate).[45] They claimed the entire credit for this improvement. However, in an earlier report the Foundling Hospital staff had attributed the improvement both to the physicians 'and the nurseries being frequently visited by an honourable Lady'. The physicians 'attended at the Workhouse month about, on Mondays and Fridays'. The Treasurer reported 'that the physicians never refused to attend, [but] cannot say that they were ever sent for [outside of these occasions]'.[46]

The year 1764 was a busy one for Denny. The children continued with their public processions and Sunday, 22 April saw them as far afield as St Thomas's Church off Marlborough Street, in the north-east of the city, where they 'made a very decent and pleasing appearance'.[47] The following day, Lady Northumberland, wife of the Viceroy, 'honoured the Workhouse with her presence'.[48] She visited the infant nurseries and different schoolrooms 'and had the goodness to express the highest approbation and satisfaction at the order and regularity of every part of the House'. Two days later it was announced that the Viceroy was donating £100 'towards fitting up a chapel in the Workhouse'.[49]

Momentum towards building the chapel continued to accelerate. In July, the governors recorded a vote of thanks to Dublin City Corporation for the donation of £100 for the building fund.[50] They also had a plan drawn up for the building.[51] In August Thomas Eaton, the register, was advertising for carpenters, plasterers and other workmen to begin the work.[52] A chapel might not strike modern eyes as the most immediate of the children's needs. However, it is consistent with Denny's deep commitment to her faith and belief in the benefits it would bestow on the children. In addition, it would play an important role in fund-raising for the charity, since potential donors could be invited to charity sermons, sometimes given by 'celebrity' preachers, an approach taken by other charities.

Meanwhile, the children continued their treks across the city. In May more than 200 of them proceeded to Dublin Castle, where they paraded in the Castle Yard, overseen by Lord and Lady Northumberland. There 'a new shilling ... was given to each of them, by order of His Excellency'.[53] If they were allowed to keep it one can imagine the excitement such a gift might have caused the children – to be spent perhaps on china 'taws' or additional food. Such gifts from the British administration based at Dublin Castle were not always as generous as they seemed, however. They were often paid for from the Irish Treasury – even when seemingly given in a private capacity.[54]

December 1764 saw the children parading to St Peter's Church, where they 'made a very decent appearance handsomely clothed in green turned up with scarlet'.[55] This is a reference to the uniforms introduced by Denny in 1762.[56] These were green with red collars and cuffs.[57]

In 1760, at the start of Denny's reign, the Workhouse and foundling hospital contained 268 children, who had been reared by nurses in the country and had returned to the Hospital at age 6, as well as 139, mostly adults, who had been admitted as 'distressed objects' including 'lunatics and idiots'.[58] Over the coming years the pattern of admissions was to change drastically.

By 1764 the numbers of children under 14 in the Workhouse had increased to 456, while the number of adults and those over 14 had reduced to sixty-seven. This was a trend that the governors, probably on the advice of Denny, wanted to see continue. The petition to parliament that year lamented the lack of separate provision for 'lunatics and idiots' and the 'aged and feeble poor of this city'. St Patrick's Hospital had begun accepting patients from 1757 but its numbers were limited to about fifty.[59] This was clearly inadequate and the Workhouse continued to experience pressure to admit people in these categories. But there was a growing awareness of the desirability of housing children separately from adults. Similarly, the 1764 petition recommends that 'beggars and vagabonds' should be sent to Bridewell rather than the Workhouse itself, and noted that the children are 'carefully educated in virtuous and Protestant principles'.[60] The MPs found that the Workhouse was unable to accept 'common beggars as a former Act directs' because of lack of space and finances. However, they recommended against any expansion, in order to prevent 'persons of dissolute and corrupt morals' from being 'admitted under the same roof with young children, trained up in innocence, industry, and virtue' and recommended that 'no additional buildings ought to be made for the reception of such persons'. This was despite the fact that, as ever, there was pressure for something to be done about the perceived scourge of beggars in the city. The MPs also recommended the building of a chapel 'for the more decent performance of divine service' and noted that the Workhouse had become 'an Hospital for Foundlings' – the first time parliament had used that term.

As well as addressing the conditions of the infants, Denny also sought to increase the employability of the older children when they left the Workhouse. In the case of girls she appears to have introduced the teaching of lace-making. This was the delicate skill of making 'bone lace' – so-called because the trailing ends of the ten or more individual strands of lace were each weighted by a piece of bone, as they were interwoven to form intricate patterns.

But perhaps the biggest impact Denny had on the Workhouse, for better or worse, was the significant increase in parliamentary funding of its operations. For its first five decades the Workhouse had relied on income from the tax on houses – amounting to roughly £2,700 p.a. at this time – and the licences and fees for vehicles – roughly £1,400 pa.[61] In 1753–54 parliament granted directly, for the first time, an additional £2,000. But this direct grant had not been repeated until 1760, when £4,252 had been awarded (although it is worth noting that in 1760 it was reported that the British parliament granted £40,000 to the London Foundling Hospital).[62] From then on, parliament made a grant in every session (roughly every two years), and in gradually increasing amounts, so that in 1765 it granted £6,750, in 1767 £9,599 and in 1769 a staggering £12,945. We know Denny was adept at using her influence with senior figures in securing substantial commitments. For example, in 1761 she successfully solicited the Duke of Bedford to secure a direct grant of £1,000 from George III.[63]

In 1770 Denny was visited by her favourite nephew, Lord Shelburne, along with his wife and eldest son, who stayed with her at Peafield Cliff.[64] Early the following year, however, Lady Shelburne died suddenly in England. Denny decided to travel there to supervise the rearing of Shelburne's children. Despite this she continued to be active on behalf of the Foundling Hospital. By 1771, as well as the chapel, 'an additional infirmary' had also been built at a cost of £1,129, raised by voluntary subscription, largely it seems under Denny's influence. Now although 'in another Kingdom', Denny remained active on the Hospital's behalf, procuring 'further aid by means of which this infirmary is almost furnished with beds and bedding'.[65]

Indeed, the degree of Denny's personal, detailed involvement in the day-to-day affairs of the Hospital even when abroad, is demonstrated by a letter written by her in May 1772.[66] In it she describes strenuous efforts to have the lace manufactured in the Hospital incorporated into the commercial sales channel (the Silk Warehouse) on an equal footing with other manufacturers, and even gives detailed instruction as to how the merchandise is to be presented.[67]

Denny considered the training that the girls were getting in lace-making as equivalent to an apprenticeship to a trade, with the hopes of providing a secure future income. However, in her letter, she seems a little defensive on the issue of the remainder of the girls' education:

> The girls engaged in the lace school I looked on as so many bound to a trade they were to get their bread by. They were therefore instructed in no other business except to work with their needle enough to know how to make their own linen and mend their clothes, and for this and to learn to read and write they had time in each day allowed by me, and this Mr Bradish [the treasurer] knows.

Later in the same letter she returns to the theme of education, again indicating her pervasive influence in the Hospital: 'I did write rules for the education of the children as well as I was able, and the book Mr Bradish has.'

Some of the girls graduated to becoming 'mistresses' in the Workhouse, training other girls and receiving a wage. It is clear Denny had an intimate knowledge of recent developments in the Workhouse, for she refers to recent events involving two girls named Bloomer and South, who had had 'fits'. It is worth quoting at length from this letter as its breathless style and attention to detail give some hint of Denny's character:

> By hearing that they are sick (I mean Bloomer and South) I fancy the prospect of their being on the 25th of March raised to be Mistresses, and put on wages and out of the uniform of the house has not been executed, and that the disappointment has disheartened them and that the fits are from low spirits, at least I hope so; it would be shocking to have any mortal overworked, and bad policy too. As I promised that advantage to them, I wish it to be performed, as it will give life to all the rest, by raising their expectations … I believe there are at least twelve of the girls in the lace school who have had each ten guineas premium from the Dublin Society so these girls are Heiresses of no small account, an advantage which has not been afforded to any other school, and as a reward to them for their not being [bound] out (which the poor innocents think to be getting liberty though they were to be made kitchen maids of). So to make these girls patiently bear the scheme formed for their advantage, as it was hoped they might by their lace making be taken as school mistresses, or by ladies to make lace at home, this money was dedicated for their use, as it might get them husbands in some of the lower trades. I left it in alderman Hunts hands in Debentures, that it might gain a little by my care of it.

The legislation levying taxes and registration fees on the carriage trade enacted in 1745 had only had a twenty-five-year lifespan. Parliament, once again failing to make timely provision, allowed it to expire in 1770. As a result 'no owner [of a carriage] or carrier of a sedan chair has taken out a license, whereby an annual loss of £630 has accrued'.[68] A direct grant had been given by the king amounting to £6,030. However due to the 'extraordinary increase of children received' the Hospital needed more. Far from being dismayed by this increase in numbers, in their petition to parliament in 1771, the governors presented it as proof they were pursuing their mission of 'strengthening the Protestant interest amongst the lower ranks'.[69] By which, of course, they meant strengthening the status quo, which maintained their own position of privilege. As a temporary measure, parliament again agreed to support the petition and granted £10,000 (while at the same time granting £15,000 to the Incorporated Society for promoting English Protestant Schools in Ireland).

But there was by now a recognition that the Workhouse and foundling hospital was no longer fulfilling the original, and long subordinated, aim of the charity – ridding the streets of Dublin of vagrants and beggars. At the same time there was, as we have seen, an awareness of the undesirability of housing such people with impressionable children. All these issues led to the enactment in 1772 of the first substantial legislation dealing with the Workhouse and foundling hospital since 1745.

The 'Act for better regulating the Foundling Hospital and Workhouse in the city of Dublin'[70] for the first time officially uses the name 'foundling hospital' in legislation, in keeping with the transformation in the function of the institution, but lagging far behind the public. A new corporation was formed: 'The Governors of the Foundling Hospital and Workhouse of the City of Dublin'.

Under the legislation, vagabonds were no longer to be sent to the Foundling Hospital but to Bridewell or other prisons. The treasurer's salary was to be increased to £150; the register's to £60. At last, by law, the two attending physicians were to be paid £80 each, ending that long-running saga. All poor children under 6 'taken up' were to be housed in the Foundling Hospital or sent out to nurse. By law the children were to be raised in the Protestant religion. With the approval of the governors they could be apprenticed 'by indenture to Protestant trades or seafaring men, or as servants'. Every such indenture was to contain 'a covenant, that every child so apprenticed, shall be instructed, educated and brought up during his apprenticehood in the Protestant religion'. This tightening of legislation to ensure continued Protestant observance by the children, even after they left the Hospital, in fact reflected a practice that was already ongoing.[71]

In the same year, 1772, parliament finally acted to make a separate provision for the adult poor, by creating the House of Industry, just as had been suggested in the 1764 petition to parliament.[72] This was a completely separate institution, which was, in effect, a workhouse. As the original workhouse was now almost completely given over to its function of foundling hospital, the recurrent pressure to rid the streets of what were described as 'hordes' of adult vagrants and beggars had continued to wax and wane. The new legislation was to deal with the usual categories of 'idle vagabonds' and 'sturdy beggars' as well as the poor 'disabled by old age or infirmities', ironically replicating the original role of the Workhouse. The project was to be managed by a new body separate from the governors of the Foundling Hospital. Under the Act, vagabonds were to be set to hard labour and beggars could be punished in the stocks or by public whipping.

This freeing up of the Hospital to allow it to concentrate exclusively on its child-rearing function was yet another endorsement by parliament of the political and religious aims of the institution. It was also another affirmation of Denny's role in the Hospital, but, as we shall see, there were some who took a far more sceptical view of her involvement.

A Christmas Visit

One winter's evening in 1772, Oliver Hely made his way through Dublin to the Workhouse on the western edge of the city. It was Christmastime and Hely had dined in town. He must have imbibed freely during dinner for, as he later admitted, he 'came home with a mind relaxed from every sort of care; with a disposition … incapable of injuring mankind' and in an 'imbecile state'.[1] Hely was apothecary to the Workhouse, and home was the apartments where he lived there with his family – on-site residence being both a requirement and a perquisite of the job. This Christmas evening he found a message waiting for him on his arrival.

At the time the post of apothecary in a hospital was usually a residential one, and required the holder to attend the rounds of the physicians and surgeons, to record in ledgers their instructions regarding drug treatments and diet for each patient, to supervise the preparation of the various decoctions, tinctures and pills, and finally to ensure that these were correctly administered by the nurses – no easy task given the often bespoke nature of the treatments, and the untrained nature of the nursing staff. A different but more common job for an apothecary, however, was as a sort of community doctor, to the poor and 'middling sort', for whom a physician, or even a surgeon, would have been unaffordable. Hely's post in the Foundling Hospital was the former, but he evidently combined his duties with the latter role.

While Hely had been out, a John Dennison had called twice, seeking assistance for his child, who was very ill. Dennison was servant to Major Butler, one of the governors. Hely duly attended the child. Perhaps because of his self-confessed 'imbecile state', the conversation turned to a preoccupation of Hely's – Dennison's employer Major Butler, the governor. Hely hinted at a corrupt relationship between Butler and the senior officers in the Workhouse. What, Hely pointedly asked Dennison, 'connected his master so much to the Treasurer?' Did it arise, he wanted to know, 'from his obliging him in money matters?' Hely later went on to accuse Major Butler of 'borrowing the Workhouse money to build houses with'.

The Honourable Major John Butler was one of the Butlers of Lanesborough who had been prominent in the affairs of the Workhouse since its inception. He was, in fact, a younger brother of the Lord Lanesborough who had chaired the 1744 meeting that heard the complaint of the seamstress Margaret Hayden. In addition to being a major in the British Army, he was also MP for Newcastle.[2] These were slanderous insinuations Hely was making, which were to have a dramatic effect on Hely himself. But in the process they allow us to glimpse an alternative view of the Workhouse to the one presented by Denny and her supporters.[3]

For this was not the first time Hely had criticised the state of affairs in the Workhouse. In October 1772 he had written to one of the governors, Dr Robert Emmett.[4] In addition to being a governor, Emmett was the state physician, and physician to St Patrick's Hospital, where he exercised a progressive influence. Hely had attended one of the governors' meetings, where he had been impressed by Emmett's 'resolution, and his extraordinary powers of speech'. Hely perceived Emmett as being 'intent on establishing ... a general reformation' of the institution.[5] 'Penetration seemed perched upon his brow,' he later wrote, and, 'I was exceedingly pleased to see a physician develop measures that I imagined very few were acquainted with except myself.'

In his letter to Emmett, written within months of Denny's letter quoted in the previous chapter, Hely paints a completely different picture to that presented by Lady Arbella.[6] For one thing, he claimed that the 'set of factories, established in 1762' had resulted in a drastic reduction in children being apprenticed out. Hely's insinuation was that the children were being retained within the Workhouse for their labour, in order to profit certain individuals. This, he claimed, was why the number of children living in the Workhouse had increased from 300 to 'near one thousand' and why the Workhouse was no longer able to survive on the taxes from houses and vehicles but needed huge funds from parliament. And this was why five, six and even eight children had to share one bed 'while spacious rooms are taken up with useless factories'. He also maintained that people who applied to take children out as apprentices met delays and obstacles, even if they were governors. He cited how at one stage Lord Glerawley had proposed taking on all the children aged over 10 in the Workhouse as apprentices, and that this had been approved by an order of the General Board, but that this order had been rescinded by the Court of Assistants because of a fear that the children 'would be brought up Dissenters'.[7]

Hely also lamented the lack of attention being paid to the children's education, it being neglected in favour of work in the factories. While they were called periodically from their work to attend lessons, these were given hurriedly by people little better educated than themselves, before the children immediately returned to their labour. The children were kept sitting eight or ten hours a day at their work so that 'our children do not look as well, are neither as tall nor as active, as the children of any other institution that I have looked into'. Hely questioned the whole viability of the lace-making enterprise: 'How ridiculous it is to persevere in the lace manufacture, when there are seven hundred pounds worth undisposed of?' He thought it was equally ridiculous to see boys 'who should be learning to read and write, [instead] learning the Canterbury Method of spinning of worsted … or that manly exercise, the knitting of stockings'. (Echoing John Vernon's criticism of half a century earlier.) Hely also alleges that the supervisors of the factories had a direct incentive to prevent the children from leaving since they received 'emoluments' from the work.

But it was his astonishing allegations against the treasurer, Wheaton Bradish, which were the most stark. He alleged that 'it has long been the misfortune of this institution to be managed by a person [Bradish], who on every occasion, sought only his own emolument, however the charity might suffer'. Hely claimed that the crisis caused by the expiry in 1770 of the legislation allowing the Foundling Hospital to collect taxes on vehicles had been manipulated by Bradish for his own personal gain. The charge was that Bradish failed to pursue the defaulters, thus encouraging others to default, in order to force parliament to enact new legislation, with the collateral benefit to Bradish of an increase in his salary (since the treasurer's salary was set down in the Act). Bradish 'sacrificed the whole carriage revenues for two years, in order that some pretext might be assigned for framing a new Act of Parliament; whereas the chief reason was to obtain a large salary for himself, to make himself more absolute, if possible, than before; and, finally to prevent the rest of the officers from getting any reasonable compensation for their trouble'. Hely was correct about the salary increase – it had in fact gone up from £60 to £150 in the new Act of 1772.

According to Hely, Bradish's self-interest prevented him from highlighting 'the miseries the factories brought on this institution', which included 'debauchery, repeatedly; the loss of limbs etc'. In all, Hely charged, Bradish's actions had cost the public purse 'upwards of thirty thousand pounds'.

As a result of his Christmastime encounter with Butler's servant Dennison and his representations to Dr Robert Emmett, Hely claims he 'incurred the implacable hatred of Major Butler'. He accuses Dennison of perjury and of being in cahoots with the treasurer 'who had him frequently, late at night, in his apartments' in the Foundling Hospital.

There is no doubt that Major Butler's dignity was highly offended by the allegations. There was a subsequent encounter between him and Hely, which led to Butler accusing Hely of 'insolence', although Hely claims Butler insulted him with an 'opprobrious epithet'. However, this was a contest of unequals – a lowly apothecary against an MP, the brother of an earl, and scion of a family that held vast estates, the levers of political power and lucrative sinecures for lesser members of the family at the expense of the Irish treasury. The Butlers were also associated with another proselytising organisation – the subsequently notorious Incorporated Society for the Promotion of English Protestant Schools in Ireland. Major Butler was a paid-up member, and his brother, Lord Lanesborough, chaired meetings of the Society.[8] This was at a time when many Protestants were embracing more liberal causes.

Hely was promptly dismissed – for 'insolence' and for accusing Major Butler of corruption. The dismissal process would probably have involved an appearance before the Court of Assistants or General Board, where Hely claims Butler acted as 'a judge, an advocate, and a juror'. After five years at the Foundling Hospital, Hely was sacked 'depriving my poor family of their subsistence' ... 'in the middle of winter' – and probably of their residence as well.

Several months later, a seemingly reckless Hely unleashed his vitriol against Butler in the newspapers, describing him as 'a despicable minion and a disgrace to an illustrious ancestry'. 'How happy it is,' he mockingly wrote, 'that his influence, his authority, and that degree of weight he derives from an illustrious ancestry, are circumscribed by the boundaries of a Poorhouse!' Hely's only crime, he declared, was to try to protect the Foundling Hospital from 'the impregnable stupidity of my persecutor [Butler]; the extravagancies of virtue in an amiable Lady [Denny]; [and] the ignominious bondage of a weak unsupportable tyrant [the Treasurer]'. The extraordinary thing was that Hely made these insults publicly in a newspaper, without even the use of a pseudonym. Had Hely not been so lowly born the affair might have ended in a duel. However, since he was not considered as belonging to the 'gentleman' class such a course would have been beneath Butler. Instead, Butler had the satisfaction of knowing Hely's career was ruined.

But what of Hely's allegations? At the start of the 1760s, as we have seen, there were 268 children in the Workhouse and roughly 1,000 with country nurses. By 1771 the numbers of children in the Workhouse had climbed sharply to almost 900, with nearly 3,000 in the country. Those in the Workhouse were looked after by sixty 'nurses and servants' and six 'officers'. While Denny's efforts had resulted in significantly increased funding, swelling numbers meant debts were rising even faster. By now a staggering £6,287 was owed to the country nurses, while £4,109 was owed for provisions for the Hospital itself.

By 1773 the picture was even more stark. There were now 1,000 children in the Workhouse, but that does not tell the whole story, since the number given is for 6- to 12-year-olds only, whereas the previous figure given to parliament in 1771 was for nearly 900 6- to 16-year-olds. Either there had been a vigorous effort to discharge all the older children in view of the ballooning numbers, or the governors were deliberately obfuscating, perhaps at last aware that the huge increase in numbers might cause alarm among their parliamentary benefactors.

In November that year, as if in response to Hely's allegations, the parliamentary committee charged with the usual scrutiny of the Foundling Hospital's business, went out of its way to praise Bradish, the treasurer, as 'a good and useful officer to the said charity' who had 'kept his accounts in a very clear, exact and regular method'. But it was not until December that a more detailed rebuttal of Hely's criticisms appeared. Again, the vehicle was a letter to the *Hibernian Journal*.[9] The anonymous writer is supportive of Denny's reforms but hints that these are being diluted or overturned – although without providing specific information. The letter is masterful in its use of biting sarcasm and scorn, while avoiding the temptation to be diverted by Hely's personal libels on the treasurer and Major Butler.

As if in response to Hely's criticisms – but more likely in response to the alarming increase of children in the Hospital – the numbers sent out as apprentices jumped suddenly in 1774 and 1775 to an average 326 for each year, compared to an average of forty-four per annum for the previous ten years. Other measures later adopted included lowering the age of children accepted to no older than 1 year in 1775–76 legislation and at some point between 1775 and 1779, raising the age at which children were drafted back to the Hospital to 8 years.

But Hely's were not the only criticisms of the Hospital. In April 1773, an anonymous complainant in the *Hibernian Journal* claimed that 'the chaplain does not read prayers above twice a week, though he ought to do so twice a day; and that he does not read the burial service over the dead above once in a fortnight, by which means the orphans lie in the dead room till they are eaten by the rats, or taken away by the surgeons [for dissection]'.[10]

Whether these complaints were motivated partly by some personal ven-
detta, or based purely on genuine concerns, is not clear but it does seem that
the Hospital was going through a period of upheaval. So much so that in
1774 the governors produced a new set of 'Rules, Ordinances, Bye-Laws and
Regulations' in response to what they called 'the anarchy and want of good
government which prevailed in the Hospital for many months, during the year
1773 and part of 74, making some plan of regulation absolutely necessary'.[11]

Denny's influence on the new rules is clear – in one area direct reference is
made to her Magdalen Asylum as a model. The proselytising mission of the charity is emphasised – as if that were necessary. For the first time it is stated explicitly
in the rules 'that no person be employed as an officer, or servant … who is not
a Protestant' – the only exception being for nurses in the infant department,
where presumably their influence on their charges would be negligible.

Particular attention is paid to the apothecary's qualifications. No apothecary
is to be 'hereafter elected without being first examined and approved of by the
physician, and who has served a regular apprenticeship to a regular Protestant
apothecary in the City of Dublin, and can produce a certificate from said master,
of his service, abilities and good behaviour during his said apprenticeship'.

Interestingly, the rules lay down that 'no child who has been apprenticed out
be ever taken back into the House on any pretence whatsoever'. Denny had
put in place a system whereby 'apprentices' were recalled to the Hospital every
three months to attend Divine service and afterwards to be examined in 'the
principles of the Christian religion', supervised by Denny herself. The children
had to bring certificates of good behaviour from their master or mistress. The
treatment of the children by their masters was also supposed to be examined,
but there appears to have been no formal mechanism for this. If they had
been found to be mistreated, in the past they had sometimes returned to the
Workhouse, but this new rule would seem to preclude this and is at odds with
Denny's assertions that the welfare of the apprentices was protected. Perhaps it
hints at tensions between some of the governors and Denny.

For the first time, the tattooing of the children, which had been the practice
since 1736, is referred to in the rules: 'To have the children, when admitted,
numbered by a separate mark for each year, that is to say, all the children admitted from the 24th of June 1774, to the 24th of June 1775, be marked with the
letter A and No. underneath, beginning with No. 1, and in the succeeding year
to be marked with the letter B and numbered in like manner, beginning with
No. 1 and so on with the other letters of the alphabet successively each year.'[12]

Just as the arrival of the infants at the Hospital was systematically recorded,
so the departure of those less fortunate was to be subject to a similar orderli-

ness. The porter, who was responsible for interments, was instructed 'to bury the dead, beginning at the N.E. corner, and digging regularly to the N.W. corner, along the north wall, keeping three feet, at least, from the foundation of the wall, and when one row is finished, to begin another as above directed, and to take care to have the graves closed immediately after every interment, and each burial day to ring the bell, to give notice of the interment'.

Turning full circle from the 1758 Rules, emphasis was placed on the primacy of the treasurer among the officers, with the 'authority to inspect, regulate and report the conduct of all the other Officers and servants'.

Denny returned to Ireland in September 1774, from her sojourn in England supervising the care of Shelburne's children.[13] Within a couple of weeks she was personally supervising the religious examination of apprentices (Lady Butler and Lady Westenra having stood in in her absence).[14] Soon a garden nursery was created on ground behind the Workhouse, and the governors advertised for sample plants to be supplied by gentlemen from their own estates.[15]

A visitor to Dublin a few years later described, after a Sunday stroll around town, following some well-dressed people into the great hall and finding himself 'in the midst of a large company of healthy looking children of both sexes, some of whom had the appearance of more importance than the rest, being distinguished by medals hung by orange-coloured ribbands; the boys who had these had also a white wand in their hands, and seemed to act in the stile of magistrats; the girls as little matrons'. At the ringing of a bell 'all this pleasing assembly marched in great order to the chapel'. He found all to be 'complete order and repair; a large convenient nursery for the reception of infants until put out to nurse, most elegantly neat and clean … a new infirmary for acute diseases, detached from the House and lately erected by voluntary donations.' And, outside, 'a large piece of ground laid out as a nursery for trees, flowering shrubs etc. for sale'.[16]

In spite of minority voices like Hely's, the general impression among the public was that things had improved significantly at the Hospital, and in some areas they had. Infant mortality in the Hospital itself seems to have improved significantly. Wodsworth – apparently based on the governors' minutes – reports that an infant mortality rate of 48 per cent in the Hospital from 1750 to 1760 had improved to 23 per cent for the years 1760 to 1770.[17] As we have seen, in the 1763 petition to parliament by the physicians Blackall and Archer,[18] they reported that a mortality rate of 52 per cent for 1755 and 1756 had improved to 36 per cent for the period 1757–61, an improvement that they ascribed to their own interventions, while others also credited Denny.[19] Remember, however, that these figures only cover the brief period (a matter of days or weeks, depending on circumstances) when the infants waited in the Hospital for dispatch with country nurses. The survival rates for children at nurse in the country were not given during the period of Denny's involvement. They had, however, been given at times before this – for example the 1737 figures indicated an 84 per cent mortality rate.

For the later period, however, it is possible to calculate the figures indirectly. For example, in June 1773 there were 1,000 drafted children aged 6 to 12 in the Hospital. If these children were aged 6 to 12 in 1773, then they had to have been originally admitted from 1761 to 1767. We have the admission figures for these years: 5,939. Only 1,000 of the 5,939 – 16.8 per cent – were drafted back to the Hospital, leaving 83.2 per cent unaccounted for.

We also know that prior to Denny's involvement, for the nine and a half years from March 1750 to September, 1760, 7,382 were admitted while during the same period only 1,336 were 'drafted',[20] a rate of 18 per cent, leaving 82 per cent unaccounted for, almost exactly the same amount as under Denny's reign. A variety of approaches can be used to roughly calculate the survival rate over the period 1750 to 1773 but the rate always works out as approximately 15 to 20 per cent. In fact, for the entire period of twenty-two and a half years, of 19,618 admitted, only 2,978[21] returned to the Hospital (15 per cent), leaving 16,640 dead or missing. And indeed this tallies closely with the reported survival rate from 1737 (16 per cent). On these figures, Denny's involvement had made no difference.

If not dead, where might these 16,640 children be? Could they have been adopted by childless couples? It is possible some might have been 'adopted' and no doubt this happened on occasions, but it is unlikely to have been on a large scale among what were the poorest of the poor, with competing mouths to feed. There was no shortage of children, and in poor communities no shortage of relatives and neighbours willing to give up children to be reared by others, therefore it is unlikely that childless couples would have to turn in large numbers to the Workhouse for children. In addition there was a stigma associated with the Workhouse child that might further reduce the likelihood of this – a stigma that could not easily be forgotten, at least in part because of the lifelong branding the foundlings bore on their arms.

It is also possible that children were retained for their labour. Contemporary accounts, however, suggest that 6-year-old children were seen as having relatively little economic value in terms of their labour, and employers often had to be paid to take on children so young, since the value of their labour did not cover the cost of their food and clothing.[22] There are anecdotal reports of children being used as beggars to attract sympathy, sometimes after being deliberately maimed, but there is no evidence this took place on a scale large enough to account for over 16,000 – or a significant portion of them – in twenty-two years. There were also reported incidents of children being abducted for transportation to the Americas to serve as indentured labourers, but it is estimated that these amounted to no more than several hundred over the course of half a century.[23]

The most likely fate of these children, other than death, was that they were 'retained' by their nurses out of 'bonds of affection'. However, the Hospital's own accounts for 1773 indicate there were only 338 such children – that is, children whose nurses were registered as due a payment but who did not present for payment, even after the Hospital advertising.[24] This averages approximately fifty-six children per annum unaccounted for, out of over 1,000 admitted per annum – or approximately 5 per cent. All other children are satisfactorily accounted for in the eyes of the Hospital – 15 to 17 per cent returned to the Hospital while 78 to 80 per cent are presumably accounted for as dead. If the 5 per cent unaccounted for all survived, the survival rate would therefore be 20 to 22 per cent. If, however, as seems more likely, they died in equal proportion to those accounted for, the survival rate calculates as 16 to 18 per cent, and consequently the mortality rate as 82 to 84 per cent.

And what of the children after they returned to the Hospital? In the entire twenty-two-and-a-half-year period, of the 19,618 admitted, only 967 were 'apprenticed' – fewer than one in twenty. A smaller number, 605, were 'discharged and given to protestant parents'. None were given to Catholic parents. And finally, of 3,849 children aged over 6 who were either drafted during the period or (a smaller number of 485) admitted directly from the streets, 1,331 died,[25] indicating a death rate among the older children of 30 per cent after they had returned to the Hospital. Taking this latter figure into account brings the overall mortality rate of the children entering the Hospital as infants, during this period, to between 85.3 and 89.3 per cent with 11 to 15 per cent emerging alive at the end of the process, only one third to one half of whom were 'apprenticed'.

★ ★ ★

The year 1778 seems to have been something of a crossroads for Denny's involvement with the Foundling Hospital. The governors' minutes contain a formal resolution enumerating her works and pleading with her to stay on[26] – suggesting that she had indicated she wished to retire from her role. And her biographer reports that she stepped down from her role in this year.[27] However, in July the governors published a resolution in the newspapers giving their 'unanimous thanks … for her obliging compliance, with their request that she would be pleased to continue her most useful care and attention to the management of the House'.[28] And certainly she continued her role in examining the religious knowledge of apprentices.[29] And as late as 1782 she is recorded as hoping to attend the quarterly examinations – although not to conduct them herself – and present silver medals to the ten best candidates.[30] It would hardly be surprising if Denny had reduced her involvement, given the scale of the task and the continuation of the high death rates.

It is debatable also, how successful her other main intervention was – that of training girls in the textile trade. Hely, in his vitriolic letters, had referred to the accumulation of unsold bone lace in the Workhouse. We have seen what efforts Denny had to go to get the lace sold through the Silk Warehouse, and in the accounts of 1775 it is notable that the output of the children's manufactory is listed by quantity rather than value.[31] Economic conditions and the state of the textile trade no doubt contributed to this and must have also seriously hampered the employment prospects of those children who had so industriously perfected their skills. If Denny had been a lesser woman, it would hardly have been surprising had she been worn out by disappointment.

In 1778, at the request of the governors, Denny gave an account of all the money she had raised or personally contributed to the Hospital, which amounted to £4,190.[32] But this was dwarfed by the funding being provided by parliament. As we have seen, this was little or nothing before 1760, rising to over £12,000 in 1769. While funds from parliament increased dramatically, the income from the tax on vehicles was to end in 1787.[33] The income from charity sermons had only ever been negligible, with perhaps 1761 being the high point,[34] and never amounting to more than a few hundred pounds a year after that.[35]

Part of Denny's strategy had been to raise the profile of the Hospital. On the streets, in church congregations, in the newspapers that were distributed beyond Dublin, the Foundling Hospital was discussed as never before. And the message was a positive one. It was a 'worthy charity'. It was improving. It offered safety and hope to countless children. It was endorsed by churchmen and gentry as a noble institution. It is hardly surprising, therefore, that desperate young women increasingly saw it as a solution to their plight, and that the number of admissions increased.

And increase they did, from an average of under 1,000 a year at the start of Denny's involvement, to nearly 2,000 by 1783.[36] But there was a fatal logic underlying the project that few seemed to have realised – or, if they had, they remained silent about it. If even half the children now being admitted every year survived their initial brief stay in the Hospital and their subsequent time in the country, to return that would mean 1,000 children being drafted every year. Even if a child only stayed six years until age 12, that would mean there would be 6,000 children living in the Hospital at any one time. And to keep the numbers as low as this would require obtaining a thousand new 'apprenticeships' for 13-year-olds every single year – when the average up to 1773 had only been forty per year. It's difficult to imagine that this granddaughter of Sir William Petty, member of the Dublin Society and enthusiastic 'improver', had not done these calculations – for the Foundling Hospital project to remain viable, infants had to die in large numbers.

As we have seen, Denny, through a combination of unremitting activity, attention to detail and simultaneous action across multiple fronts, was able to profoundly affect the Foundling Hospital. Apart from the Viceroy, she was able to influence parliament, the Board of Governors and the Archdiocese of Dublin, all of them unwieldy, male-run political entities, and seemingly bend them to her will. Her connections to Lord Shelburne, and the wider elites in both Ireland and Britain, were a significant advantage, one that she exploited vigorously. She was widely admired, not to say venerated,[37] during her lifetime, yet there were some contemporaries willing to cast a cold eye on her 'extravagancies of virtue'.

But what was her ultimate legacy? In 1760, just as the processions of children navigated the busy junctions of the city, so the Foundling Hospital had been at something of a crossroads. Just as Denny was beginning her involvement in the Dublin Foundling Hospital, a disastrous four-year experiment at its London equivalent was coming to an end. In a period known as the 'general reception', that hospital had admitted all comers, just as the Dublin institution had always done. In 1760 the British parliament brought the scheme to an end, appalled by the spiralling costs and death rate.[38]

In Ireland, it appears, the mission of the Foundling Hospital was considered too important to allow a similar change. Undoubtedly well-meaning, Denny allowed her name to be closely and publicly associated with the Hospital, greatly enhancing its public acceptability, enabling its viability through 'reform', helping to prolong its life and swelling the numbers of children who passed through its doors, to meet whatever fate awaited them.

A Letter from the Matron

On 4 April 1797 Mrs Alice Hunt, matron of the Foundling Hospital, addressed a letter to the governors.[1] In terms laden with deference she outlined her concern: the infants arriving at the Hospital doors were dying in even greater numbers than before. The difficulty, she respectfully suggested, was in recruiting sufficient numbers of country women to act as wet nurses. She pleaded with the governors for help.

The reason for the scarcity of applicants was clear to Mrs Hunt: 'the rumour of the threatened invasion'. For the past few months rumours had been sweeping the country that had shaken the confidence of the wealthy in the banking system and of the poor in the likelihood of receiving their paltry wages.[2]

There was good reason for some to fear and others to long for the invasion to which Mrs Hunt referred. Britain had declared war on revolutionary France in 1793, but the war was not going well. In December 1797, just three months before Mrs Hunt composed her letter, an invasion force of over thirty warships and 14,000 French troops had set sail for Bantry Bay in the south-west corner of Ireland. They had arrived on a fair wind and all had boded well for an unopposed landing. The force merely had to wait a day or two for the arrival of their commander, General Hoche, whose ship had become separated from the main fleet. In the course of two days, however, the wind had changed and the fate of Ireland along with it. A storm blew up that had scattered the fleet and ruined the chances of a landing. The fleet had limped back to France in scattered groups.

Rather than despairing, however, those in Ireland who had hoped for the success of the invasion seemed to draw more hope. If the French had been prepared to throw so much into the enterprise, then surely they would come again. The United Irishmen were organising and arming themselves with renewed vigour. Raids were carried out on private houses for the purpose of acquiring weapons.[3] Government forces responded with equal vigour, and even brutality. Pro-government newspapers incited violence against suspected United Irishmen.[4] A few days before Mrs Hunt sat down to write her letter, a detachment of Dragoons had arrived in the north.[5] These heavy mounted troops were to be used against the civilian population to instil terror. Ships departing from Irish ports had been ordered to sail in convoy to deter French attacks.[6] Meanwhile, fears of (or hopes for) another invasion had shattered the complacency of the ruling elite and given hope to those who longed to overthrow them.

Mrs Hunt, who although matron of the Hospital, had the status only of an upper servant, framed her letter as a 'humble petition' to the governors, addressing them as 'your honours'. So concerned was she about 'the number of infants which are daily dying in this Hospital' that she urged the governors to write to every relevant parish minister and to have printed notices circulated throughout the parishes to reassure potential wet nurses that if they applied for work, they would get paid.

She also raised another issue: since the infants were not being put out to wet nurses they were being sustained only with 'panada', which was little more than bread soaked in water, with a little flavouring added. She tentatively suggested that something more nourishing would be required. She did not specify the number of children who had died, nor did she refer to any long-standing problems in the Hospital.

The governors may have been alarmed by Mrs Hunt's letter. They may also have been in receipt of additional information of concern. Whatever the cause, a delegation of five governors was dispatched within a few days to inspect conditions at the Hospital. The conditions they found there, during their visit on 11 April, as described in the prologue, were to set in train a series of events that would lead to a national scandal and accusations of murder on an almost unimaginable scale.

One day after this visit, Sir John Blaquiere rose to address parliament.[7] Around him rose the benches of the House of Commons, its opulent chamber rising to a magnificent dome 60ft overhead. From a lofty gallery, visitors could peer down, between columns, at the drama in the chamber below. The Speaker, through whom Blaquiere addressed the House, sat on a richly adorned and canopied dais, in a long white wig and elaborate robes, his golden brocade reflecting the light from above.

Constitutionally, Ireland was a sister kingdom to Britain, sharing a king but with its own Houses of Lords and Commons. In reality, political control lay with the British Cabinet in London that ruled Ireland in England's strategic and economic interests. The Anglo-Irish often chafed under this rule, in which their economic interests were subordinated to England's. But their dreams of greater independence were trammelled by a fundamental problem. For their fear of the Catholic majority was greater than their resentment of English interference. Catholics, though forming at least three-quarters of the population, at that time were still excluded from power. Inevitably, politics was dominated by the Anglo-Irish.

A group had emerged, largely from the ranks of the Anglo-Irish Protestants, but allied where possible with Ireland's Presbyterians, and with whatever nascent political organisation the Catholics had. This group saw Ireland's future as an independent nation, where Catholic, Protestant and Dissenter would live in equality. They saw no prospect of achieving this through the existing political structures. They believed that Britain would never allow this. Like the Americans prior to the revolutionary War of Independence, they had gradually come to the opinion that Britain's stranglehold could only be loosened by military force. Abandoning parliamentary means, they had organised themselves into the Society of United Irishmen. As they swelled in numbers the tension grew between those who favoured immediate revolution and the more cautious. In response, military activity was increasing. Infantry and cavalry units patrolled the city at night. Units of part-time soldiers performed military exercises and manoeuvres in Phoenix Park, enthusiastically supported by Blaquiere.[8]

Today, however, he focussed on other matters; rising from his seat, he called the attention of his fellow MPs to a subject that he feared 'would excite in the House as much horror in the hearing, as he felt in the recital', namely 'the abuses which prevailed in the Foundling Hospital'.[9] He reminded the House that he had raised the issue some years previously, without success.[10] He had been approached again, he said, some days ago 'in the interests of humanity'. He pressed on his listeners the gravity of the situation and urged them to action.

Blaquiere had arrived in Ireland as a landless and relatively obscure outsider.[11] Born in 1732, he was the son of a French Huguenot merchant who had emigrated to Greenwich, England. His first job was in a London merchant's counting house but in 1759, perhaps tiring of a sedentary life, he purchased a commission in the British Army and became a major in the 18th Dragoons.

He rose through the ranks, becoming a lieutenant colonel by 1763, no doubt again through purchase, as was the norm. Around this time his regiment was stationed in Ireland. Here, the social affability and skilful self-promotion, which he was to polish to a high art in his career, first became evident, and he became friendly with Earl Harcourt. After Harcourt was made English ambassador to the French court, he was sufficiently impressed with Blaquiere to bring him over to France as his secretary, in 1771.[12] At the French court, Blaquiere proved invaluable to his patron, including, it was rumoured, by spying on the pretender to the British throne, Prince Charles Edward – Bonny Prince Charlie.[13]

When Harcourt was appointed Viceroy to Ireland in 1772, so confident was he in Blaquiere's abilities that he made him Chief Secretary – a remarkable elevation for a man with little experience of politics. If the Viceroy could be considered the king's proxy in Ireland, then the Chief Secretary was his Prime Minister. The Viceroy represented the king and ensured Ireland was governed in Britain's interest. Dublin Castle was the seat of the Viceroy, his Chief Secretary and the British administration in Ireland. Given the constant tension between the Castle and parliament – where Anglo-Irish interests could clash with purely British interests – the role of the Chief Secretary was to ensure the Castle retained a majority in the Irish parliament and to shepherd legislation through the House of Commons.

As Chief Secretary, despite his lack of experience Blaquiere quickly rose to the challenge. He proved himself adept at using the main political tools of the time – patronage and 'places' – what today we would see as outright corruption. Even for the times, Blaquiere practised corruption so audaciously that he inspired widespread mistrust, even among his friends. It was said that the chief benefactor of Blaquiere's largesse was Blaquiere himself. For example, at one point he was made 'Bailiff' of the Phoenix Park, the vast estate on the edge of the capital. This post was typical of the 'places' that were one of the chief tools of political patronage. These were posts with obsolete or redundant functions, often dating from the Middle Ages, but with salaries attached, funded by the Irish public purse. In this case there was a small salary of £40, a modest house and grounds, and the right 'to graze cattle' in the park. Not content with this, Blaquiere quickly increased the stipend to £500 per year, a respectable amount. But this was merely the beginning. Feeling the need for a gentleman's residence to match his status, Blaquiere annexed 62 acres of the park for his own use, and greatly expanded the house, at the cost of £8,000 to the public purse, a stupendous amount for the time.[14] So grand was the edifice that the government subsequently bought it from Blaquiere to use as the residence of all future Chief Secretaries (and it remains today a landmark building – the residence of the ambassador of the United States to Ireland.)

In another spectacular coup, in 1775 Blaquiere acquired the position of Alnager. In the 1600s the Grand Alnager of Ireland had been responsible for checking and certifying the quality of woollen cloth. One may assume that Blaquiere had never examined any cloth, except perhaps for his own clothing; nevertheless, the position came with a salary of £3,000 per annum for life – a substantial fortune for the time, and one that Blaquiere was subsequently able to pass on to his son and heir.[15]

Requiring, as a gentleman, a country seat, Blaquiere purchased a property in County Westmeath. This was a mansion in a beautiful wooded demesne overlooking Lough Owel, a richly stocked trout lake, only 50 miles from the capital and a few miles from the prosperous county town of Mullingar. The estate was named Port Loman after the sixth-century ascetic saint, but Blaquiere, with an impressive indifference to the ancient Irish heritage of the area, renamed it Port Lemon. Here he entertained lavishly, no doubt on the public purse where possible, and where not through mortgaging his legacy.

Some 14 miles away lived the famously eccentric Richard Lovell Edgeworth with his daughter, the novelist Maria. They must have met socially, for Blaquiere is said, somewhat scurrilously, to have been the model for the lavishly convivial and notoriously spendthrift Sir Ulick O'Shane in Maria's novel *Ormond*.

Following his brief but immensely profitable period as Chief Secretary, Blaquiere had continued as a member of the powerful Irish Privy Council, and as an MP. He invariably supported the pro-British Castle faction, notwithstanding a role in the reform of the prisons in the 1780s. As an MP he opposed the admission of Catholics to the political process in the 1790s and was a supporter of aggressive military suppression of dissent.

Such was the man who had risen to address the House, and on whom depended the fate of the foundlings. Now, furnished with the report of the deputation who had visited the Foundling Hospital, he reminded the House that he had raised the issue some years previously, without success. At that time, 'such facts as had come out had astonished and appalled every man who had heard them,' he stated. Cleverly, he reminded them that in relation to the past proceedings there was a 'report upon their Journals' i.e. a published account – what we would now call a 'paper trail'. This should act as an incentive for action, he implied, if compassion and the horror of what he was about to relay did not.

Two of the most powerful members of the House, the current Chief Secretary, Thomas Pelham, and commissioner Beresford in support, 'called on him to move instantly for an enquiry'. This he duly did and a committee was convened to 'enquire into the state and management of the Foundling-hospital'. As a sign of the seriousness of the matter, the committee was to sit 'notwithstanding any adjournment of this House'.[16]

Even two hundred years later, what this committee uncovered still has the power to shock.

14

A Dangerous Journey

Although it was called College Green, there was not a blade of grass nor a leaf to be seen. Its wide expanse was bounded on one side by the college, with its seeming hundreds of windows, on bright days glinting in the sun; on the other, parliament, its entrance shaded amongst the cool pillars of its deep portico.

The staff of the Foundling Hospital, summoned to give evidence, would have climbed the steps between these great columns. Mrs Hunt the matron, who by now may have been regretting her letter, and Annslie Bailie, the register, along with other staff members would have entered a great hall called the Court of Requests, before proceeding through enfiladed arches, down corridors floored in chequered marble, to the committee room where they were to be questioned.

Within two days of Blaquiere addressing parliament, the committee of enquiry had begun its meetings, probably in one of the rooms set aside for that purpose to the west of the Commons chamber. The committee rooms were grand spaces, 20ft in height, richly upholstered in green damask, and lit from above by glass domes – not spaces where servants would feel at home. From the outset the committee was sparsely manned – just three or four MPs showed any interest. Blaquiere was the chairman and almost certainly did most of the questioning. The other regular attendees were his older and eccentric brother James, referred to as Colonel Blaquiere; David La Touche, the ultra-wealthy banker; and Richard Annesley, a fellow member of the Paving Board.[1]

It seems the first witness to be examined was Annslie Bailie, the register and effectively second-in-command at the Foundling Hospital. Bailie had taken over the role from his father five years earlier, having assisted him for about two years before that as 'coadjutor' while the latter was ill.[2] The role of register was central to the running of the Hospital, requiring a detailed familiarity with all the activities of the organisation, and keeping records of these. Especially important to the inquiry was the register's responsibility for recording all admissions to the Hospital, and all subsequent information relating to each child's course through the institution. Another crucial aspect of the role was the register's attendance at the governors' meetings and the taking of minutes at these. As one of the few permanent staff attending these meetings, and with his detailed knowledge of the Hospital, Bailie would have been in a key position to influence the agendas and manage their outcomes, given the haphazard and inconsistent nature of the governors' attendance and their likely very superficial knowledge of the institution. In a sense, the role of register could be very much what the incumbent wanted it to be, and was no doubt influenced by the personality of the post holder. To all appearances Bailie seems to have been unassuming, punctilious and rather lacking in imagination.

He was first asked about the number of children admitted in the quarter-year ending on 'Lady Day', 25 March, 1797.

'Five hundred and forty as per Returns,' came Bailie's reply.

'How many have died in the Hospital in that period?' he was asked, probably by the chairman, Blaquiere.

'Four hundred and fifty-four.'

'What number have been admitted and have died since the 25th day of March last?'

'From the 25th of March to the 13th April instant there were one hundred and sixteen admitted, and one hundred and twelve died.'

'Do you know the reason of this extraordinary mortality in this period?'

'I cannot give any reason for it; but have heard from the matron that the causes were the nurses not coming up for the children, and the food not being sufficiently nourishing.'

Bailie was asked how many infants had died in the quarter up to December 1796.

'Two hundred and seventy three,' he answered.

The committee pointed to an 'anomaly'. Bailie was required to notify the Foundling Hospital governors of the number of deaths at the end of each quarter. But instead of notifying them of 273 deaths, he had informed them of just three. Asked to account for this, he explained that 273 was the number of infants who had died, but that three was the number of those who were over 8 years old.

'How comes it that no notice is taken in the printed account sent to the governors … of the two hundred and seventy three Infants who have died in the Hospital in that quarter?' he was asked.

'Because it was not in the form that was handed down to me.'

The committee then pointedly asked Bailie how long he had held the office.

'I was appointed coadjutor with my father 22nd May 1790 and elected 7th April 1792.'

'In that period have you ever made any return in the quarterly accounts to the Governors of these deaths?'

'I have not.'

Following these revelations, and after answering some more questions, Bailie was allowed to stand down.

* * *

Next to give evidence was Mrs Alice Hunt, the matron, who may have set things in motion by her letter of 4 April. (Her daughter, *Miss* Alice Hunt, was the deputy matron.) Mrs Hunt lived in the Hospital and according to another member of the staff she lived 'on the same floor with the children, and if she hears the cries of any of them she goes out immediately to assist them'. However, these were likely to have been older children sleeping in the dormitories of the main building, not the infants in the nursery and infant infirmary.

It was the matron's role to receive the newly arrived infants from the porter, who brought them from the gate. Previously, Mrs Hunt had given testimony about the extraordinary mode of arrival of some of the infants at the Hospital. They were often brought either on foot or by 'car' – heavy wooden flat carts whose two wheels were made of solid wood. As to their condition on arrival, 'three are frequently brought in the skirt of one woman's gown, sometimes living and dead together. At other times seven or eight are brought up together on a car, some of them dead, and so bruised and flattened that it is imagined that the person who has been intrusted with them has sat upon them'.[3]

On another occasion she reported that 'two cars arrived yesterday from the town of Galway with eleven children, one of them dead, three dying, and in short but two of the number likely to go out' (i.e. survive to be taken on by country nurses).[4] She had also revealed that, of sixty-four children received in the previous five days, twenty-five were already dead.[5] A journey from Galway to Dublin on an open cart pulled by an ass or donkey would have taken at least seven days. With five or six infants on each cart, tended by one woman who likely also drove the cart, how could they have been fed?

Now this new enquiry was going over the same ground.

'Can you give any reason why there is such a number of deaths in the Hospital in the last quarter?' Mrs Hunt was asked.

'Many have died for the want of nurses,' she replied. She had 'heard that the nurses were afraid they would not be paid on account of the landing of the French, and therefore would not come up'.

'Are the children that came up from the country in as bad and unhealthy a condition as when you gave your examination before a committee in the years 1791 and 1792?'

'They are as bad now; they cannot be worse. In winter the children are brought in in a worse condition than in summer.'

'Are those that were brought in in the last winter worse than those who were brought to the House in the preceding year?'

'They are much in the same condition as those of the former year.'

The committee then enquired about the nutrition of the infants. They asked Mrs Hunt a leading question: whether she thought a better diet would have saved lives. In this they probably wished to build on her letter to the governors, which they had clearly seen. Mrs Hunt duly obliged: 'I believe it would,' she answered.

When asked what she would have given the infants by choice, Mrs Hunt, seemingly unambitious when it came to their diet, replied, 'I would have given a little wine or broth.' Not as a 'common food', she hastened to add, but only 'when the children come in in a weak state'. Mrs Hunt confirmed that she had brought her proposals for 'a little wine or broth' – strictly for the weakest infants only – instead of the habitual bread soaked in water, to the attention of the physician and surgeon, who 'neither approved or disapproved of it'. She had also brought it to the attention of governors, although individually when they happened to visit the Hospital, and not to the Board.

Next to give evidence were the porter, William Kellet, and his wife, Elizabeth. Based on records of wages paid, Elizabeth was one of the lowliest members of the Hospital staff, with a salary of just £2 10s per year for assisting her husband.[6] Part of her job was to 'receive the Children at the Gate and bring them to Mrs Doyle the head nurse; she carried them sometimes to the matron, but oftener to Mrs Doyle'. For each child her husband gave a receipt to whoever had delivered it to the Hospital. This was the case for infants delivered from country parishes, whose carriers required the receipt to obtain payment from the parish. It did not apply to infants deposited anonymously, principally from the Dublin area.

William Kellet's other role was that of grave digger. There were three regular 'burying days': Monday, Wednesday and Friday. The burials took place after the older children had gathered for morning prayers in the great hall between seven and eight o'clock in the morning. If a child died after 'the burying hour' on a Monday, it would 'be kept 'til the next burying day'. Burials were never carried out on other days. Kellet also gave evidence about some infants who had arrived the day before his appearance. One of them had come from Roscrea and was 'in such a wretched state that it appeared more like a liver than any human thing'. He reported burying up to thirteen children in one day.

✳   ✳   ✳

Within twenty-four hours, Blaquiere stood again in the chamber of the House of Commons to report progress.[7] He complained that the committee of enquiry 'was so thinly attended, that little good could be expected from their labours, unless gentlemen would condescend to attend a little better'. He updated them on the mortality figures and added, 'If gentlemen did not think these facts sufficiently enormous to call for inquiry and redress,' he hoped 'that they would release him from the mortification of sitting in the chair of a committee without members, and [that] after having promised so much support, and given so little, they would rescind the order for the inquiry, or attend to give it effect.'[8]

Then his brother, the colonel, rose and 'having dwelt with much force on the enormity of the abuses prevailing in the institution', reported how 'a woman who had been executed at Cork, had confessed herself the murderer of ten of these children'. And there was evidence from another woman, 'that the children died in such numbers from the want of food and necessaries'. In response, the Chief Secretary Thomas Pelham, at this stage still supportive of Blaquiere, agreed that a committee of the whole House, not just of certain members, would be convened.[9]

Outside parliament, military activities continued apace. On 17 April, Easter Monday, there was a large show of force in the Phoenix Park. Infantry corps and troops of cavalry paraded and engaged in manoeuvres in different areas of the vast park.[10] Militia troops patrolled the city at night. The papers also described fighting between the Armagh militia and civilians in Monaghan, during which six civilians were killed.[11]

The Nurses Speak

In the committee chamber the questioning of staff members continued. When Mrs Mary Doyle was asked, 'What is your employment?' she answered, 'I am counted Head Nurse,' as if she were unsure of her role, and relied on others' description of it. Or perhaps she was in an 'acting' or unratified position – although she had 'attended' the infant nursery for 'six years last June' at a salary of £8. As we have seen, nurses at the time were untrained attendants, merely servants who worked with the sick or dependent. As evidence of their status, the infirmary nurses, on wages of £3 10s per year, were paid less than half the porter's wage.[1] In addition to payment they were provided with accommodation, in the dormitories and infirmaries, where they slept with the children, and meals – taken either in the great hall or the nursery, depending on the age of the children they were looking after. They probably also still received a quantity of cloth annually from which to make their own clothes.

There was a stipulation in the regulations that the ordinary nurses had to be able to read and write, mainly so that they could follow and administer the prescriptions of the physician, surgeon and apothecary. However, it is not clear to what extent this was enforced. There is some evidence that many of the nurses were in fact older girls from within the ranks of the foundlings, in which case they would probably have taken up their duties at the age of 15 or younger.

Mary Doyle gave some further details of the transport of infants to the Hospital, prior to their coming under her care. Contrary to popular belief, at this time the vast majority of infants were not deposited anonymously at the Hospital. Mrs Hunt had testified that this happened 'not so often as one in a fortnight'. In fact, the majority arrived with a 'certificate' from the Anglican clergyman of their local Church of Ireland parish (regardless of the religion of the parents) stating the name of the child – whose surname might be that of the father or the mother, or neither. It was usually the parish that arranged for the transportation of the child to Dublin, if it was born outside the capital, acting in many ways as an arm of local government.[2]

Now Mary Doyle testified that 'sometimes the children are stripped on the road by the person that brings them up'. She knew this because 'there is a note sent with the children specifying the clothes sent with the child'.

'Does the physician attend regularly at the Hospital?' Doyle was asked.

'He does. Mondays and Fridays,' she replied.

'Mention the person whom you call the physician?'

'Surgeon Woodroffe.' Either nervousness had led her to confuse the titles, or, despite her role as head nurse, she did not have a clear grasp of the distinctions between the roles of physician and surgeon.

'Is there no other physician attends the Hospital but Surgeon Woodroffe?'

'None, except him or some person who attends for him.'

'Does Surgeon Woodroffe or some person for him regularly attend every Monday and Friday?'

'In general they attend. They might have missed some days.'

'Is the surgeon sent for on any other days but the attending day?'

'He is not to the infant side of the house.' She had 'nothing to say to any other part of the house'.

'Do you know Dr Harvey? How often does he attend?'

'I never saw him [in] the infant nursery.'

As we have seen, the infant nursery and infant infirmary were located in the same building, set slightly apart from the main buildings, with the infirmary being the 'dark and gloomy apartment' seen by the visitors on 11 April.

'How long have you attended the nursery?' Mary Doyle was asked.

'Six years last June.'

'Do you know anything of the state of the children who are sent into the infirmary upstairs?'

'The children are stripped and other clothes put on them when they are sent to the infirmary.'

'Before a child is sent to the infirmary, who makes the report of the state of the child?'

'Surgeon Woodroffe, and sometimes the matron if she sees it very bad.'

'Did you ever know Surgeon Woodroffe or any other person [on his behalf] go to the infirmary after the children are sent there?'

'I do not know. I do not attend that department.' Doyle's work was clearly confined to the nursery as opposed to the infirmary.

'Do any children ever return after they have been sent to the infirmary?'

'Never in any one instance.'

The Foundling Hospital, Dublin. (With permission of the National Library of Ireland)

Propoſals for the Taking in Boys into the King and Queens VVork-Houſe in Strand-ſtreet near Capel-ſtreet, Dublin, agreed on by the Maſter, Officers, and Senior Workmen of the ſaid Houſe.

1. They muſt reſolve to be conformable to the Rules and Laws of the Houſe, during their abode there, otherwiſe they muſt be dealt with as ſturdy Beggars and Vagrants are uſed, by the Authority of the Government.

2. They muſt be Bound to *John Collis* for ſeven years at the leaſt, or till they be twenty three years old, if they reſolve to be Preferred to farther Employments in the ſaid Work-houſe.

3. Their Parents or other Diſpoſers of them, are to give with them, Three new Suits of Apparrel; (*viz.*) three Frocks, three Coats, three pair of Breeches, three Hats, ſix pair of Stockings, ſix pair of ſhooes, ſix Cravats, ſix Handkerchiefs, ſix Shirts, a Bible, a Knife, a Comb, a Thimble, a Porringer or like diſh, and a Penner. Not that theſe muſt needs be given on their Entrance, but it's to be underſtood, before the ſaid *John Collis* will be at any charge on them for theſe things; and after the Receit of the ſaid Apparel, the ſaid *John Collis* will provide for them during their ſtay in the ſaid Work-houſe.

4. That at their coming into the ſaid Houſe, they are to give to the Stock of the ſaid Houſe, a piece of Plate to the value of twelve Shillings at leaſt, but more if they pleaſe, with their Names Engraved on it, which Plate they are to leave behind when-ever they leave the Houſe.

5. That this Admittance is by Auction, and no Bidding for any Boy to be leſs than 5 *l.* and riſe what they pleaſe at each bidding; and of all thoſe that expect to Enter, they that bid moſt, are the perſons that will be only taken in.

THE POOR HOUSE

John Collis's *Proposal* for a workhouse on Strand Street, Dublin (1690)

The Workhouse as depicted in 1728 on Brooking's map. (With permission of the National Library of Ireland)

The Royal Barracks , Dublin, across the river from the Workhouse,
and begun around the same time, would eventually become the
largest in Europe. (With permission of the National Gallery
of Ireland)

Christchurch Cathedral before its nineteenth-century renovation.
(With permission of the National Gallery of Ireland)

THE
C A S E

Of the Foundlings of the City of Dublin; *humbly recommended to the Confideration of the* Parliament.

T HE Cafe of the Foundlings or expofed Children in the City of *Dublin*, is very deplorable : The Law has provided, that they fhould be maintained by the refpective Parifhes, in which they are found, by a Cefs to be levied upon the Parifhioners in Veftry, in Proportion to the Minifters Money, and in fome Parifhes they are honeftly maintained as the Law directs.

But in many Parifhes, to avoid the Expence of this Cefs, Care is taken to have the Children lifted out of the Parifh where they happen to be dropt into other Parifhes, by which Means they often Perifh : Or if they furvive, the Parifhes into which they are lifted, are burthen'd with more Foundlings than belong to them ; which is no Doubt, the Reafon why fome Parifhes have a vaft Number to maintain, while others, who are more careful to avoid the Cefs, have very few.

Besides the Lifters of thefe Children from Parifh to Parifh, for Fear of being difcover'd put *Diacodium*, or fome other unwholefome Stuff, into the Mouth of the Children to doze and ftupify them, that they may not by their Crying, alarm their Neighbours, and detect the Lifters. This appear'd lately before the Committee of the Houfe of Lords, and, by this Means, Children are often poifon'd to fave Charges.

It has alfo appear'd before the faid Committee, that in one Parifh of this City, and that a very fmall one, the Parifh-Nurfe, who was retain'd by the Parifh at 3 l. a Year, did, by the Direction of the Church Warden, lift out of the faid Parifh no lefs than 17 Children, and when fhe was asked what fhe did with them ? Her Anfwer was, that fhe run them into St. *Paul's* Parifh.

A   But

A shoe Boy at Custom-House Gate?

The Case of the Foundlings of the City of Dublin (1730)

A Dublin shoe-boy c. 1760. (Courtesy Churchill House Press/Irish Georgian Society)

Tholsel, Dublin (1793)

The Tholsel, meeting place of the governors of the Workhouse and Foundling Hospital.

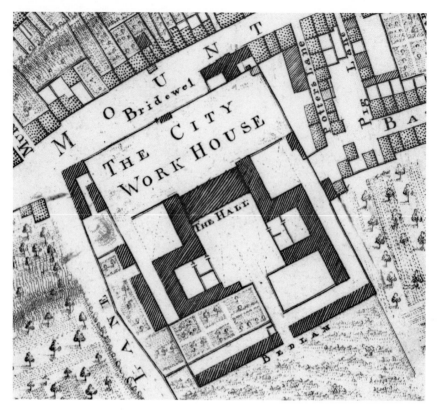

A detail from Rocque's map of 1756 (the year after Emy French died) showing the location of Bedlam. Note the gardens adjacent to the Bedlam yard, into which Emy allegedly threw stones. (Courtesy of Andrew Bonar Law)

One of only two known contemporary depictions of the Dublin foundlings. Taken from the seal of 1749. (With permission of Dublin City Library and Archive)

The seal of 1772 showing a female foundling. (See endnote 57, p. 247 for details of dress.).

The east wing of the Foundling Hospital, where the officers' apartments were located. (With permission of the Irish Architectural Archive)

The old Irish Parliament. (With permission of the National Library of Ireland)

Entrance to the Parliament, with Trinity College in the background.

This building to the west of the main building may have been the site of the infant infirmary in 1797. (Courtesy of the Bureau of Military History)

The entrance to the previous building. (Courtesy of the Bureau of Military History)

L'Allaitement des Nourrissons par les Ânesses à l'Hospice des Enfants Malades.

Direct feeding of infants from asses, Hospice des Enfants Malades, Paris, nineteenth century. (Courtesy of the Wellcome Collection)

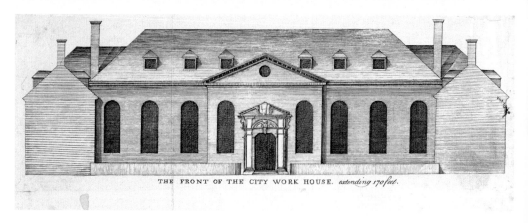

THE FRONT OF THE CITY WORK HOUSE. *extending 170 feet.*

The Workhouse and Foundling Hospital in 1762. (With permission of the National Library of Ireland)

Elevation of part of the former Bedlam drawn *c.*1797 by Francis Johnston. Note the visible relieving arches indicating the presence of cellars. (With permission of the Irish Architectural Archive)

The Foundling Hospital in 1803. It shows the side ranges which are excluded from other illustrations. (With permission of the Irish Architectural Archive)

*   *   *

When Catherine Maquean was sworn she described herself as 'nurse over
the sick infirmary' and testified that she had been in that role for seven years.
As we have seen, she, along with one other nurse, Esther Wiggan, most likely
provided all the care the very sickest infants received. It's worth contemplating
how two women, unaided, could carry out even the basic tasks of feeding and
toileting, day after day and night after night for that number of supposedly sick
infants. Perhaps in recognition of what must have been one of the grimmest
jobs in the Hospital, their wages were marginally higher than the other nurses,
at £4 per year. One wonders what attributes meant that they were considered
suitable for such a role.

Unlike the previous nurse witnesses, Maquean appears to have been unmarried. There is no clue as to her age but when the surgeon, John Creighton,
visited the infirmary in July of that year he described it as being under the care
of 'an old woman of eighty'.[3]

Maquean described how after admission to the infirmary, the clothes of
the infants were washed and exchanged for their own 'linen and flannel' in
which they had arrived at the Hospital.[4] This ensured the Hospital was not at
any loss when the infant came to be buried. However clean the clothing may
have been at first, as we shall see, other evidence attests to the 'filthiness' of the
children's 'rags' in the infirmary.

When asked about the bedding and covering of the children, Maquean
replied that they had 'straw in their cradles, and … old blankets that are cast
[off]' as not 'decent' enough for the nursery.

'Have you known any children to recover that have been sent to the infirmary?' Maquean was asked.

'I have known two children to have been recovered; afterwards they were
sent out to nurse, but died from the weak state they were sent out in.'

In such circumstances the two nurses working in the infirmary must have
had an expectation that every infant who came under their care would die,
which must have shaped their attitude and their practices towards those in
their care.

'Do you know anything of the attendance of the physician?' Maquean
was asked.

'Surgeon Woodroffe attends; [I] never saw Doctor Harvey at my side of the
House; I have seen the apothecary attend, but very seldom.'

'Have you seen the apothecary visit the infirmary once in a week?'

'No.'

'Have you seen the apothecary visit it once in a month?'

'No.'

'What medicines do you give the children in the infant infirmary?'

'There are medicines which come from the apothecary; there is a bottle which Mr Woodroffe calls a medicine bottle.'

'Is that bottle administered to all children in that infirmary?'

'Yes, except to children in a dying state; I supposed it a composing draught, for the children were easy after taking it for an hour or two.'

'When the surgeon calls on you does he make any enquiry as to the effect that bottle has had upon the children?'

'The surgeon asked me if I gave the bottle, but not as to the effect it had on them.'

The term 'composing draught' needed no explanation to the committee members, or indeed anyone else at the time. Dozens of different preparations – either proprietary, or mixed by individual apothecaries according to their own recipes – existed to promote sleep and 'soothe' both adults and children. One virtually universal ingredient was opium, usually in the form of laudanum. For example, William Buchan, in his *Domestic Medicine* of 1784 – perhaps the most widely read medical text of the time, and one that ran to many editions – gives the ingredients for a 'composing draught' as follows: 'liquid laudanum twenty five drops; simple cinnamon water, an ounce; common syrup(i.e. sugar and water), 2 drachms.' Laudanum was essentially opium dissolved in alcohol. East India or Turkey opium came in cakes of resin that were first 'bruised' using a mortar and pestle, then soaked in alcoholic spirits for up to fourteen days, before the liquid was strained and considered ready for use. While there was much variation in the strength of laudanum produced, there was some attempt to standardise the strength through the use of 'pharmacopeias' or formularies, produced by various physicians' bodies. Consulting these, it seems a common strength of laudanum was one grain of opium to every twenty-five drops of laudanum. One grain of opium is equivalent to 64 milligrams in today's measure, which in turn contains 6.4 milligrams of morphine, the main active ingredient of opium. Medical authorities in the early nineteenth century recommended doses of five drops for an infant. Today morphine is hardly ever given to infants, because of its many side effects, but where it is given (for example where the mother is addicted to opiates) the doses used appear to be roughly equivalent. We can't be certain what dose of opium was given to the infants in the infirmary of the Foundling Hospital, but we do know the effects it was likely to have had. The first is obvious: sedation. The children 'were easy after taking it for an hour or two'. Clearly it was given to silence the desperate cries of starving babies. However, in a newborn infant who was already starving, the effect must have been catastrophic, for it would further reduce the drive to feed and hasten the downward spiral to death. Catherine Maquean testified that 'the Bottle' was given to all 'except to children in a dying state'. By that time the children were so weakened by starvation no sedative was needed.

Another effect of opium is to reduce the movement or 'motility' of the bowels. As one writer of the early nineteenth century, George Sigmond recorded, 'it renders the intestinal canal so exceedingly sluggish, that the most active purgatives lose their power'.[5] So much so that opiates were (and still are) used to treat diarrhoea. But even then there was awareness of the dangers of such treatment: 'Three drops of laudanum, in chalk mixture, administered for a diarrhoea, to a stout child fourteen months old, has caused death,' Sigmond warned.[6] Although this may well have been due to the variation in strength outlined above, or other unknown factors, it illustrates that there was an awareness of the hazards involved. Severe constipation may account for the second notable omission from the visitors' report – any reference to smell. Despite the delicacy involved, it is unlikely that the gentlemen would have ignored this issue, since they were keen to emphasise the plight of the children, and at the time, predating the germ theory, it was believed that bad smells themselves, or 'malodorous airs', were the source of contagious diseases – an additional reason to highlight it, if it had been present.

Starvation in itself does not cause absolute constipation, since the gut continues to secrete fluids even after food intake has ceased. However, it is likely that a combination of opium and starvation rendered the infants severely constipated. Severe constipation is a dangerous condition, leading to intestinal obstruction, inflammation and rupture, with poisonous bacteria from the gut being released into the abdominal cavity, causing rapid death, especially in an era before antibiotics. However, perhaps few of the infants survived long enough to die in this manner. In a further tragic irony, it is possible that 'the Bottle' used to administer the laudanum was the same 'bottle shaped like a human breast' designed with such good intentions by Catherine Fitzmaurice, Lady Denny's cousin, back in the 1760s.

In fact, whatever the manner of their deaths, the evidence was to show that of 5,216 infants who entered this room in the previous six years, only one emerged alive.[7]

✳   ✳   ✳

The treasurer, Eugene Sweny (or Sweeney), was the most senior of the full-time foundling hospital staff to be interviewed. But by now the physician William Harvey was firmly in the sights of the committee, or at least of its chairman, as evidenced by virtually the first question put to Sweny.

'Do you know the physician to the Foundling Hospital and what is his name?' he was asked.

'I do: His name is Doctor Harvey.'

'Do you see the physician, Doctor Harvey, in the yards of the Hospital very often?'

'There are two stated days for his attendance, Mondays and Fridays.'

'Has Doctor Harvey visited the Hospital once a week?'

'He has.'

'Do you believe that Doctor Harvey has attended the infant infirmary?'

'I am told he has not attended.'

'Do you think he ought or ought not to have attended it?'

'My opinion is, that he ought to have attended the infant infirmary. I often turned it in my thoughts, and I supposed it his duty to attend the infant children.'

'Did you ever state to Doctor Harvey that he ought to have attended?'

'I never did.'

The Visitors' Report

By Thursday, 20 April 1797 the committee, consisting of Blaquiere in the chair, his brother the colonel, David La Touche and Richard Annesley, were ready to examine the Reverend Doctor Murray and Sir John Trail, two of the five gentlemen who had visited the Hospital on 11 April.[1]

The Reverend Samuel Murray was vicar of St Anne's Parish in the fashionable south-east area of the city and a governor of the Hospital, who had been dispatched there on behalf of the governors, apparently in response to Mrs Hunt's letter. As we have seen, the visitors had drawn up a report immediately after their visit that had not equivocated in its condemnation of the infant infirmary. It was to the contents of this report that the committee now turned its attention.

'It appearing in this report,' began the member of the committee – most likely Blaquiere – 'that no human effort was ever made use of to save the lives of the children, except administering the common food of milk, bread and common water, I want to know how or where the [gentlemen] got that information?'

'From the matron,' replied Murray.

'As to the treatment of the children, did you get that information from the matron?'

'I did.'

'Did it appear to you that no care or exertion through the physician, surgeon or apothecary to recover them was ever made?'

'I think [it] did. The physician thought from the situation of the venereal diseased children that any exertion to recover them was unnecessary.'

'Did it also appear that no medical assistance or advice was ever given to recover the children?'

'I think so for those that were infected.'

'Did you make any enquiry as to the apothecary's attendance … ?'

'We did; I think his attendance was seldom, because his powers were very much circumscribed by his superiors.'

'Who are the superiors who circumscribed the apothecary?'

Murray replied that he believed it was Doctor Harvey and Surgeon Woodroffe.

'Did you enquire whether any medicines were administered to the children in the infirmary?'

'I understood there was not any. Very near one half of the children sent to the infirmary were afflicted with venereal complaints.'

'Who did you get that information from?'

'I got it from the matron and the nurses.'

'Did you examine the apothecary?'

'I did. He gave the same information as the matron, and … that he could not administer medicines without orders from the surgeon, and that no medicines were ordered.'

At the time, as we have seen, apothecaries practising independently often made diagnoses and dispensed treatments on their own authority; however, those practising in hospitals were usually 'circumscribed' as Reverend Murray outlined. That is, they were confined to dispensing only medicines prescribed by the physicians or surgeons working in the Hospital.

Next to give evidence was Sir John Trail, architect of the fortress-like Kilmainham Gaol recently completed not far from the site of the Foundling Hospital. He was also a governor, one of the deputation dispatched by that body to visit the Hospital. Again the committee sought to clarify the nature of the treatment the children in the infirmary received.

'Did it appear to you that any medicines were administered to the children on their being sent to the infant infirmary?'

'By the information of the matron there was no medical assistance or extraordinary sustenance given either in the nursery or infant infirmary to ailing children. While the matron gave this information the treasurer and register were both present,' came Trail's reply.

'Did you enquire whether any medicines were brought into the infant nursery or infirmary?'

'The matron said there was none.'

As can be seen, the matron, in the presence of senior officers of the Hospital, had told the deputation of governors that had visited the Hospital that the infants in the infirmary were neither visited by the medical personnel, nor had any medicines prescribed for them. This is subtly but significantly different from the evidence later given by the matron herself, and several other staff to the sworn parliamentary enquiry, as outlined above. The latter was to the effect that neither the apothecary nor the physician ever visited the infirmary, but that the surgeon *did* visit from time to time and that there *was* medicine prescribed, albeit only the 'composing draught'.

'When you examined the children in the infant infirmary, had they clothing sufficiently warm on them?' the MPs now asked of Trail.

'In my opinion they had not, and what there was appeared to be filthy and dirty: the blankets that were on them were dirty, and the cradles where the children lay, according to the information received from the nurses, were swarming with bugs.'

'Was there any difference of opinion between the gentlemen who composed the [deputation] and you?'

'There was not; every gentleman was unanimous as to the wretched state of the infants.'

After asking about the visitors' conversation with the porter at the gate, the committee then went on to ask Trail:
'Did you have any conversation with the apothecary relative to his attendance at the infant [infirmary]?'

'Yes, he informed the gentlemen that he always attended when sent for to the infant infirmary, but that he did not consider it his department.'

'Did you ever enquire whether any medicines were sent to the infirmary?'

'He, the apothecary, said that he could not prescribe a dose of physic without the prescription of the physician, as the bye-law specified.'

'Did you examine the physician?'

'Yes, he said he always attended [when] sent for – he did not consider the infant infirmary as in his department. This last question was put to Doctor Harvey at a subsequent period.'

'Did it appear to you that Surgeon Woodroffe attended regularly?'

'When I first examined them, the matron said that there was no medical assistance given at all, but at the next meeting of the committee, at the re-examination after the business had made some noise, she prevaricated, and did acknowledge that Surgeon Woodroffe attended twice or thrice a week or some person for him, and that the apothecary constantly attended.'

Did Mrs Hunt bow to pressure and give incorrect evidence to save the medical men? After all, criticisms in the report of the visitors to the governors had precipitated frenetic behind-the-scenes activity, eventually resulting in an amendment to their report.[2]

A more favourable interpretation would be that in the heat of the moment Mrs Hunt's passion caused her to speak unguardedly in her initial evidence, and while not completely accurate, the weight of her evidence was correct – that little medical effort was made to save the children. And yes, while Surgeon Woodroffe did visit the infirmary, there is little evidence of any active intervention on his part, other than prescribing the 'Bottle' to ease their passing.

✳ ✳ ✳

James Shaughnissy, the apothecary, was now called to give evidence, and placed under oath. At the time, the training of apothecaries was under the control of Apothecaries Hall, a body itself under the control of the College of Physicians. A young man wishing to become an apothecary would first undergo an examination to determine whether his 'basic education' (including in Latin) was adequate. He was then required to undertake a seven-year apprenticeship. Shaughnissy's role required him to 'wait upon the physician and surgeon with a book where all the prescriptions are to be regularly entered by them', and to 'obey at all times the directions of the physician and surgeon'[3]. He also had an important role in recording all cases admitted to the infirmary, including their diagnoses, and, in fatal cases, the cause of death. Indeed, the duties as laid out in the Hospital bye-laws placed far more emphasis on his clerical duties than any therapeutic role. In addition, Shaughnissy was required to live in the Hospital.

After confirming his position in the Hospital, the committee (again probably led by Blaquiere) started by showing him a document that Shaughnissy himself had submitted – 'a return, signed by him of the number of diseased children in the infant infirmary'. This dealt with admissions over the previous twenty-one months.[4]

'What disorders are meant by diseased?' he was asked.

'According to the surgeon's report, they were venereal.'

'Are the number one thousand nine hundred and seventy-five in the infant infirmary, stated in the said return as diseased, the whole of the sick children that were in the infirmary?'

'Yes.'

'Are there two infirmaries for the infant children in the Hospital, or are they all sent to the same room?'

'There is but that one room.'

'Am I to infer from thence that there are in that infirmary no children sick of any other complaint?'

'Not that I know of.'

'Are you sure that those children are or were all afflicted with that disorder?'

'They were returned so to me by the surgeon.'

Shaughnissy was then asked if he knew 'what effect the Lock Hospital in Townsend Street has had in respect to the preventing the ravages of that disorder?'

Lock hospitals specialised in the treatment of venereal disease. Patients could be detained until their symptoms had resolved. The Townsend Street hospital had opened a few years earlier.[5]

'I have heard it said that it has had a great effect in preventing it in Dublin, but it has not prevented it in the country.'

'Do all the children that are sent to the infant infirmary go there on the report of the surgeon?'

'The visiting days of the surgeon are twice a week, sometimes three times; in the mean time if children supposed to be very much diseased should come in to the nursery, and if I find them in a very bad state, I send them up to the infirmary, to prevent their being fed with other children.' (Mary Doyle had testified that the apothecary attended the nursery when sent for, but not otherwise.)

'Is the surgeon's report verbal or written of the state of the children to the matron?'

'The method is, the surgeon visits the foundling nursery, and each child has a badge about its neck, the number of which is returned to me as a certificate of the child's being infected with the venereal disease and sent to the infant infirmary, where none are admitted but such as are supposed to be infected with the venereal disease.'

'How long have you been the apothecary in the hospital?'

'Between eight and nine years.'

'During that time have you known any child sent from the infant nursery to any other infirmary?'

'I [have] not.'

'Am I then to understand that during that time no child in the infant nursery was so ill of any other complaint as to require being sent to any other infirmary but those who were affected with the venereal disease?' In other words, in those eight or nine years was venereal disease the only condition ever requiring treatment in an infirmary in the infants who entered the Foundling Hospital?

Shaughnissy's reply, although indirect, appears to be in the affirmative: 'I know of no other infirmary for infant children.'

'State to the committee how many diseased children have been admitted into the infants infirmary in the last six years ending 24th June.'

'I cannot without examining my books.'

Here, the report records, a 'return' was produced, 'of the diseased children in the infirmary for six years, amounting to five thousand two hundred and sixteen'.

'Does the return you have now made include all the diseased children?'

'I cannot tell.'

'Have you attended the infant nursery [infirmary?] once a week?'

'No.'

'Have you attended it once a month?'

'No.'

'Have you visited it once a quarter?'

'I have not.'

(Here the parliamentary clerk may be confusing the nursery with the infirmary, as Mary Doyle had already testified that the apothecary visited the *nursery* when sent for. However, it is clear from Catherine Maquean's testimony that the apothecary rarely, if ever, visited the *infirmary*.)

'Have you administered medicines in the nursery [infirmary]?'

'I have not. Medicines were sent there by me to the matron, who administered them at her discretion.'

'What authority have you for knowing when the children die in the infant infirmary?'

'I have no authority for knowing the children had died but from the return of the matron.'

'Five thousand two hundred and sixteen children are said to have died in the infant Infirmary of the venereal disease in the last six years, have any other children been admitted in that hospital afflicted with any other illness or complaint?'

'I cannot recollect.'

'Have there been admitted in that infant infirmary no children except those who have been afflicted with the venereal disease?'

'None that I know of.'

'Have the infant children in that hospital no other complaints or no other sickness but the venereal disorder?'

'The answer to that would come better from the persons who attend the infant nursery.'

'Are there any medicines whatever administered to the children in the infant infirmary besides the bottle which appears to be handed around indiscriminately to all?'

'There has not.'

Again, apparently struggling to comprehend what he is hearing, the committee member asks: 'Is there any other room or place where children are sent to that are sick except to the infirmary?'

'There is not.'

The members of the committee clearly found it astonishing that no child had ever been admitted to the infirmary for any complaint other than a venereal one.

The committee then called as a witness the eminent surgeon Samuel Croker-King to testify as to the duties of an apothecary. He testified as to the apothecary's tasks in Dr Steeven's Hospital (where he was a senior colleague of Harvey and Woodroffe.) Here it was clear that the apothecary's duties included a daily visit to the wards. This was the rationale behind creating a residential post. However, Croker-King's evidence was rendered redundant by the ever-efficient Annslie Bailie, who produced an extract from the Hospital's own bye-laws as outlined above.

* * *

Mr Philip Woodroffe was a venerable surgeon who held a leading post at Dr Steeven's Hospital, perhaps the leading general hospital at the time. He had been associated with the Hospital since 1766. He was said to have been the 'last of the barber surgeons' – that is, at the beginning of his career, surgeons were still associated with the medieval guild of barbers, although they had already long diverged in practice. However, the status of surgery had evolved radically since then. Woodroffe had been in the vanguard of this development and had been one of the founder members of the Royal College of Surgeons.

In recognition of his seniority and experience, he sat on the board for examining candidate surgeons for appointment to county infirmaries. He was consulting surgeon to the Houses of Industry, Chanel Row (where he gave his services gratis).

'Can you account for the extraordinary number of children who have died more than usual in the last quarter?' he was first asked.

Woodroffe answered that 'it being the severest season', more had died.

'Compared with the corresponding quarter of former years, how does it stand?'

'More diseased children I think were taken in in the last quarter.'

'By diseased children, do you mean venereal children?'

'I do.'

'Do you examine any other children not afflicted with the venereal disease?'

'I do if any other surgical complaint occurs.'

'Do you confine yourself to surgical complaints alone?'

'I do; nothing else comes within my department.'

'Whose department do the other disorders come under?'

'I think the medical.'

'Who is the physician?'

'Doctor Harvey.'

'Has he the care of the infant nursery?'

Woodroffe's reply is recorded in the truncated style of the parliamentary clerks: 'He attends whenever he is sent for: believes the apothecary is in the way to answer any other call in his absence.'

'Do you know Doctor Harvey's salary?'

'Believes £80 per annum; understands there were some additional fees which were struck off by the Imprest Commissioners; believes it was previous to the session before last.'

'Was not that a quarterly allowance of £20 per quarter?'

'No it was an additional fee to make up his salary one hundred guineas annually.'

'Were you ever called on to go into the infant infirmary?'

'Yes, very often.'

'What situation did you find the children in as to clothing and care?'

'As to clothing, I think that the clothing is as warm as necessary, but I have found fault with the children being crowded in the cradles; the children were kept as cleanly as they possibly could.' This seems to be at odds with the testimony of both the nurses and the visiting deputation of governors.

'Do you know of any medicines being administered to these children?'

'Yes, constantly; the place was never without medicine by my direction, and the apothecary informed me that he sent them, and the nurse told me she gave them.' Here he is undoubtedly referring to 'the bottle' containing the 'composing draught'. 'Nothing,' he went on, 'can recover venereal diseased children but breast milk impregnated with mercury, which cannot be got, as no nurse will suffer herself to be salivated for the purpose, and even if the child recovered it would be a burden to the state.'

'Is the food sufficient for the children?'

'I always understood it was.'

'What effect has the establishment of the Lock Hospital in Dublin had upon the state of the children admitted into the Foundling Hospital?'

'Not any as yet, for the majority of the venereal diseased children come from the country parts.'

It is a mystery why greater attention was not paid to this fact, for it surely points to starvation and neglect during the long journey to the Hospital, and not venereal disease, as the main cause of the poor condition of the infants. However, according to the record, the committee had no further questions for Woodroffe.

✻　✻　✻

Like a theatre director saving the climax to the end of his production, the committee saved their prime witness until the very last. In recounting Dr Harvey's testimony, however, the inquiry process demonstrates its inherent bias, for after what must have been prolonged and detailed questioning, the committee report allocates his evidence only a single paragraph. Nevertheless, what evidence it does record is significant and does not reflect well on Harvey. After detailing that Dr Harvey was sworn, the parliamentary clerk records his evidence in the truncated style we have already seen: 'Says he never visited the infant side of the house unless when sent for; he did not consider it as belonging to his duty to visit it, but never failed to go when sent for.'

Harvey testified that 'the former matron used to send for him to visit the infant children, but does not recollect that he had been sent for by the present matron, except to visit her own children; believes that the present matron has had that appointment about seven years.'

Harvey was asked: 'Whether you know is it the duty of any medical person to attend the children in the infant nursery?'

'I conceive it to be the duty of the apothecary, and if he sees any occasion to call on me, that it is his duty to do so.'

And that is where the record of Harvey's evidence ends. After its long and careful preparation the committee was perhaps demonstrating its disappointment in failing to deliver a decisive blow. Nevertheless, as we shall see, Harvey was not to escape so lightly.

Meanwhile, outside parliament, military activity continued. On Thursday 27 April, the Liberty Rangers, a unit of yeomanry, marched to the Phoenix Park, where they practised their marksmanship. The four most accurate shots were awarded silver medals. Afterwards Blaquiere and others joined the officers for an evening of 'pleasing sentiment and conviviality'.[6]

Cross-Examination

On 3 May, when Blaquiere presented the report of the committee's enquiry to the House of Commons, his brother James, the colonel, commented bitterly on the 'negligence of the honourable gentlemen around him' while the report was being read out in the chamber.[1] The report called for sweeping changes in the Foundling Hospital, but by now the lack of interest by most of their fellow parliamentarians in the subject was palpable. Blaquiere called for a full debate on the issue and significantly he called for the report to be printed – the only reason we have access to it today – so that there could be no doubt as to the findings they had unearthed.[2] The mild-mannered Chancellor of the Exchequer (John Parnell) 'deprecated as much as anyone the idea of such a subject being treated lightly' and supported Blaquiere's request.

Colonel James Blaquiere also commented on another development that had occurred a week earlier. On 27 April a meeting of the governors had been held in the Hospital's grand boardroom.[3] At this, fifteen leading female members of society had volunteered their services to the Board to act as visitors and supervisors to the Hospital. Now, the colonel implied that this was a cynical move, pointing out how their 'humanity lay dormant until the business was brought before parliament' and that he could not 'reconcile this sudden benevolence' with their 'former neglect', implying it was merely designed to protect others. In response, the Right Honourable Sackville Hamilton 'denied that any motive short of an exalted charity influenced the conduct of the ladies'.[4] (Lady Sackville Hamilton was one of the ladies.)

In any event, Blaquiere was granted his wish for his report to be considered by a committee of the whole House. This meant that the House sat as a committee, with a chairman, rather than a Speaker. It could then summon and question witnesses, rather than just debate.

On Monday, 8 May Blaquiere again rose to address the House of Commons. He began by criticising those 'gentlemen who quit the House the moment the subject was entered, as if its very mention acted as a pestiferous blast'. He was referring to 'crimes of the most inhuman kind', he claimed.[5]

This was the first chance the committee had to bring the more detailed figures they had heard in oral testimony to the attention of the public. But there was worse to come. For in addition, the committee had sought, and been given, more detailed written returns covering the six years from 1791 to 1796. These revealed the full scale of the horror. In these six years 12,786 infants had been admitted. At the same time 7,807 had died in the Hospital (5,215 in the infant infirmary, and the remainder in the infant nursery). A further 1,997 were known to have died with wet nurses in the country (and a further 252 older children also died). In other words, during the period that 12,786 were admitted, 10,056 were confirmed dead. In addition, a staggering 2,847 were unaccounted for, possibly dead.[6] So that, in the words of Blaquiere, out of nearly 13,000 'in six years only 135 children were saved to the public and to the world'.[7]

When the returns for the twelve years from 1784 were considered, the numbers were even more horrifying. Of the 25,532 admissions in that time, 17,253 were confirmed dead with a further 6,442 missing, giving a total of 23,695 dead or missing.[8]

Blaquiere promised that he would 'bring proof of the most foul and horrid murders having been committed by women … who were employed to bring children from the country to the Hospital'. He mentioned two instances. One was of a woman who had been executed in Cavan for such murders after allegedly engaging in the practice for fifteen years;[9] the other was of a woman who 'confessed at the gallows, to which she was brought by other offences, that she pursued this traffic in blood for twenty-four years'. What's more, he 'could also bring proof that those infernal wretches, not unfrequently formed of the unfortunate infants committed to their care, an easy seat on the car which brought them to town'. He also claimed that: 'many of those infants' throats are cut, the barbarous perpetrators thereby saving the journey to town'.[10] Unfortunately (other than the 'easy seat' allegation) the source for these claims is not given. There is no evidence touching on this area in the printed report of the enquiry.

Blaquiere also drew attention to the 'vast annual expense' of 'a charity not merely ineffectual, but wholly perverted [by] the negligence of the physician, surgeon and apothecary appointed under salary to attend the Hospital'.

The Solicitor General then rose, and said 'that till now he had considered Dr Harvey a man of the most distinguished character' both for his 'humanity' and skill in his profession, 'but if the charges made against him by the report were founded, he was a man whom no person should admit within his doors'.[11] However, he advised caution and forbearance from making a decision until

Harvey himself had had a chance to speak in his own defence. And, although praising the diligence of the committee, he alleged the report was inaccurate 'in many instances'.

Now the Chief Secretary, Thomas Pelham – the most powerful member sitting in the House, whose role was to ensure parliament toed the British government line, just as Blaquiere's had been twenty-five years before – poured some cold water on Blaquiere's fervour by pointing out the natural attrition occurring in childhood, and the virtual impossibility of treating syphilis in the newborn. He also expressed doubts about Blaquiere's proposal in the report to extend foundling hospitals to every county in the country.

Blaquiere expressed some surprise at this, indicating that he had discussed the details of his bill in advance with the Chief Secretary 'on Monday last' and had understood him to be in support. 'The opposition of the Right Honourable Secretary he knew must be fatal,' Blaquiere declared. He therefore hoped that 'that gentleman would send him about his business without giving him any more trouble'.

Pelham 'denied that he had expressed a full assent to his plan – he had advised him to continue the enquiry, but he did at that time suggest to him the doubts which he entertained on the utility of such institutions in any shape – he did no more now'.[12]

After further discussion, the members (sitting as a committee of the House) agreed to all the resolutions in the report except those relating to the physician and surgeon. A decision on these would have to await the appearance of Woodroffe and Harvey to be questioned by the whole House.

Blaquiere concluded by outlining some details of his proposed bill, which he hoped would remedy existing abuses and prevent future ones. Similar to a bill he had presented in 1791, the main thrust of this was to establish a foundling hospital in every county, thereby removing the need to travel long distances. These would be annexed to the county infirmaries and under the care of a certain number of guardians or directors.

The House then ordered the appearance of the physician, surgeon, and apothecary for questioning the next day.

Thus it was that on Tuesday, 9 May, Dr William Harvey MD, one of the most prominent and senior physicians in Dublin, having already appeared before the committee, was ordered to appear at the bar of the House of Commons, to be examined by the members.

Measured in terms of his public profile, Harvey would have to be accounted one of the leading physicians of the day. From a relatively humble background, as the son of a Strabane Anglican clergyman, Harvey had entered Trinity College at the age of 16 or 17.[13] From the college records of the time he was largely educated by his father. The clergyman had done a good job in laying a solid foundation, which, combined with Harvey's hard work, led to him being elected 'Scholar' in 1769 – a prestigious award granted on merit to leading students. The subjects of course were the 'classics' – Latin, Greek and Rhetoric. These were the principal subjects that any university undergraduate studied at the time. In 1771 Harvey obtained his BA from Trinity and shortly afterwards made his way to Edinburgh, where he enrolled in the university to study medicine. While it was technically possible to graduate in medicine from Trinity, as with most universities, tuition in medicine there was neither well organised nor attractive to potential students. Would-be doctors tended to concentrate on a small number of academic centres in Europe where there was a commitment to teaching medicine in a relatively structured way, preferably combined with access to a teaching hospital where students could obtain vital practical experience. In the 1770s, leading centres included Leyden, Paris and Edinburgh. The latter was the most important centre for the study of medicine of the universities in Britain, but it had yet to gain the pre-eminence it achieved by the end of the century – which saw the number of Irish students there grow until they outnumbered even the Scottish and English. To this extent, then, Harvey was in something of a vanguard.

Teaching in Edinburgh consisted of structured lectures combined with practical experience at the Royal Edinburgh Infirmary, over the course of two years.[14] By today's standards this is a very short period during which to master the theory of medicine as well as to gain a broad enough experience to be useful to patients. Students could pay an additional fee to become 'dressers' at the Hospital within the two-year period – a busy role providing much desirable practice treating wounds and sores under supervision. As part of the requirement for obtaining his MD degree, Harvey completed a fifty-page thesis in Latin – 'De Venenis' (On Toxins), which he dedicated to his father as his 'best teacher'.[15]

A year later Harvey registered at Leyden and shortly afterwards returned to Dublin. In 1779 he married Catherine Scott, of a well-connected Wicklow family, and in the same year was appointed physician to Dr Steeven's Hospital. As we have seen, this was the leading general hospital in Dublin at the time.

On Friday, 29 September 1780, the *Hibernian Journal* contained the following announcement: 'Last Tuesday Dr Wm. Harvey of Stafford-Street was unanimously elected by the Governors of the Foundling Hospital, physician to said Hospital, in the [place] of Doctor Archer, (resigned).'[16] That appointment was to be followed by many more prestigious advancements. In 1783 he was elected one of the governors of Dr Steeven's Hospital, where he was already the senior physician. The role of governor, while unpaid, allowed the possibility of mingling with the nobility, as well as publicly demonstrating the refined quality of charity.

The following year he was appointed as the physician to the Lying-In Hospital, then governor of the same as well as being elected as a governor of another charity, the Blue Coat Hospital, before being elected as President of the College of Physicians for an annual term. His ascent continued and by 1794 he was living in a grand new house on North Great George's street, fast becoming one of the most prestigious addresses in Dublin, only a stone's throw from the Lying-In Hospital and its fashionable pleasure gardens. In the same year, as if to cement his status as the leading establishment doctor, he was appointed joint Physician-General – the chief medical advisor to the British army in Ireland with a staff of at least five physicians and thirteen surgeons, responsible for the medical welfare of 42,000 men as well as 20,000 yeomanry.[17] The post included an appointment to the Royal Military Infirmary (with a salary of £300), an elegant neoclassical hospital recently built for the treatment of soldiers, situated in a delightful location in the Phoenix Park. It's likely that this responsibility would have entailed a daily visit to the Hospital. Combined with his responsibilities to the Lying-In and Dr Steeven's Hospitals, along with a no-doubt thriving private practice, this would have meant that Harvey was a busy man.

There is some evidence that he had a bluff, no-nonsense, even brusque manner, which may have appealed to patients and inspired confidence.[18] There is also evidence that he was respected clinically by colleagues, for at least one senior physician consulted him as a patient.[19]

Facing a man with such formidable accomplishments, even the powerful politicians had had to lay some careful ground work. However, accomplished and wealthy as Harvey was, he still ranked clearly below his opponents, many of them with vast personal wealth, hereditary titles and political connections. Furthermore, parliament had considerable power. For example, only a few weeks later, one newspaper publisher who had 'the insolence to print a false account of the proceedings of this House' was to be summoned for interrogation by parliament before being fined and 'confined for three calendar months … in the prison of Newgate'.[20]

At first Harvey was questioned by the Attorney General, Arthur Wolfe. His evidence covered the fact that there were three infirmaries: the medical and surgical infirmaries – for older children – and the now notorious infant infirmary. Harvey made it clear that he believed his responsibility was to visit the medical infirmary only – unless specifically summoned to one of the other two by the surgeon or apothecary. He outlined how for his first fourteen years he had been in the habit of visiting all three infirmaries, but for the last six he 'gave up the practice – he never declined going to the infant infirmary when his aid was solicited, but cannot charge his memory with having been there frequently in the last six years' and he was clear that the infant infirmary was under the care of the surgeon. The surgeon could call for his assistance, and had done so frequently for the first fourteen years, but not since.

He was asked about the nature of venereal disease in children. (At the time, while some practitioners were beginning to recognise syphilis and gonorrhoea as distinct illnesses, the majority saw them as one condition.) Venereal disease, Harvey testified, could be contracted in three ways by infants – in utero, during delivery, or through the mother's milk. Children infected during delivery, he reported, were generally considered incurable, whereas those contracting it at the breast 'may be easily recovered in eighteen months'.

The Right Honourable Denis Browne MP asked about 'the different symptoms in different stages of the disease'. The doctor 'answered him with some medical precision, protesting that his skill in that disease was not however very acute.'

He was then asked about the accuracy of nurses in diagnosing the condition. (Remember the nurses were untrained women, paid less than a maid.) Out of 6,000 children, for example, could a nurse make an error in say 400 cases? Harvey thought that impossible. The error rate he suggested might be fifty out of 6,000, or less than 1 per cent.

Sir Frederick Flood then 'interrogated him respecting the bye-laws of the Hospital' – a copy of which he held up in his hand. Harvey acknowledged that he was familiar with these. Flood had done a little homework. The bye-laws were very specific and detailed about the role of the physician and surgeon in supervising the diets of the children – which we have now seen were grossly inadequate. They were less specific about the areas to be visited – specifying that the physician should visit the Hospital regularly, Monday and Friday, 'and at all times when sent for' 'to attend carefully to the health of the children, giving his advice to and prescribing proper medicines for all such officers, servants, nurses or aged poor as shall have occasion for his assistance'.[21]

Flood questioned Harvey as to whether his responsibility to monitor the infants' diet necessitated him monitoring the infants themselves. Harvey believed it did not. 'He however did inspect their diet, of which he kept a register which could be referred to.' In any event, a 'skilful woman generally superintended the … health of the infant children, to which he thought her competent'.

According to the *Freeman's Journal*, 'the Doctor's examination lasted for a considerable time, but it was too minute and too professional for public attention'.[22]

Harvey's testimony was followed by that of Woodroffe and Shaughnissy, the apothecary, neither of which are reported in detail. But the thrust of the evidence is summed up in the *Dublin Evening Post*:

> That the infant infirmary is peculiarly and exclusively under the care of the surgeon, who attends twice or thrice a week – that the infant nursery is never visited either by physician or surgeon, but left to the sole care of the matron – that the physician considers himself bound only to attend to the medical infirmary, unless particularly called on – that tho' scarcely any of the children have ever come alive out of the infant [infirmary], yet in no instance in the course of the last six years, has it been thought necessary to consult either the doctor or the apothecary – nor has either of these persons, in that time, ever paid a voluntary visit to this place, notwithstanding the excessive mortality – that the children who come in are, one half of them at least, on an average, infected with the venereal disease, and the others are generally exhausted with hunger or cold – that in this case the venereal patients are sent to the infirmary, and the others left to the mere care of the nurse, without any medical aid – that they are frequently put to lie four in a cradle, about six feet long by 2½ broad.[23]

'When the last witness withdrew,' reported the *Freeman's Journal*, 'Mr Annesley … declared that their united testimonies only confirmed him in his former opinion respecting the degree of their criminal neglect.'[24]

Syphilis Considered

The following day the House again 'resolved itself into a Committee of the whole House' to further consider the report on the Foundling Hospital.

Annesley raised the resolution of the select committee 'which fixed a censure on Doctor Harvey for a criminal neglect of his duty as attending physician at the Hospital' and invited the whole House to concur.[1] He reviewed the numbers of the dead previously reported. He restated some of Harvey's arguments and while conceding that Harvey's salary for the post was inadequate for the duties entailed, nevertheless, he argued, as long as Harvey had accepted the duty, he was 'reprehensible in omitting to perform it'. In a telling phrase he stated: 'beside his medical aid, his countenance and attention would have been useful.' Humanity 'should impel him to afford any assistance which could conduce to preserve the lives of so many helpless children thrown on the public for protection,' he concluded, before calling for support of the censure.

According to the parliamentary reporter, the colourful Sir Boyle Roche 'shewed great sensibility at the horrid details of deaths and murders which he heard during the discussion of this unhappy business'.[2] If guilt, he said, could be traced to those who were responsible in the Hospital, he 'wondered that gentlemen would content themselves with mere censure'. They should mount a legal prosecution, 'so that the lives of the delinquents may be … forfeit'.[3]

At this the Speaker intervened. He pointed out that all the charitable institutions of the city were attended by physicians of the first eminence, without fee or reward – but then perhaps recollecting that Harvey *had* received a fee, he hastily pointed out how inadequate this was. Undaunted, he continued in his argument that it therefore followed that such work was carried out 'from benevolence and humanity' and questioned whether a doctor in such a position should be forced to 'run a gauntlet of enquiry and investigation, for not obtruding into a department which appeared to be no part of his duty?'[4]

The Speaker also argued, more cogently, that the purpose of the report and debate was the reform of the institution of the Foundling Hospital, not the censure of the medical men, which was, in fact, a distraction.

As it was then observed that there were fewer than forty members in the House, the matter could therefore not be decided upon and was adjourned until the following day. In fact, it seems the issue of the censure of the medical men was never raised again in the chamber.

Furthermore, the following day (12 May) when Blaquiere raised his bill for consideration in the House, it was pointed out to him that since it involved the spending of public monies, it would have to be considered by the Committee of Supplies. Blaquiere had no choice. The bill was withdrawn.

✳   ✳   ✳

But were the MPs right to condemn the medical men as 'delinquents' whose lives should be 'forfeit' because of their 'criminal neglect'?

In fact, despite suggestions to the contrary, all three medical men attended the Hospital frequently, if not exactly in accordance with the regulations. The evidence is that the surgeon attended twice, or sometimes three times a week; Harvey himself attended 'Mondays and Fridays' and 'at all times when sent for'; and the apothecary lived on the premises.

The surgeon, Woodroffe, had pointed out that 'nothing can recover venereal diseased children but breast milk impregnated with mercury'. There was universal agreement on this point. Mercury, having first been used in the treatment of leprosy from the thirteenth century, became the accepted treatment for syphilis in adults from the sixteenth century — for almost as long as the disease had been recognised in Europe. (Whether it had reached Europe in the ships of the explorers returning from the New World was — and is — still a matter of debate. The first descriptions of the illness spreading in Europe date from within a few years of Columbus's ships returning). Although doctors and patients were convinced of mercury's effectiveness, they were also aware of its shocking side effects. According to the theory of the time, mercury worked by ridding the body of excess disordered fluids. This it did by causing diarrhoea, sweating and copious salivation (up to four pints of saliva per day). These were considered desirable effects. Unwanted effects included loosened teeth and weakening of the bone structure, causing the nose to collapse and jaws to disintegrate. Different compounds of mercury were tried in an effort to decrease side effects and increase effectiveness, but few of these could be taken by infants.

In France, which led the way in this area, usually only palliative care was given to infants. A putative treatment recommended by the Paris Faculty of Medicine was the inhalation of mercury fumes, supplemented by one half grain of *mercure doux* (mercurous chloride or calomel) alternating with purges of rhubarb water.[5]

In the Paris foundling hospital – the Enfants Trouvés – children with syphilis were assigned to a special room. Care consisted of bathing the infants and feeding them with goats' milk, along with the application of mercurial ointments – a hopeless gesture. These infants rarely survived more than ten weeks.[6] There was no known way of having infants ingest mercury, other than through impregnated breast milk. And the only way to achieve this was to have the nurse consume the toxic medicine – an impossible ask. As Woodroffe had commented in his evidence to the committee, 'no nurse will suffer herself to be salivated for the purpose'.[7]

Extraordinarily, however, the French authorities did in fact attempt to do just that. In 1780 the government opened a hospital at Vaugirard, on the outskirts of Paris, exclusively for the experimental treatment of infants with syphilis. New mothers with syphilis were treated with mercury and in addition to feeding their own child, also each fed one foundling with syphilis. In a variety of experimental approaches, mercury was also administered to the mother through mercury-containing baths and skin rubs, the treatments continuing for two to three months. The infant could also be administered mercury directly, including by mercury fumes – powdered vermilion or cinnabar could be sprinkled on coals and the infant suspended above in a woven hanging basket to be 'smoked', initially for four to five minutes, the time gradually increasing.[8] Mercury ointments could also be applied, though these tended to destroy clothing and bedding and smelled unpleasantly.[9] Detailed records were kept of the various treatments and their effects, in what was a heartfelt effort to find a cure for a devastating illness. Initially the results seemed promising, with as many as 25 per cent of infants seeming to survive.

Ultimately, however, the research was in vain, defeated by the sheer complexity of the illness and the need to control for many confounding variables – which still bedevils medical research today – and was brought to an end in 1790. Since many Dublin doctors trained in France, they may well have been aware of the experiment. Even if not, the consensus was that such infants were untreatable, and as Woodroffe commented 'even if the child recovered it would be a burthen to the state'.[10]

The suspected presence of syphilis caused another difficulty. There was widespread fear that the suckling child could pass the infection to the wet nurse. This compounded the difficulty in feeding these children. We have seen the problems and dangers associated with artificial feeding (p.54). This was due to the twofold challenge of obtaining safe and hygienic milk, and a satisfactory mechanism for feeding. Direct suckling by animals was a solution adopted in some countries, particularly France, where feeding of infants by asses and goats was used, particularly in the Foundling Hospital in Aix from 1775, but continuing to the twentieth century in some institutions.[11] This approach might have saved many lives but was not adopted in Ireland or Britain.

But the extraordinary fact that so many infants were diagnosed with venereal disease, and that no infant was ever transferred to the infirmary with any other condition, cannot be overlooked. It seems the diagnosis was made by Woodroffe himself, and by the apothecary, but was principally delegated by Woodroffe to the matron, Mrs Hunt. Such a diagnosis was not straightforward since the symptoms or signs in infants were sometimes completely absent, and if present, could be quite mild and could easily be confused with other conditions, such as oral thrush, scurvy (from vitamin C deficiency) and many skin diseases. The Dublin surgeon William Dease, in his *Observations on the different methods of treating the venereal disease*, found it difficult to distinguish from scurvy and scrophula (tuberculosis of the skin).[12] The most common symptom was 'snuffles' – congestion of the nasal passages. Another sign was a dark red to coppery colour skin rash appearing after one to two weeks. Contemporary writers described a bewildering variety of symptoms, many of which overlapped with other diseases.[13] But modern writers describe most affected babies as appearing normal after birth. Therefore it would appear that diagnosis is far from simple. Yet Harvey, when asked, had asserted that it would be a straightforward task for the matron – a woman with no medical training. He estimated that her error rate would be only 50 out of 6,000, or 0.8 per cent. Out of 12,786 infants admitted to the Hospital in the previous six years, 5,216 had been diagnosed with venereal disease and sent to the infant infirmary (from where only a single one emerged alive) – an apparent incidence rate of 40 per cent. In fact, the surgeon who took over from Woodroffe found a rate of one in eleven (9 per cent).

Although the focus of the enquiry, and of parliament, was on Harvey's role, the unanimous testimony of the three medical witnesses was that responsibility for the infant infirmary lay with the surgeon, Philip Woodroffe. This was partly because syphilis manifested with external lesions, which could be treated and dressed – a surgeon's area of expertise, whereas physicians concerned themselves with putative 'internal' disorders treated with diet, purging and bleeding. Although socially the physician was of higher status than the surgeon, and commanded higher fees, clinically they acted independently. There was no suggestion that Woodroffe reported to, or was in any way subordinate to, Harvey. Thus, technically, Harvey had no direct responsibility for the infant infirmary, although it might have behoved him to enquire into the extraordinary death rate there.

Account must be taken of the two other infirmaries, where such a sense of fatalism did not prevail. The medical and surgical infirmaries admitted older children (and a small number of adults who might still have been resident in the Hospital). During a period of eight years there were 3,450 admissions to the medical infirmary, under Dr Harvey's care, and only 298 deaths, with 91.5 per cent discharged recovered. The admissions included cases of smallpox, whooping cough and measles – all potentially fatal diseases. The surgical infirmary, under Woodroffe's management, was even more impressive. Of 3,864 admissions over the previous six years, there had not been a single fatality, and all patients had been discharged 'cured'.[14]

Some of the witnesses hinted at the real reason for the appalling death toll in the infant infirmary: the grueling journey endured by new-born infants en route to the Hospital, which left them close to death. Faced with this, and the impossibility of helping such fragile patients with 18th century medical technology, a terrible fatalism seems to have taken root.

The final question that arises is this: would the infants have survived if they had not been incorrectly diagnosed as having venereal disease, and had remained in the infant nursery, and perhaps been sent out to country nurses? To answer that we must continue to examine events in the Hospital over the succeeding years.

On 20 May Blaquiere again presented a bill to reform the Foundling Hospital. This was a modified bill, for there is no mention of a requirement for it to be considered by the Committee of Supply. After some wrangling, a frustrated Blaquiere 'declared himself as disinterested as [a] man could be in the business, excepting from motives of humanity, and stated it to be a mockery in appointing a committee to investigate the abuses of the institution, which consisted of 37 members, when two only attended; and declared from the most accurate calculation, that each day's procrastination produced the murder of five children. He concluded by declaring, whatever might be the state of the bill, he had acquitted himself of a duty which he thought he owed to his God and his country.'[15]

Opposition to change didn't only come from within parliament. On 31 May a petition to the House on behalf of Dublin City Corporation asserted that it had 'by a grant of land ... [been] constituted permanent governors' of the Foundling Hospital and opposed the bill. However, a compromise was reached whereby two aldermen would always be nominated as governors in the event that the bill progressed.[16]

Outside parliament, tensions in the country continued to escalate. On 20 May for example, private houses in Mullingar were raided for arms, probably by rebels, and a unit of the army was despatched to protect Blaquiere's country house at Port Loman outside the town.[17] Evidently he was regarded as a prime target. In Belfast, meanwhile, the army ran amok, as described by the French traveller De La Tocnaye.[18] An 'illumination' had been ordered to celebrate the king's birthday on 4 June. In Belfast, under martial law, this took on sinister connotations. Householders were expected to honour the king by placing candles in their windows. As De La Tocnaye reported, 'the soldiers ran through the streets armed with sticks, breaking the windows of those who had not lit up their houses'. De La Tocnaye noted that the military even went to the trouble of 'breaking back windows and the fanlights of doors', under the supervision of their officers and their commander, General Lake, who seemingly did little more than prevent even greater excesses. Although by no means unsympathetic to the government cause, De La Tocnaye found the largely Presbyterian inhabitants of Belfast, many of whom supported the United Irishmen, 'in a sort of stupor hardly distinguishable from fear' induced by the army's activities. 'I imagine the people of Belfast will not for long forget the terror in which I found them,' he wrote.

Hurrying from Belfast the following day, he 'was much surprised to see that the soldiers had taken the trouble to break windows as far as two or three miles from the town'. He found Lisburn, Hillsborough and Dromore 'full of soldiers' and pervaded by an atmosphere of fear. The 'troops went through the country, burning the houses' of suspected United Irishmen. 'Not a day passes without murders or the burning of houses,' he reported. In Banbridge, while he was there, the military 'promenaded through the market-place and obliged women who wore anything green, ribbon or otherwise, to take it off'. De La Tocnaye took the sensible precaution of removing from his umbrella a ribbon that happened to be green. None of this appeared in the newspapers, which were largely loyal to the ascendancy, and ultimately the British authorities, or were too cowed to publish it.

Blaquiere was an enthusiastic and active supporter of the military, and a staunch opponent of rights for Catholics and Presbyterians, but the turmoil in the country at large failed to penetrate the calm of parliament's debating chambers where Blaquiere's bill continued to make slow progress. On Wednesday, 7 June it was debated in the House of Lords.

The Earl of Clare, the Lord Chancellor, started by graciously commending the intentions behind the bill, but then went on to expound in great detail on how certain technical aspects of the bill made it legally inconsistent and how it could not be remedied without 'striking out every clause and inserting others' – to such an extent that it would not then be passed by the Commons. He had spent 'two hours' working on it that morning but was convinced of its fatal weaknesses.[19]

He again protested his support for the aims of the bill, admitted the horrors that it was intended to correct, and praised Blaquiere for his efforts, while firmly restating the impossibility of the bill being passed. Instead, he referred to reforms undertaken by the governors of the Hospital themselves, changes that he was confident would end the abuses and meet the aims of the bill. The governors had 'that morning', he declared, decided to give the 'utmost powers' to 'thirteen humane ladies' who had agreed to 'superintend and watch over the children of that charity'.

The vastly wealthy Lord Altamont then commented on the plight of the 'poor diseased infants' in the Foundling Hospital. It 'would be a humane act' to 'put an end to [their] existence with a pistol,' Altamont sensitively declared.[20]

His Lordship also condemned the practice of accumulating bodies 'in a putrid state before they were interred'. He went on to say that 'he had been informed that some of the persons who attended that place, instead of being affected [by] the mortality of the poor infants, made their charnel house a place of amusement'.[21]

As we have seen, at one stage the infant nurseries were located over the part of the Hospital named 'Bedlam' – the vaults where the insane were housed. In London, the original 'Bedlam' – the Bethlem Hospital – was a notorious tourist attraction. However, there is no evidence, other than Lord Altamont's allegation, of this happening in the Foundling Hospital. On the other hand outsiders – potential donors – did visit charities such as the Foundling Hospital, often to attend charity sermons, and it was noted that visitors could often be seen in the wide central aisle of the great hall, surveying a scene of one thousand children sitting down to eat.[22]

A number of other Lords spoke, both for and against the bill, until finally the Earl of Clare reiterated his objections, and the House moved on to other matters.

On 13 June Blaquiere reported back to the House of Commons on the fate of his bill in the Lords – how it 'contained many clauses which the Upper House thought proper to reject'.[23] He therefore undertook to modify the bill to make it 'less objectionable', and also to limit its duration, as an 'experimental act', to one year. This was agreed to and in short order Blaquiere reappeared in the chamber with the altered bill, apparently having prepared it in advance.

Perhaps the production of the altered bill so quickly was unexpected, as the Solicitor General now 'expressed his surprise at the introduction of such a bill at so late a stage of the sessions, and in so thin a House – particularly as the subject had undergone a very ample discussion ... and as the opinions of gentlemen both within and without parliament were far from being unanimous and well collected on it'.[24]

Blaquiere 'thought it extraordinary the honourable Gentleman would not permit the bill as usual to go through the first reading before he offered any objections, weighty as they might be'. Blaquiere got his way and the bill was 'read a first time'.

The next day, the bill was back in the Commons for its second reading, again sponsored by Blaquiere. By this time, however, it was obvious that whatever slender support Blaquiere had once enjoyed, had by now totally ebbed away. The Solicitor General again turned on his former ally. He 'hoped Blaquiere would withdraw his motion and not force him to divide the House'. He savaged the bill as 'wholly inadequate to the purposes for which it was framed' and 'without reflecting on the talents of his right honourable friend', hinted that Blaquiere was out of his depth, and expressed the hope that relevant legislation would come from the 'Minister' (i.e. the Chief Secretary), at the beginning of the next parliamentary session. In the meantime he was confident the 'institution would experience all the correcting care which honour, talent, and humanity could bestow, as some of the first characters in the country had made it the object of their humane and benevolent solicitude'.[25]

And anyway, he argued, the 'great mortality' of the infants for which the institution had been blamed, had not reduced despite all the recent attention from parliament, and the particular care and attention it had been subject to, 'so that it would appear that the mortality was not forced but natural and inevitable'.[26] He also objected to the considerable extra expenditure that the new bill would impose on the public, and for 'many other reasons which he enumerated' hoped Blaquiere would withdraw the bill. Gone were the elaborate tributes to Blaquiere's magnanimity. Gone also was the polite but qualified support.

Blaquiere retorted angrily that 'had the honourable and learned gentleman attended to the progress of the subject in the House' he would not now be blocking the proposal.[27] Referring to the Solicitor General's assertion that since the mortality had not decreased it must be natural and not amenable to any reforms, he asked, 'what did it go to prove?' – 'that without the coercion of law, the evils complained of' would continue, notwithstanding any 'humane and benevolent solicitude' which might be expressed in the House.

Further mocking the Solicitor General's use of the term 'humane and benevolent solicitude', Blaquiere referred to 'bills and advertisements ... stuck upon posts and pillars,' seemingly by the governors, 'descriptive, and, he was sure, consequent of this solicitude'. Nevertheless, he was no more hopeful 'of the abuses being diminished, and was only reminded of the zeal and activity of the Black Cart, while the Committee of Supply is sitting'.[28]

In emotional terms, Blaquiere expressed strong regret that the Chief Secretary, Pelham, then sitting in the chamber, had not taken up the issue, as his support would have been critical. However, Blaquiere refused to withdraw his bill: 'as he would consider it little less than consenting to ... the murder, on an average of four or five children a day'. What's more, referring to Pelham, 'he was sure that ... [the] bold and manly opposition to what he considered wrong, which characterised his honourable and learned friend on all occasions, would prevent him from recommending the withdrawing of a bill which ... was opposed to one of the most shameful and barbarous abuses, which could disgrace any country'. According to the *Freeman's Journal*, a firm supporter of Blaquiere, 'the Right Honourable Baronet seemed inclined to say more, but sank into his seat, evidently overpowered by the pressure of his feelings'.[29] Another MP then rose, but the Speaker intervened, ordering a count of members present, and there being insufficient members in the House should a division be called, he adjourned proceedings.

The following day Blaquiere attended at the bar of the House of Lords with the 'new Foundling Hospital bill'. However, it was 'ordered to lie on the table'. No further action would be taken by parliament before the session ended.[30]

Shortly afterwards, the parliamentary session was adjourned and many of the members returned to their country properties.[31] Blaquiere, whose country mansion was located outside Mullingar, was one of the Grand Jurors for the midsummer assizes in the county town that June.[32] As already mentioned, a military detachment had been ordered to guard his house. Incidents reported just 12 miles from Blaquiere's home illustrate the brutal unfolding of events. In the village of Moyvore, on 19 June, an elderly blacksmith who had handed over illegal weapons was sabred to death on the spot by the officer commanding the Wicklow militia unit. The blacksmith's three sons, also United Irishmen, were then killed by the troops. The family home was set on fire while the wife and child of one of the dead men remained inside. She was dragged outside, verbally abused as a 'bitch' and threatened. The four dead bodies were then piled on a wooden cart. Three other men were arrested nearby and tied to the same cart, which was then escorted by the military unit 3 miles to the village of Ballymore. It is reported that during the journey, the entrails of the butchered men protruding through the partially floored cart, became entangled in its axle. Meanwhile, a fifer and a drummer marched beside the cart, playing loudly to drown out the voices of the female relatives of the still-living men bound to the cart, who pleaded for their lives throughout the journey. (No males would dare to do the same for fear of summary execution.) It was fair day in Ballymore, as the military well knew, and they proceeded to the fair green, where the bound men were ordered to kneel. They were then shot dead in full view of the crowd. The militia then proceeded to brutalise those attending the market, slashing at them with swords and inflicting serious injuries on sixteen, some of whom were permanently maimed. The targeting of market fairs, it seems, was a deliberate tactic, since it allowed maximum dissemination of word-of-mouth reporting of the brutality – intended to intimidate any who would challenge the regime. (In an era before mass media and when the largely pro-establishment newspapers were unlikely to report it.)

Later, the military unit returned to the village of Moyvore, setting it alight in the dead of night, destroying thirty-four out of forty houses, and rendering the inhabitants, men, women and children, homeless.

A few days later, at the midsummer assizes, the local Grand Jury – made up of the leading ascendancy figures of County Westmeath – voted to award a 'service of plate' to the militia unit involved, to reward their 'splendid services'. On the Grand Jury, as we have seen, and considering his political connections, perhaps the most influential member, was none other than Sir John Blaquiere.[33] A gesture such as this would have a number of functions, as Blaquiere would have known. The most obvious was to encourage the military in their brutal techniques. Another, more subtle, purpose might be to force wavering members of the gentry to declare their hand – to either back repression or risk alienating themselves from their peers, and risk being labelled as rebel sympathisers. (In a nearby town, Richard Lovell Edgeworth was to learn the danger of this when he was almost lynched by a loyalist militia for perceived laxity towards the rebels.) The public backing of such a gesture by any figure would have a further effect – exposing the individual to potential revenge attacks from the rebels, and thus binding him further to the side of the regime.

What are we to make of Blaquiere's unsuccessful bid at reform? One of the ablest politicians of his day, few knew better how to manipulate the levers of power. He had been a governor of the Foundling Hospital since at least 1784.[34] Opportunistic and adept at self-enrichment, he was an entrenched opponent of rights for Catholics and condoned atrocities against civilians. When the interests of a section of the ascendancy and those of the British government diverged, he was firmly on the side of the government. And here may lie at least a partial motivation for his approach to the Foundling Hospital. For at least one historian saw the Hospital as an indictment of ascendancy rule in Ireland, and an argument for full Union with Britain – soon to become the most heated political topic, with Blaquiere firmly on the pro–union side.[35] Exposing the Foundling Hospital conveniently supported this agenda. But a full consideration of this complex character is outside the scope of this book.

Following its adjournment that summer, Blaquiere never again raised the issue of the Foundling Hospital in the House of Commons. He spent the remainder of his political career in Ireland working for the demise of the old Irish parliament, while simultaneously furthering his own prospects, insisting on both a peerage and the right to sit in the British parliament after the Act of union. As Lord de Blaquiere, he continued to oppose rights for Catholics until his death in 1812, still drawing enormous pensions from the Irish revenue.

A Fallow Field

In the Foundling Hospital, meanwhile, the 'lady governesses' had been active since their nomination in April 1797. The women had no formal role or position, despite their informal title.[1] From the start they had asked the governors for certain powers. These included the authority to suspend lower-level staff and suppliers' contracts. They also looked for the apothecary, matron and housekeeper to be placed under their control, the power to make repairs and improvements not exceeding £10 in value, as well as the ability to request a meeting of the Board of Governors if more significant actions were required. The governors declined to give the women powers to dismiss any staff or terminate contracts, but did instruct staff to otherwise obey their directions.[2]

In July 1797, three of the 'lady governesses' led a young surgeon, John Creighton, around the Hospital. He had just been appointed as resident surgeon. Born in Athlone, Creighton was only 29 years old, and was just five years qualified. But he was a rising star and had been made Professor of Midwifery in the Royal College of Surgeons at the age of 26. In addition to developing what would become a very successful private practice, he also carried out charitable work at the Dublin General Dispensary in Temple Bar. This charity aimed to provide medical and surgical treatment to the labouring poor rather than the destitute.[3] He would also go on to pioneer the vaccination of children for smallpox in Ireland at the Dispensary for Infant Poor.[4] Through either his college work or his private practice, Creighton had come to the notice of the Speaker of the House of Commons, John Foster, who had recommended him to the governors. They had previously advertised for candidates but without success.[5] Creighton allowed himself to be appointed, rather than actively pursuing the post.[6] But he turned out to be a good choice. Significantly, the post was now a residential one and he was given handsome apartments in the Hospital for himself and his family.

Recalling his first visit many years later, Creighton described his tour of the Hospital on the day of his appointment.[7] Although parliament had heard of the appalling conditions the previous April (and indeed in 1791 and 1792, and any of the many MPs who were governors could have investigated conditions at any time they chose), by July it seemed little had changed. The 'infirmary or dying ward', as Creighton termed it, was located in a building separate from the main establishment , as we have seen. There, Creighton saw thirteen children lying in cradles. An 'old woman of eighty' was in the room. He 'looked about to see where the nurse tender slept', expecting her to sleep in the same room as her charges, as was the normal practice. It then dawned on him that the children were under the care of the old woman and that the infants 'were left [alone] there all night, and the place swarming with rats, and everything that was abominable.'[8]

Creighton was also able to inspect the notorious 'Bottle' or 'composing bottle'. It contained 'simple water with tincture of opium, at the mercy of the head nurse tender' to make up as she pleased. In other words, the concentration of opium administered was entirely at the discretion of the head nurse. The consequence of this was that 'the child was thrown into a state of stupor, or into convulsions'. When later asked if 'this composing draught was in fact a killing draught?' he replied, 'It could not be called anything else.'[9] On that same day, the day of his appointment, Creighton also visited the burial ground at the back of the Hospital. He described it as 'just like a fallow field, all turned up – the burials were so rapid that there was not a blade of grass allowed to grow upon it'.[10]

Work soon started on rectifying matters in the Hospital. The wooden bedsteads that served as cradles 'were found to be so alive with vermin that they could not be carried down the stairs', so they were 'broken up and thrown clean out of the window and burnt'.[11] The men employed to carry out the work were so overcome that they had to be given 'stimulants' (more likely alcohol) to continue the work.[12] Wodsworth relayed how 'the yards and back premises of the buildings were found full of holes, stagnant water and filth, and were forthwith cleaned out, levelled, and purified'.[13]

Creighton immediately turned his attention to the medical care of the infants. Again recalling the events years later, Creighton confirmed some of the details that had emerged in parliament just a few months before his appointment: 'The gentlemen who were my predecessors did not take any pains in examining the children,' he recalled. They 'never saw them at all, they left them to the head nurse to decide upon … as she thought proper'.[14] 'There was no medical treatment I could perceive; those gentlemen did not attend.' And although 'the apothecary was resident in the house ... according to his own report, he visited merely once in three weeks or a month'.[15]

Creighton found it necessary to emphasise the 'advantages which may justly be expected to arise from an accurate inspection of the infants on admission, and from a skilful and unremitting discharge of medical duty'. He began to personally examine every infant on admission. After being received at the gate by the porter, the children were 'brought up immediately to the Foundling Department, and washed and dressed and cleaned' before being examined 'uncovered' by Creighton himself – essential to a thorough examination but by no means the norm at the time.

From the start, Creighton carefully classified the infants he examined into several groups according to their state of health and began to publish monthly figures. He was very conscious of the shockingly high rates of venereal disease reported in the Hospital, on which most of the deaths had previously been blamed. However, his own meticulous examinations seemed to indicate a much lower level of infection. In fact, of 802 children admitted in the first six months he found just seventy-six who might have had venereal disease – a rate of roughly one in eleven. But even of these he was sure in only nineteen cases – the other fifty-seven he classified as 'Doubtful Eruptions', i.e. skin lesions of uncertain type. All but two of these fifty-seven died, lending weight to the inclination to consider these as venereal cases.

Encouragingly, however, infants began to survive for longer in the nursery. Under the old regime no infants had survived in the Hospital beyond the first month, whereas in the first six months under the new arrangements, at least forty-nine did so.[16] Before, any child who spent longer than one week in the Hospital ultimately died there, whereas now children were being sent out to nurses after three and even after up to six weeks.[17]

However, quite dispiritingly, even though they were surviving for longer, and in spite of Creighton's daily attendance, of the 802 admitted in the first six months of his tenure, 418 eventually died in the Hospital. Creighton carefully tabulated the causes of death. The commonest was 'complaints in the bowels', of which 329 died. Creighton conceded that these children were likely to have died of a variety of illnesses, of which bowel upsets were only the most prominent signs. Likewise for the fifty-one who died of 'convulsions'. The two deaths arising from 'accidents', he later revealed, resulted from the infants 'being overlaid by the House wet nurses'.[18]

The other change that Creighton made, apart from detailed examination of the infants on admission, was to provide them with appropriate, although rudimentary, treatments, whereas before the only treatment given was 'the Bottle'.

Another crucial change was the provision of more wet nurses in the Hospital itself, to feed infants between the time of their arrival at the Hospital and the time they were taken out by country nurses. Creighton was able to calculate that, assuming each nurse could feed two infants, the Hospital would need twenty-six such women, and it appears these were duly engaged.[19] Experiments with a greater child-to-nurse ratio were unsuccessful, for as it was reported, 'whenever three infants were put to the breast of one House nurse, the event was, that on the sickness of one of them calling for her [individual] care, the other two, by being unavoidably neglected, very frequently pined away and died'.[20]

In February 1798, a committee of parliament praised the 'extraordinary and unremitting diligence' of Creighton and the new apothecary, William Lindsey. Creighton later recalled that his salary was doubled to £200 on the recommendation of parliament that year. The committee also praised 'the ladies of high rank and character who in the last year humanely undertook the superintendence of this charity' whose conduct 'reflects the most distinguished honour on themselves, and confers the most essential benefits on the institution and on the nation'.[21] Another investigation in September 1797 had found that one of the tax collectors, Joseph Whitty, had embezzled at least £124 from the Hospital.[22]

There was still a rearguard action being fought in relation to Blaquiere's proposal regarding county foundling hospitals – that a foundling hospital would be opened in every county, thereby removing the need to transport newborns over long distances. This is unlikely to have found favour with conservatives, concerned that the children would be more open to influence by Catholic parents. After all, removing children to distant and even secret locations had been a recurrent practice throughout the history of the Foundling Hospital and other proselytising organisations such as the Incorporated Society for Promoting English Protestant Schools in Ireland.

MPs interviewed senior surgeons Gustavus Hume and Samuel Croker King, as well as senior physician Dr Boyton. Each was pointedly asked about the desirability of local institutions, which would reduce the need for long cart journeys. Each agreed that this would be beneficial.[23] Despite the medical evidence, however, conservative supporters of the Hospital were determined its mission – to take in the children of poor Catholics and raise them as loyal Protestants – would continue unchanged, albeit with reform of its day-to-day operations. Accordingly, in 1798 a new Act of Parliament reduced the number of governors from 171 to nine, but made few other changes.[24]

Notwithstanding the disappointing mortality figures for the first six months of Creighton's involvement, efforts continued at the Hospital to increase survival rates. Efforts were made to increase the availability and quality of the country nurses. To this end wages were increased from £2 to £3 per annum and the premium payable to nurses at the end of the first year if the child survived was increased from £1 to £2.[25]

Plans were also made to increase the supervision and improve the selection of country nurses by establishing a system of 'county inspectors' who would recommend nurses to the Hospital and supervise the care of the children in the countryside. Furthermore, this system would allow the nurses to be paid locally without having to make the arduous annual journey to the Hospital with their child in order to receive payment. However, there is no evidence that this system ever got off the ground (at least not until the 1830s) and, instead, the Hospital continued to rely on references for the nurses from 'some respectable resident gentry or farmers in the neighbourhood from whence they come'[26] or from the local Anglican clergyman.

Finally, Creighton and the 'governesses' turned their attention to the transport of the infants from the country, who appear to have been swaddled and placed in baskets either on the nurses' back or on carts. A number of new regulations were made. Firstly, the women conveying them were not to bring more than one infant at a time. Secondly, if the 'nurse' had not 'discharged her trust with care and humanity' or 'if any abuse of carriage appears on the body of an infant, or there be reason to suspect from its weakly state that it has been neglected by its nurse on the road, the certificate entitling to payment is withholden, and the circumstances of such abuse and misconduct immediately made known to the proper officer in the country'.[27] It was, however, acknowledged that this approach was completely reliant on the co-operation of the relevant 'officer' (almost invariably the local Anglican clergyman or churchwarden, who had arranged the transport in the first place).

From the outset, Creighton carefully analysed his results and fearlessly published them, even when, for reasons beyond his control, they were not flattering. His aim was to bring the light of science to bear on the problems of the infants. He applied a profound scientific scepticism to the problems confronting him, and cautioned that 'we must beware of drawing general conclusions from a hasty and superficial view, however forcible, and however authentic certain facts may appear'.[28]

Over the next few years the mortality rate in the infant department fell from a peak of 76 per cent in 1797 to 25 per cent by 1802. However, the rate continued to fluctuate up to 40 per cent.[29] This, of course, includes deaths in the Hospital only, and says nothing about the survival of infants while in the care of country nurses under the governance of the Hospital.

But by now the governors had begun to learn a fundamental truth underlying the Foundling Hospital – a truth that had emerged again and again, but had often been ignored: for the Foundling Hospital to function, children had to die in large numbers. If even a modest proportion survived, it quickly ran into a financial and accommodation crisis. The lesson was about to be learned yet again.

A Severe Malady

By 1803, the governors realised the enormity of the challenge that was facing them. Based on an anticipated increase in the survival of infants, thanks to the reforms after 1797, they were expecting a surge in the numbers of children being drafted back into the Hospital from 1805 onwards, when these children would reach drafting age. They calculated that this would result in a requirement for 1,200 places in total in the Foundling Hospital.

Now that the crisis in infant mortality appeared to have abated and the institution had been preserved, its proselytising *raison d'être* was beginning to be reasserted. The ideological and political motivation underlying the Hospital was never far from the surface. In particular, the governors were gravely concerned about the length of time children were remaining in the country with their nurses – usually, at this point, until 10 years old or later. The governors' principal concern was that frequently 'a strong attachment had been formed, not only to the religion of their nurses – almost exclusively Catholic – but to their vicious habits and modes of life, and which too often baffled subsequent attempts to eradicate and amend'.[1] As far as the governors were concerned 'habits of theft, lying and other vices [were] acquired at nurse'.[2]

Therefore, there were two reasons why the governors wanted to expand the accommodation. One was because of the anticipated increase in numbers due to increased survival of infants thanks to the improved standards of care. The other was to reduce the number of years the children spent with their (mostly Catholic) nurses, by drafting them at an earlier age. They petitioned the British parliament and managed to secure an addition of £5,000 to the annual grant.[3] This, they calculated, would allow them to accommodate 1,200 children, to draft them at 8 years of age, and apprentice them at 12, after four years in the Hospital.

With the increase in funds secured, the governors set about expanding the accommodation and enlarging the chapel. Plans drawn up by the architect

Francis Johnson and subsequent images of the Hospital show, over the succeeding years, a considerable aggrandisement of the façade, with the addition of decorative battlements and a central clock tower to the great dining hall.[4] The more liberal-minded inhabitants of Dublin must have silently shuddered to see this symbol of the penal days being so significantly augmented.

But the driving force behind this expansion – the need to cater for the supposed increase in survivors, along with the urge to separate the children from their nurses at an earlier age, resulted in another catastrophe. For, as a report by the governors outlines, 'out of this measure … circumstances arose which were altogether unexpected, which could neither be foreseen nor provided against … A severe malady (chiefly dysentery …) broke out among the younger children in the two years in which this early drafting took place, which spread among the grown children and also the adults of the establishment.'[5] With the new buildings still not finished, 'the former Infirmary accommodation was found utterly inadequate [and] several of the dormitories … were converted into temporary hospitals for the sick'. However, 'in spite of vigilance, attention, and care, the mortality … was considerable and alarming in both years'. The illness struck the younger children, who had just been drafted, first and was thought to have been triggered by the traumatic changes in their 'diet and mode of living' upon returning to the Hospital.[6]

To make matters worse, by 1809 the Foundling Hospital was once again in a financial crisis. The increased accommodation had still not been finished and the new infirmary was 'roofed, but the inside work not completed'. The hospital was in debt to the tune of over £9,400. The age of drafting was increased again, but this was still not enough. In a dramatic reversal, the governors suspended all building work and ceased drafting of all children from country nurses.[7]

An outside observer, the writer and statistician Edward Wakefield, visited the Hospital on 5 May 1809 with three female companions, and was struck by the 'wretched' appearance of the girls whose 'countenances [were] disfigured by disease and hard living'.[8] Visiting the boys' section, he 'could not perceive that their looks [were] in the least superior to that of the other sex'. Elsewhere, he reported, he was 'struck with the wretched appearance which the children in general exhibited; the majority of them had sore fingers, scalded heads, and inflamed eyes, or were afflicted with tumours or ulcers, the effects I believe, of confirmed and inveterate itch' (most likely scabies).[9]

Although in general negative about the Hospital, he reported that the 'dormitories were spacious and clean; the hall in which they dine had a noble appearance', and other areas were well whitewashed.[10] However, he also related how, on an earlier visit, his companions had particularly noticed 'two beautiful infants, which had that day been sent in'. On their subsequent visit, on asking after the infants, they found one 'was in the most wretched state I ever beheld any infant; the truth is, this child, as well as the other children in the ward, was covered with the itch.' The second infant was dead.

Wakefield could hardly be considered as having a preconceived hostility towards the Hospital, since his work was undertaken at the suggestion of Lord Oriel, John Foster, a conservative supporter of the institution and the individual who had recruited John Creighton to his role in 1797.[11]

When Wakefield published the report of his visit a few years later he made an eloquent plea for the closure of the institution. Noting its proselytising function, he commented that 'when I take into consideration that the trustees, the governesses, and the commissioners who have inspected it are all of that faith, I perceive the spirit with which it is conducted, and what must be its ultimate object and aim'. He argued that 'extending a system which adds misery to misery, spreads wretchedness and encourages vice, even if it should answer the end of conversion, ought not for a moment to be entertained. It has failed of its purpose in every respect'[12] Sadly his pleas fell on deaf ears.

In contrast to Wakefield's experience, two months later, on 20 July 1809, the Hospital was visited by commissioners of the Board of Education in Ireland. This was a body established by the British parliament to examine education throughout Ireland. As part of their work, the commissioners carried out the first substantial enquiry into the Foundling Hospital since the Act of Union. The commission included such leading figures as the Anglican Archbishop of Armagh, the Dean of St Patrick's Cathedral, the Provost of Trinity College, and Richard Lovell Edgeworth, inventor, and father of Maria. Although the group carried out an extensive enquiry, and published a fifty-seven-page report, they appear to have only visited the Hospital on this single occasion.

The impressions formed by the commissioners on their visit were at odds with those of Wakefield two months earlier. They were 'struck by the order and regularity which everywhere prevailed, as well as the neatness and healthy appearance of the children in the schools and workrooms'.[13] Although aware of the high death rate, the Board strongly endorsed the continuation of the Hospital. Indeed, they appeared to emphasise that the saving of lives alone, without the specific educational formation provided by the Foundling Hospital, was of relatively little value, even though they were well aware of the proselytising nature of that education.[14]

The commission went so far as to endorse the long-planned extension to the accommodation to increase the capacity for children returned from the country to 1,200, and advocated their return to the Hospital at an earlier age.[15] On the other hand, they recognised that admissions of infants should be kept to a maximum of 2,000 per year, or the institution would become unviable.

✱　✱　✱

Following the relatively positive report of the commissioners in 1809, admissions continued to climb. And in the wake of that report, the parliamentary grant was increased dramatically from £21,825 in 1810 to £37,575 in 1811, further strengthening the institution.[16] (In addition, income from the tax on houses continued to average approximately £8,000 per annum.)[17] In 1813, 2,664 infants were admitted. In that year nearly 1,000 died in the infant nursery alone, while a further 1,700 had to be found places with country nurses.[18]

Alarmed by these increases, this time the Foundling Hospital governors themselves took action. Perhaps they were motivated by a new liberalism, or pragmatism, as the membership of the board slowly evolved, due to death or resignations. They initiated their own 'solemn enquiry upon oath'.[19] As if discovering it anew, they found the principal cause of death to be the condition of the infants on arrival at the Hospital.[20] No amount of improvement within the Foundling Hospital itself could address this. The 'scantiness of their clothing' was found to be even worse than in previous years. The distance of the journey was sometimes 150 miles or more (this could take eight or nine days in an open cart). The governors cited the lack of care by the 'carrying nurses', who were described as 'hired carriers, generally of the lowest description and most abandoned character and rendered callous by the practice of the trade at all times of the year and under every inclemency of weather'.[21] Finally, the early age at which the infants were conveyed was identified as a significant factor. In the previous year alone, of the nearly 1,000 who had died in the infant infirmary, more than 180 had done so within a few hours of reaching the Hospital, having arrived 'in a state incapable of deglutition' (swallowing). The governors, who by now included two senior medics, felt that even a delay of ten or twenty days after birth before transporting the infants would help, allowing them to gain a little extra size and strength before the trip.[22] 'The heaviest mortality is found to take place in the winter and spring months,' the governors also found.

The governors began to argue for some control on admissions. To support their arguments, they produced some disturbing mortality figures. Of 4,334 infants admitted in the first four months each of 1810 to 1814 (a total of twenty months), 1,971 had died in the nursery, a mortality of nearly 50 per cent, which represents a considerable regression from the last previously published figures from 1799 to 1808.[23] Again, it should be noted that these are the deaths in the nursery alone and do not include further deaths that occurred with the country nurses.

To bolster their case for a limit on admissions, the governors pointed to existing Acts of parliament that allowed parishes outside Dublin and Cork to raise a 'cess' to maintain infants locally for the first year of life. They also pointed out that the Hospital was only intended to be for the destitute, and therefore they should only accept an infant where the parish had demonstrated every effort to confirm that its parents were unable to support it.

The governors were careful not to resile from the oft repeated (and still unachieved) plan to increase the accommodation to 1,200 places – a model that assumed the drafting of 400 children, and the apprenticing of 400 per year. But they pointed out that the 'failure of an adequate demand for apprentices, or of any other mode of providing for the children (particularly the females)' meant that no amount of expansion in the accommodation would be enough 'so long as the outlet continues to be obstructed'. To their credit the governors wrote formally to the Viceroy, recommending the most radical change to the operations of the Foundling Hospital in many years – its closure. But only to new admissions, for short periods of time, and only in the 'inclement season'.

As a result, in 1814, the first substantial change in many years was made to the legislation underpinning the Foundling Hospital.[24] There were two main provisions in the new Act. The first was that the governors were given powers to suspend all admissions for up to six months at a time, after giving 'due notice' to the parishes. The second was that before any infant was accepted, a certificate signed by a minister and/or churchwardens of the parish from which the child came was to be provided, indicating that a diligent search had been made for the parents of the child and that either they could not be found, or it had been established that they were unable to support the child.

And so the first closure of the Foundling Hospital to new infant admissions in its 100-year history commenced, after due notice, in February 1815 and lasted for two months.[25] However, the closure was restricted to country parishes only. The governors, perhaps anticipating a reaction from Dublin Corporation, continued to admit infants from that city and county. This action resulted in a reduction in admissions by about 400 compared with the previous year. Correspondingly, the death rate for those two months fell sharply. It is likely that many infants were simply held onto by the parish authorities, in the temporary care of a nurse paid for by the parish, and then transported at the end of the closure period. But it is also likely that even this, as the medics had anticipated, would aid the survival of the child, by allowing it to gain a little extra maturity before the trip.

Despite its limited nature, the temporary closure (which was repeated in 1816 for four months) was vehemently opposed by Dublin Corporation, exercising its traditional proprietorial attitude to the Hospital, long conscious of its donation of land and central role in the foundation of the original Workhouse back in 1703. The Corporation wrote to the Viceroy in 1816 alleging an increase in infanticide resulting from the closure.[26] The reply of the governors to this charge was robust: the Corporation had not instanced a single case of infanticide as evidence of its claim, they stated, and only one case incidentally linked to the Hospital had been reported in the newspapers since the measure had been introduced. Furthermore, the Hospital, in its frequent communications with the Anglican clergy all over the country, had not been made aware of a single case of infanticide linked to the closure.[27]

However, despite the temporary improvement, soon the overall number of admissions began to rise again and by 1817–18 had reached 2,210.[28]

The next change to the legislation was in 1820, allowing greater flexibility to the Hospital in its periodic closures. But the change that was to have most effect of all was the imposition in 1822 on the parishes of a £5 charge, payable for each infant on admission.[29] The effect would be dramatic. From 1,640 admissions in 1821, admissions were to plummet to 419 by 1823.

21

The Foundlings Speak

When the Hospital was visited in 1819 by the American Quaker, educationalist and writer John Griscom, he described the long-standing practice of tattooing the newly arrived infants on the arm: 'When an infant is brought in it is stripped, washed, and one of its arms is tattooed … by pricking into the skin, an ink composed of a mixture of India ink, indigo, and a little gunpowder.'[1]

A separate report from the same period confirms that the children were 'marked with an alphabetical letter denoting the year of admission, and the number they stand on the books, on the upper part of their arms with ink and gunpowder, by means of needles fixed in a handle for that purpose'.[2] The number was then recorded in the registers of admission along with the child's name, its state of health, distance carried to Dublin, and details of its sending out to nurse.[3] (These registers, which together with the governors' minutes amounted to over one hundred volumes, survived into the twentieth century, but not to the present day.)[4]

After tattooing, the infant waited a number of days in the Hospital before being dispatched with a country nurse to grow up in the countryside. Little information survives about their lives there. The voices of the poorest and most marginalised are rarely heard in the historical record.

Yet, remarkably, details of some foundlings do survive from this period. After 100 years of admissions, apart from the brief glimpses described in Chapters 8 and 10, we at last gain a fleeting picture of the lives of the foundlings with their country nurses. They emerge as wary, resourceful, intelligent and above all, supremely loyal to, and protective of, their country foster mothers.

For example, the foundling Eliza Stroaker believed she was just 3 days old when she was given to her nurse, Margaret Burns. Burns lived a mile from Wicklow town, a two-day round trip on foot from the Foundling Hospital.[5] To Eliza, her nurse was her 'mother', the only one she had ever known. Eliza felt she was treated better than her nurse's own two older daughters. At first her nurse worked as a servant, then after her husband died, she cared for an old woman who was 'doating' and the woman's husband who had had a stroke. Burns 'washed and mended' for them. According to Eliza, her nurse was 'always sewing' to support the family. In addition she kept a pig and a 'cabbage garden' and a 'potato garden'. Eliza reported that she had had a happy childhood. Her nurse managed to delay Eliza's drafting back to the Foundling Hospital for a number of years by persuading the local Anglican clergyman to write to the institution on her behalf. Although the nurse was a Catholic, when a letter arrived from the Hospital instructing that all foundlings had to be brought to 'church' (i.e. the Protestant church) and attend a Protestant school, she complied, even lending Eliza 'her old cloak to go to church in'. Indeed, it is likely the Protestant clergyman would have had to convince the Hospital authorities of Burns's compliance in order for them to allow Eliza to remain with her nurse longer.

Eventually, at the age of 13, under a new, stricter regime, Eliza was drafted back to the Hospital. When interviewed nine months later she was still 'always crying' and longed to return to her 'mother'– Burns – with whom she was not allowed to have contact. However, although she admitted this longing, she declared that she would not return, as to do so would place a burden on her foster mother, and she feared that if she once returned, the latter would never let her leave again. Instead, she vowed to secure an 'apprenticeship' as a servant so as not to be an encumbrance to her.

Another foundling, Mary Birch, lived a mile and a half from Wicklow town with her nurse, and her nurse's own five children, before being drafted into the Hospital at the age of 12. Two years later, she still longed to return to her nurse. In the Hospital she was friends with Eliza Stroaker, whom she had known from Wicklow, where they had attended school for a year together. Mary reported having been well treated by her nurse, better even than the nurse's own children, and although neither the food, nor the clothing, nor the bedding were as good as in the Foundling Hospital, she still longed to return to her nurse.[6]

Anne Burgh, on the other hand, in the thatched cabin that she shared with her nurse and nurse's family, was not allowed to 'dine at her [nurse's] table',[7] but instead had to eat by the fire along with another foundling, Biddy Neil. She contributed to the household by sewing and 'making frocks'. She reported preferring the Foundling Hospital and had no desire to maintain contact with her nurse after her return there. However, this seems to have been an exception. The fact that Anne was fostered by her nurse at 3 years of age may have impaired the bonding process.

The occupation of most nurses is not known for certain, but most were probably farm labourers with smallholdings for subsistence, who took on a variety of additional roles to make ends meet, like Margaret Burns. However, Jane Maxwell's nurse in Ballymore Eustace was a mantua-maker, or dressmaker, as was Bridget Haywood's.

The foundlings formed strong bonds with both the natural children of their nurse and with other foundlings in the same household. For example, Jane Coghlan described fellow foundling Sarah Lewis as 'my sister', since they had grown up in the same household, and this seems to have been the norm.[8] Mary Everett reported that when she was living with her nurse in Leixlip, 'I had a little sister and brother that were out of the same house, the Foundling Hospital,' as well as nine other siblings, her nurse's own children.[9] When 11-year-old Patrick Henley was asked, 'Who among the boys [in the Foundling Hospital] is your best friend?' he replied, 'My brother ... John Hutton.'[10]

In such poor country households sleeping arrangements were basic and cramped. Esther Wade, who must have been with a relatively well-off family, described the house she grew up in as 'a large thatched house', on the basis that it had an upstairs and two rooms downstairs. Nevertheless, her 'father and brother' shared one of the two beds, with 'my mother and us three in the other'. While in Thomas Garder's household 'there were three [beds]; my mother and father lay on one bed [with] two little children, and the four girls in another bed, and I and two brothers laid in a turned up bed' (possibly a settle bed).[11]

We even learn a little of the hopes and ambitions of the foundlings. Their frequent fate was to be 'apprenticed out' when they reached the appropriate age – usually from 12 to 16 depending on circumstances in the Hospital and, crucially, the availability of employment. The majority of the apprenticeships were as servants or labourers – effectively bonded servitude. Some hoped to be apprenticed out to the district in which they had been raised, or even to the same family (if the family was well off enough to afford a servant.) Jane Coghlan hoped that, 'I could get apprenticed; my mother's people, some of them, are very rich; I dare say some of them would take me.'[12] The most common employment awaiting the foundling was that of servant , sometimes within the Hospital itself. Mary Everett became a 'servant in the dormitories'. Anne Calvert, 15, was a 'cook in the preparatory [school].'[13] And Mary Rider, 15 or 16 years old, and Ann Bryan, 16, also worked in the 'preparatory'. Bridget Haywood reported that the schoolmaster in her country village 'was saying he would take me as an apprentice', but whether that was as servant or as teacher is not clear. As we have seen, Eliza Stroaker's ambition was to be apprenticed 'as a servant'.

Other work destinations included a textile factory at Buncrana, which received at least forty-five boys from 1802 to 1809.[14] Reportedly up to 380 boys and girls from the Foundling Hospital and 'certain of the charter schools' worked in the factory, which was near the 'country lodge' of the Bishop of Derry. He supported the factory and was a governor of the Foundling

Hospital. Although the factory was reported to have failed by 1810, records show foundlings being sent there again from 1814 to 1819.[15] Many were also sent to a cotton-spinning factory at Nantwich in Cheshire, Britain.[16]

While we can hope that a group solidarity may have helped the foundlings in this situation, they would have lacked any network of support from family or village should things go wrong. In an era before any system of state welfare or support, the wider family network was crucial to survival. Yet that is the one thing the foundlings lacked. However, those who conformed to the regime in the Hospital had at least one advantage – they were Protestants. Those who did benefit from the 'social capital' of their adoptive families (if they did manage to return to the area they were raised in) suffered the disadvantage that these families were among the very poorest.

At one stage, the foundlings left the Hospital as apprentices 'without any species of bonnet, shawl, or cloak', wearing only the blue and red uniform of the Hospital, which they continued to wear until it 'wore out' (as would be common for the poor of the time).[17] Understandably, this was 'considered a mark of reproach'. The practice appears to have been discontinued between 1822 and 1824.

Only a small minority of children who were drafted back into the Hospital were ever apprenticed. The record is silent on the fate of those who weren't. Religious affiliation may have played a role. Even as late as the 1840s this publicly funded institution required masters taking apprentices from the Hospital to be Protestant and to sign an indenture committing them to raise the apprentice as a Protestant.[18] This may have been unpalatable to any foundling unwilling to conform. It is likely, therefore, that the small number of apprenticeships available went preferentially to those willing to conform. Although every child leaving the Hospital was highly vulnerable, there is no evidence the institution took any steps to ensure those leaving without apprenticeships returned to their foster homes, where they would at least have benefited from family support.

Although the death rate of the foundlings while with country nurses was shockingly high, the majority of deaths occurred in the early months and years. There is strong evidence that deep ties of affection sprang up between those who survived and their carers.

For example, the Reverend Robert Daly of the parish of Powerscourt in Wicklow reported that, 'I can state that almost all the women in my parish that have foundlings to nurse, if they were sure that the children would be taken from them, they would not go up for the salary – they would lose their £3 or £4 to keep the children.'[19] And, 'I know poor women who … have said, "When that child is five years old I will not take it up to the Hospital, I will lose the money."' Rather than enforce the rules, Reverend Daly claimed he was 'inclined to wink at it, when a child has a good parent'. He reported that the nurses 'treat them exceedingly well, they treat them in fact as their own' and develop 'a very wonderfully strong affection for them'. He could hardly think of a single exception to this.

The foundlings almost always informally went by the surname of their nurse's family, while living in the country, unless there happened to be two foundlings of the same Christian name with a family, in which case their formal surname would be used to distinguish them. Strong affection also existed between the foundlings and the natural children of the family, whom they regarded as their brothers and sisters, and, as we have seen, with other foundlings if they were in the same household. Reverend Daly recalled that 'the unhappiest scenes I have ever seen were separating the children from those who had taken care of them for eight or nine years'. The commissioners enquiring into the Hospital in 1826 reported that following drafting the children's attachment to their country nurses and family was 'so strong that even for years after their admission they eagerly avail themselves of every possible opportunity to escape for the purposes of returning to them'.[20] Even Archbishop Magee (see Chapter 23) reported, 'we have found this sort of artificial affection very strong.'[21] Reverend John Pomeroy, one of the governors, reported that if a child was drafted the nurse would often plead with the Hospital to be allowed to take the child back immediately as an 'apprentice', even offering to forego the fee that was normally paid to the apprentice master. Such was the pressure on places in the Hospital that this was sometimes granted, but 'to Protestants only'.[22] Often, if apprenticed in the normal way, the children would abscond 'and go to their nurses, and [the nurses] harbour them and provide for them. The attachment of the nurses to the children that have been reared by them is prodigious.'

Life in the Hospital

June, July and August were the hectic months in the annual cycle of the Hospital, which saw thousands of country nurses make the long round trip with their children for 'the pay'. The officers in the Hospital worked twelve-hour days from 6 a.m. to deal with the press of business.[1] Descriptions recount heart-rending scenes when children were unexpectedly removed from their foster-mothers. They and their foundlings rarely knew accurately the age at which the child would be drafted, as this varied from year to year, depending on vacancies in the Hospital. Since the nurses rarely knew the state of vacancies, once their child reached a certain age they could never be sure if this trip would be their last.

This led to a cruel game of chance. If the nurses were too cautious, and stopped attending too early, they risked foregoing many years of wages – wages that, given their level of poverty, were essential not just for the maintenance of the foundling, but for the viability of the entire family. If the nurses were less cautious, they risked their loved child being abruptly removed from their care forever. Often the women, having made the annual trek to Dublin with their child, would wait in the environs of the Hospital so that they could hear from other nurses and try to divine what the current age of drafting was. 'Scenes of deep distress' were reported, 'which take place when the period arrives for the ultimate separation of the nurse from the child.'[2]

And what was life like for the children when they returned to the Foundling Hospital? Girls on arriving were dispersed among ten or more 'schools' of about forty girls, each one under a mistress. These were akin to modern-day classes except that the children were not divided by ages, each school having girls from the drafting age up. This made eminent sense as it allowed the older girls to assist the younger ones, when paid staff were few. It meant, however, that the welfare of the younger inmates was dependent on other children. The mistress was allowed to choose, from among the girls, one or two to act as monitors: 'to represent to the mistress any improper behaviour or language of the rest which may escape her notice; to assist her in the care of the children; and if at any time she should be absent, to conduct the school, and hear the lessons in her stead; the monitors to be distinguished by wearing a cap and a head ribbon the colour of their school trimmings' while the children of each school were to be 'distinguished from the others by their clothing being trimmed with a particular coloured tape'.[3]

The children slept in large dormitories that they shared with their mistress. According to the 1800 Rules, in theory, no children were to share a bed. This would have been a hardship for children who were used to sharing a sleeping space with 'siblings' in their country cabins before their drafting. As one of the officers commented, 'the children have to sleep in large dormitories; their cabins [in the country] are generally very small and warm, and the large dormitories being exposed to the air more than they were in the country' were a cause of the high rates of illness amongst recent draftees.[4] But by 1813, crowding in the Hospital meant that the dormitories, particularly on the upper floors, were long, low rooms, crammed with bunk beds, without spaces between them, and two or three often shared a bed.[5] The windows had to be left open at night to reduce stuffiness. There was a high rate of sickness among the recent draftees. One common affliction was trachoma, affecting the eyes, with many of the children reporting prolonged stays in the infirmary within a short time of admission.

From April to September the children rose at 5 a.m., when they were supposed to be 'well combed, their hands and face washed' before getting dressed – the mistress, her maid and the older girls assisting the younger ones.[6] Then, according to the rules, each child 'was to say separately and slowly to the mistress the Lord's Prayer, the 3rd morning Collect, and the Grace', a process that would have been impossibly long were it not for the fact that 'the monitor may assist the mistress by hearing some of the children in another room; but that no two children say their prayers in the same room at the same time'.

At 6 a.m. teaching began in the schoolroom and continued until the chapel bell was rung at 8, at which time all were to 'go decently to chapel, accompanied by the mistress'. After prayers they breakfasted in the great hall, following which they were allowed to 'play in the hall or courts' until 9.30. At this time most of the children returned to the schoolroom, where they were given tasks to perform under the supervision of the monitor, while the mistress then left, locking the door of the schoolroom behind her 'lest any should absent themselves without leave', while she attended to her own breakfast. Some of the girls, rather than going to the schoolroom, instead returned to the dormitory, where they had to change their clothes in order to work in the laundry, to where they proceeded accompanied by a monitor.

Education focussed on reading and writing – taught almost entirely from religious texts – the Psalter, the Collect, and Mrs Trimmer's Abridgement of the New Testament. Only some of the girls were taught to write. A writing master visited each school for one hour, three times per week. It was at the discretion of the visiting lady governess which girls were to be taught writing. Reading was considered a useful skill for a servant, but writing was treated with some wariness.

At any one time a proportion of the girls were involved in textile work. When first drafted, the younger girls would start with picking wool, before progressing to knitting. When they had progressed sufficiently to knit cotton stockings 'perfectly' they moved to the 'learners' spinning wheel' and 'when perfect in spinning wool for the factory' they progressed to 'plain work'. When they had mastered this, along with reading and religious knowledge, they were ready to be apprenticed out of the Hospital, or so the theory went. The effect of the rotation between the laundry, the spinning school and the schoolroom was that the children received the equivalent of three days' education per week.[7] However, as one visitor makes clear, spinning took place in the schoolroom itself, while the other children were at lessons.[8]

Early in the century there were twelve schoolmistresses and six schoolmasters, while at the same time there were 819 children in the Hospital itself, giving a crude teacher–pupil ratio of one to forty-five. However, bear in mind that at any one time, only half the class attended school while the other half were trained in trades (at least in theory). This would bring the ratio down to one to twenty-three approximately, not a bad ratio, albeit the pupils were only taught three days per week. In addition, there was a Superintendent Mistress of female schools and a Superintendent Master of the male schools as well as two writing masters and a singing master (for accompanying the liturgy).

Teaching continued in the schoolroom until 'the first great bell rings for dinner' – which was eaten at 2 p.m. At the sound of the bell, each girl was to 'wash her hands, smooth her hair, tighten her clothes, and be ready to walk decently with the mistress to dinner'. At the ringing of the second bell they were to leave the schoolroom and, being joined by the laundry girls, already changed out of their laundry clothes, the girls were to walk 'two and two thro' the court'. An eyewitness described the scene in 1813:

> In favourable weather the boys are paraded in front of the Hall immediately before the hour of dinner; the girls, at the same time, assemble in the interior court, (i.e. behind the Hall) and the children of the various schools, distinguished by their appropriate badges, and conducted by their

respective masters and mistresses, enter the Hall on the proper signal, [and] with a decency, silence, and regularity extremely pleasing, repair to their appropriated seats.

When finished, the children sang 'a hymn by way of grace' and left the hall 'in the same order without the smallest symptom of confusion'.[9]

After dinner the girls were allowed to play again in the 'hall, court or garden' supervised by two mistresses who were to 'watch strictly that none of the girls go into the kitchen, laundry, or any of the buildings; that they make them play about and take exercise, and especially prevent their running into corners in parties'. At 3.15 p.m. 'when the butler's bell rings' the mistress was to round up her charges and escort them to the schoolroom again, where she was to lock them in and where 'they may divert themselves as they like' while she retired to her own room to eat her dinner. At 4, on the ringing of yet another bell, lessons resumed with the reading of the psalms, and continued until 7, when they went for supper. Following this, in the summer months, the girls could play again until 8, after which they returned to their dormitories and, after yet more prayers, retired to bed. The mistress was to wait in the dormitory for half an hour 'till they are asleep', after which she could retire to her sitting room until 11, if she had the energy, by which time she must return to the dormitory, when 'all fire and candle must be extinguished'.

This routine continued for six days of the week. On Saturday evenings 'after the Psalms are read and the [girls] have said the catechism' they were to carry out any repairs needed on their clothes and, after supper, 'each shall tack on the tucker of her own gown' ready for Sunday.[10]

On Sunday, throughout the year, the girls rose at 7.30 a.m. and, after the usual prayers and breakfast, returned to the schoolroom, where they learnt by heart a chapter of *Crossman's Explanation of the Catechism* or hymns, before proceeding to chapel. Forming part of the southern range of buildings, the chapel was located on the far side of the vast interior courtyard, directly opposite the great hall, to which it was linked by a flagstone pathway. Following its rebuilding by the architect Francis Johnston, the chapel had an impressive interior with an elaborate ceiling and Gothic pillars and windows. Rising tiers of benches ran lengthways, facing the central aisle. An upper gallery was accessible directly from the first floor of the new nursery, so that nurses could attend services discreetly and without straying far from their stations.[11] In a separate gallery a seat was reserved for the 'governors and governesses'. The chapel also contained two large fireplaces, over the eastern of which was the inscription, from Matthew 19:14: 'Suffer little children to come to me and forbid them not, for of such is the kingdom of heaven'; and over the western, from Matthew 25:40: 'Inasmuch as ye have done it unto the least of these little ones, ye have done it unto me.'[12]

After chapel on Sundays, the children were allowed play until 3.15 p.m., only interrupted by dinner. They then returned to the schoolroom for religious instruction, following which they returned to chapel for evening service. From there they returned to the schoolroom, where the mistress was to read them a lecture from *Mrs Trimmer's Sunday Scholar's Manual*, until 7, after which the evening followed the usual routine.

The mistresses had to be 'qualified to teach reading, spelling, knitting, plain work and making the children's gowns, and especially to be capable of instructing them in the principles of religion, and decency of manners'. The mistress was entitled to employ a maid – who also had to be a Protestant – for which she was given £6 yearly.[13] The mistress herself was paid £20 per year – a reasonable salary – plus accommodation and associated perks, which consisted of coal (2 tons!), 2½ dozen candles, and 21lb of soap per year, plus diet, including 14 pints of beer per week.

Few of the girls could hope to become schoolmistresses, and it is clear that initially these were recruited from outside the Hospital.[14] Foundling girls could perhaps aspire to be school maids, since most were destined to become servants or farm labourers.

The duties of the school maid make clear how arduous life as a servant could be. The school maid was to rise before the children, to be ready to assist them with washing and dressing. When the children went to school she was to sweep out the dormitory and make the beds (for forty children), then to carry down 'the tubs' and ashes and empty them. In the dining hall she had to 'arrange the porringers and get the bread and milk ready' and have breakfast prepared for the children on their return from the chapel. While they were eating breakfast the maid had to go to the mistress's sitting room to light the fire, then return to the dining hall in time to 'collect the porringers, wash them, and clean the hall tables and forms'.

Following a brief interlude to eat her own breakfast she was to 'scour her tubs and pails, bring up a tub of clean water, and leave it ready for the children to wash their hands before dinner; then to sweep or scour the stairs or passage, dust and sweep the mistresses' room; wash her own and mistress's clothes; bring up her meat or other allowances; and when the small bell rings at half past one, be ready to arrange her trenchers or porringers for dinner, bring in the bread, then the broth or meat, cut it on the trenchers, and have all ready against the last bell rings for dinner.'

After dinner she was to 'collect the utensils, scour them, and as soon as the children leave the hall, clean the tables and forms; then empty the tub the girls washed in before dinner, and leave two tubs filled with clean water ready for washing feet, faces, and necks at night ... at half past six to begin to prepare in the hall for supper at seven; after supper to scour and put by the things as after dinner, and at eight o'clock assist in combing, washing and getting the children to bed; when they are in bed she must sweep out, dust, and prepare the school-room, and leave it ready and clean against morning.'

Only then could she go to bed. In addition, all the maids were 'once a week to unite in scouring the Great Hall, and every one to attend chapel with her mistress on Sunday, both in the morning and afternoon [probably a welcome break] under penalty of a fine to be levied at the discretion of the chaplain'.

The boys followed a similar routine, governed by bells, of early rising, schoolwork and prayer services.[15] The three days not spent at schoolwork were spent at 'Trades' – that is, the boys were trained as 'broad weavers, narrow weavers, winders, wool scribblers, wool pickers, stocking menders, [assistant] tailors, shoe-makers, carpenters and gardeners'.[16] Sunday was spent in a combination of religious instruction in the schoolroom and attendance at chapel.

But for boys and girls alike, for masters and mistresses, for monitors and maids, life in the Foundling Hospital was about to change drastically.

The Arrival of the Magees

The year 1822 saw the appointment of the new Archbishop of Dublin, William Magee. Magee was a brilliant scholar and one-time professor of mathematics and of Greek at the university, before resigning to become a full-time cleric and preacher. Sadly his brilliance was marred by what has been described as 'obsessive anti-Catholicism'.[1] While Dean of Cork he had notoriously caused the burial service of a Catholic in his churchyard to be halted. Prior to this the practice had generally been tolerated since Catholics had had few other options under the penal regulations.

Magee was described as a 'pillar of orthodoxy' and an opponent of Catholic Emancipation (the granting of full civil rights to Catholics).[2] He was an enthusiastic supporter of the 'Second Reformation', a renewed effort to convert the Catholics of Ireland to the Anglican Church. Evoking memories of the original Reformation in Ireland by Henry VIII, this was hardly likely to inspire enthusiasm in Catholics. Over the following decades, rather, there was increasing polarisation along religious lines. (The cross-denominational United Irishman movement having ended in disaster, Catholics were now organising around the single-denominational issue of Catholic Emancipation). Although he was said to have donated £2,000 a year to diocesan and charitable funds, as an Anglican archbishop, Magee was still enormously wealthy with a salary variously put at £7,000, £12,000 or £14,000. This was at a time when the Catholic Archbishop of Dublin had an income of no more than £500.[3] As Archbishop of Dublin, Magee was also a governor of the Foundling Hospital and he took to his duties with great enthusiasm.

By some contemporary accounts, however, Magee's role in the Hospital was overshadowed by that of his wife, Elizabeth. Mrs Magee, a woman of great energy and firm principles, became one of the 'lady governesses', a role that she was soon to exercise almost singlehandedly.[4] Mrs Magee was accused of assuming powers far beyond those of any legitimately appointed governor. According to her critics, she was 'the busiest and most bustling Governess that ever was seen'[5] who 'breaks down, builds up, dismisses and appoints at her pleasure, and conducts herself to all as if they were her domestics'.[6]

The Magees found many shortcomings in the running of the Hospital. Probably under the pressure of increased numbers, the system of education appears to have deteriorated. According to Archbishop Magee, by the time he took up his role the children were taught in 'an exceedingly large room, in which from four to five hundred children were assembled at school, and in which noise and irregularity, from want of method, continually prevailed'.

As if from a Dickens novel, the whole scene was presided over by the headmistress, Mrs Innes, a 'gentlewoman, who is also of delicate health', who, 'in that immensely large room, and amidst so great a number of children ... sat at one end, not raised upon any eminence, scarcely seeing or being seen by any ... of the children'. The unfortunate Mrs Innes 'had no other mode of attempting to enforce order ... than by calling, at the utmost exertion of her lungs, to the disorderly children, and also to the under-mistresses by name. This call was followed by reply and rejoinder ... at the fullest stretch of voice, by all parties, so that even the very attempts at order only produced more confusion and greater clamour.'[7]

Mrs Magee was not impressed with the 'under-mistresses' either. These, she described as 'either persons in a low situation of life' or – even worse – they had been appointed from among the grown-up foundling children. Some of these were appointed mistresses or masters simply, she felt, because no one knew what else to do with them, since they 'were unfit and unqualified to earn their living anywhere else', because the majority had 'a bodily deformity, or a sickly constitution'. And they 'were too nearly upon a level with the children to be regarded by them with due respect'.[8] This seems a little unfair. All the visitors' accounts from this period attest to the high degree of order they witnessed in the Foundling Hospital. It seems likely that it was the more able foundlings who were appointed monitors and then teachers (at age 18, 19 or 20), albeit that they might have had some physical disability that barred them from physical labour.[9]

There may have been another motive for Mrs Magee's antipathy to them. This is hinted at in the following: 'To a bystander, the Foundling mistresses seem to teach well; they spoke fluently what they had learned from Mr Murray, the chaplain; and the children, or rather some few of them, answered readily what they had been taught; but of the true meaning of the words, and the comprehension of religious doctrines and religious principles, they were lamentably ignorant.'[10]

In any event, these young schoolmistresses and masters were all dismissed from their posts by the Magees. They were given the option of going on the 'poor list' – that is, of going to reside permanently in the care of a country nurse, as the invalid foundlings did – or receiving a one-off severance payment of £4 and making their own way in the world. None chose the former voluntarily, but some were forced to accept this arrangement, as the governors found that 'taking the £4 and going away was only throwing them into distress'.[11]

In the atmosphere of heightened polarisation exemplified by the 'Second Reformation', Reverend Murray had fortified his teaching of religious doctrine, increasing the number of catechisms the children were taught from to no fewer than six, including some of the more stridently anti-Catholic editions.[12] However, the shortness of the children's stay in the Hospital often frustrated his wish to complete their instruction. Nevertheless, he felt that 'you ought to treat their persons at the same time with kindness, as our Lord did when he told the woman of Samaria her religion was nonsense'.[13]

Reverend Murray, one of the longest-serving officers of the Foundling Hospital, and as superintendent of the schools, one of the most senior, was profoundly suspicious of the children on arrival, believing they were 'imbued deeply with Popish principles' by their Catholic nurses. He was never quite convinced of the success of his teaching, believing 'some [children] may be hypocritical enough to say they are convinced of the truth of the religion of the Bible, which is the Protestant religion, and when they go out they may prove to have been acting the hypocrite' and 'they pretend to be convinced when they are not'.[14] He particularly noticed opposition among the girls: 'the girls would not take broth on Friday', he reported. Reverend Murray was quite open about the fact that the children were purposely fed meat broth on a Friday, in order to thwart the Catholic practice of refraining from eating meat on that day. Those who refused it were given no alternative food. In order to prevent the children subsisting on their bread allowance alone, this was crumbled into the broth by staff, although this practice had reportedly ceased by 1824.[15] Reverend Murray reported seeing thirty to forty girls refuse to take the broth at any one time. It is not clear if, or how, the children were further punished for these acts of rebellion. In general in this period, punishment for girls consisted of solitary confinement, or 'occasionally' by whipping, whereas the boys were punished by whipping 'occasionally, not often'.[16] However, Surgeon Creighton had had occasion to complain of the boys being punished 'too severely'.

One of the first things that had struck the Magees on assuming their new roles was 'the great evil [of] … the prodigious accumulation of children at nurse, kept to a very late age, much too late an age for the purposes of beneficial instruction afterwards'.[17] The belief was that the later it was left, the harder it was to convert the children to Protestantism.[18] This belief was to lead to one of the last great acts of cruelty associated with the Foundling Hospital.

Foundling W 149

By 1822 there were a staggering 7,185 children with country nurses. Children could only be drafted as places became free in the Hospital. This eventually led to children not being drafted until they were as old as 12, or even older.

The vast majority of country nurses, as we have seen, seem to have been Catholics. The Magees were of the opinion that this was to a large extent due to the misconduct of the foundling clerk, responsible for the placing of the children, 'who exercised every species of contrivance (being himself a Roman Catholic) to prevent the placing [of] the children with Protestant nurses'.[1] The register, Thomas Finlay, did not seem to agree,[2] and the Magees themselves conceded that even without the alleged conspiracy, 'there would naturally be a greater number of Roman Catholic nurses to offer themselves ... because there is a greater number of the lower orders of that religion [and] persons of that description are willing to accept of lower wages, not only from their greater poverty, but also from being under an influence urging them to receive the children ... on any condition'.[3] Nevertheless, the clerk was dismissed.

But that was only the beginning. When the Magees learnt that a few of the children had allegedly received the Catholic sacrament of the Eucharist while with their country nurses, a sort of panic seems to have set in. On 10 June 1824 the governors issued a fateful instruction:

> Ordered
> That at the ensuing pay, all the children above the age of four years, and who are now with Roman Catholic nurses, be transferred to Protestant nurses.[4]

Since Archbishop Magee was by far the most senior, influential, and active of the (official) governors, there can be no doubt that the resolution was largely his doing, whatever the influence of his wife.[5] He was later quite clear in his defence of the policy. But the resolution, cruel as it was, was also ill-considered, for within a week it had been calculated that there were 4,200 children over the age of 4 with country nurses. Given the almost certain impossibility of finding enough Protestant nurses to meet the injunction, the order was modified and reissued a week later by adding the words 'so far as may be practicable'.[6]

In order to effect the transfer, the plan was to take the children from their foster mothers without warning during their annual visit for 'the pay', and lodge them in the Hospital for a number of weeks. This was to deter desperate women from waiting in the environs of the Hospital in order to follow their child to its new destination, or even try to seize it back, as sometimes happened. Few poor country women could afford to stay in Dublin for such a length of time. When this period had elapsed, the children were to be given to Protestant nurses in another part of the country. As the commissioners themselves conceded, 'it is impossible to expect the same affection and care towards the foundling from a woman to whom a child of four or five years of age has been transferred, as if she had reared it from its infancy'.[7] To compound the issue, despite the protestations of the governors to the contrary, it is unlikely the supply of poor Protestant women willing to undertake this work for such low wages was as plentiful as that of Catholics, and in fact 'in some cases there have been as many as six children transferred to one nurse'.[8]

What had started as a trickle in 1823, before the formal resolution of the governors, soon began to accelerate. From four children seized in June 1824, the number increased to over 200 in July and over 500 in August, as the payment season peaked.[9] The numbers tailed off over the winter and began to rise again the following summer as, unknowing, nurses attended the Hospital during 'the Pay'.

At first the public seem not to have been aware of what was going on, but by 1825 reports were beginning to appear in the newspapers. On 6 August 1825 a correspondent to the *Morning Register* reported distressing scenes at the Foundling Hospital a few evenings earlier, necessitating the calling out of a police guard to restore order. The witness described 'sobbings and wailings and all the other indications of mental agony' and that 'all the police of James's Street' were called out when nurses tried to retrieve or prevent seizure of their children. 'No riot however occurred but the people in the streets and from the windows were looking on in wonder and indignation.'[10] Such scenes did not dissuade the governors or officers of the Hospital. On 16 August ninety-five children were seized – the highest number on a single day.[11] Within eighteen months, 2,150 children had been reassigned.

The degree of distress caused by the premature sundering of the nurse–child bond is illustrated by a number of court cases that later reached the newspapers. Catherine Hannan (or Harman) had nursed her foster child, Henry Lifford, for seven years until he was taken from her by the Hospital in July 1825 and given to a Catherine Philips, who lived in Dunganstown. Somehow Hannan managed to discover Philips' identity and location and visited Henry at Dunganstown. The following year, when Philips was obliged to bring the boy to Dublin for 'the pay', Hannan was in wait. She must have followed the pair when they left the Foundling Hospital. In Thomas Street she 'seized' the boy and together they fled. However, an informer tipped off the Foundling Hospital as to their hiding place. The house where they lay hidden was searched thoroughly, but nothing was found of either the woman or the child. The search party was about to leave when a movement, noticed through a dormer window, alerted them. The pair were found hiding on the roof, Catherine Hannan in tears and Henry 'with a two penny loaf in his little fist'.[12] When the case came to trial, 'all the witnesses for the prosecution admitted the kindness which the prisoner displayed towards the child'. The case was seen as a demonstration of 'the affection of the Irish nurses for their foster children', which was described as a 'peculiarit[y] of the natives of this country'. Both the magistrate and the jury showed considerable compassion and Hannan was acquitted. It is most unlikely, however, that the governors allowed her to keep her child.

Another case reveals the apparently reckless desperation to which country nurses could resort to retrieve their foundling child. In March 1820 Sarah Beaghan received a week-old girl, Mary Humphries, from the Foundling Hospital to nurse. Beaghan reared Mary at her home in Rathangan, Kildare, near the Bog of Allen. However, in August 1826 the child was taken from her by the Hospital and placed with a Thomas Dickinson in County Wexford, along with at least three other foundlings. Apparently distraught, Beaghan managed to visit the child, despite the distance involved. In July 1829, however, after Dickinson had returned to the Hospital for the annual payment, and he was proceeding across Baggot Street bridge, his cart containing the now 9-year-old Mary and the three other foundling children was held up by 'six or seven men' along with a woman he recognised as Sarah Beaghan. Mary was seized and driven off in a jaunting car with Beaghan. Dickinson reported the incident to the police and within ten days Beaghan had been tracked down to a house in Portobello, Dublin, not far from the scene of the seizure. Beaghan was arrested, although the child was not located until the following day, hidden in the neighbourhood. At Beaghan's trial, a foundling hospital official who testified was able to confirm the identity of the child, her date of admission and nurse from her tattoo, W 149 (the 149th child admitted after 6 January 1820, the start of the accounting year). Identification of a foundling was always possible, since as Surgeon Creighton confirmed, 'they are always marked upon the right arm with the letter of the year, and the number of the child'. By this period it was done, he explained, with 'a spring instrument something like … you use in cupping and scarifying'. It was 'struck in and rubbed in with a little gunpowder'. But the mark could fade. As Creighton explained, it was 'just as you would cut … the bark of a tree, the incision will expand, and in grow-ing, one part will become farther removed from the other; the indentation of the points with which the arm is marked will appear farther distant, so that it will be more difficult to distinguish it'. And then 'we are obliged to do it over again'.[13] Helped by Mary's tattoo, Sarah Beaghan was convicted of abduction and sentenced to one month's imprisonment in Smithfield penitentiary.[14]

So anxious were the Magees to remove the children from Catholic nurses that they even established their own facility near the archbishop's 'palace' in Tallaght, which Magee called a 'small country seminary'. Here thirty children lived under the care of a Mrs Powell, who was supervised by Mrs Magee and her daughters.[15] Another response was the creation of a 'preparatory school' within the Hospital for the reception of up to 200 younger girls. This was specifically the idea of Mrs Magee, to allow the drafting of girls at an earlier age – as young as 6 or 7. The Reverend Henry Murray explained the background: 'The origin of that school was this: it appeared [at] the drafting before last, that some children belonging to us had, at the age of six or seven, been given the sacrament [i.e. communion] by a Roman-Catholic priest in the country; this shocked everybody who heard it … it was this made Mrs Magee think of the preparatory school.'[16]

Another response was the sending of 500 children from the Foundling Hospital to the charter schools – the notorious schools of the Incorporated Society for the Promotion of English Protestant Schools in Ireland. These chil-dren 'were walked off, [from the Hospital] in batches of thirty and thirty two, to the Society's house in Aungier Street',[17] from where they were dispatched to schools all over the country. The Magees also toyed with the idea of having some of the children 'disposed of in some of the foreign settlements'; however, this seemingly came to nothing.[18]

After being admitted to the Hospital the children continued to pine for their nurses. It was reported that 'their attachment is so strong, that even for years after their admission they eagerly avail themselves of every possible opportunity of escape for the purpose of returning to them'.[19] There is evidence that the minority of children who had had Protestant nurses were allowed contact with them, by an occasional visit, but this was not allowed with Catholic nurses. Archbishop Magee believed that 'as we are an establishment of the state, and bound to bring up the children in the religion of the state, we were not only obliged to transfer the children from their Popish nurses, but also to keep them separated from all connection or intercourse with them, after they returned to the Hospital'.[20] According to the Reverend John Pomeroy, one of the governors, 'if they have been reared till six or seven years old with one nurse, and are transferred from that nurse to another, they very frequently elope to the first nurse, because their attachments are there, and in the Hospital they would do anything to escape. We have been obliged to raise the walls, and fortify it in every possible way, and put guards upon the doors.'[21]

Some of the children were able to communicate with their nurses by letter. The nurses were too poor to afford the cost of postage but had the letters 'conveyed by persons coming to town, and they are left [in] at the gate'. But in May 1824 the 'Governesses' (i.e. Mrs Magee) 'put a stop to the writing'. The elderly headmistress, Mrs Innes, reported that the children 'used all to write on paper, now it is confined to slate-writing' to prevent the smuggling out of letters. However, according to the Reverend Henry Murray, the children eventually became resigned to their situation.[22]

Under the new regime, segregation of the sexes was enforced rigorously. This meant that foster siblings – boys and girls raised together by the same nurse – would be separated on entry to the Hospital. Any windows in the boys' section overlooking the female courtyard were bricked up after the Magees' arrival and since the female courtyard had to be crossed to reach the dining hall from the kitchens, all boys were removed from the task of conveying food from one to the other.[23] As Archbishop Magee reported, 'the galleries and passages also had places where the children might be concealed, so … if improperly associated, to escape detection. We have got rid of all this entirely.' And 'thus we expect to have the two sexes cut off from every kind of communication, even from that of signs'. Referring to foster siblings, Mrs Magee observed, 'I find if there be any window or door, or anything by means of which they can communicate with one another, in spite of every rule and regulation they will do it.'[24] She added, 'I find them all set at defiance and the boys and girls caballing together.'

An example of the Magees riding roughshod over the regulations of the Foundling Hospital and the legislation underpinning it was their establishment of a separate training school run by the Association for Discountenancing Vice on the Hospital's premises. This evangelical proselytising organisation was totally separate from the Foundling Hospital and its purpose was the training of young men (not foundlings) as parish clerks and schoolmasters. It was clear these were to benefit from all the resources of the Hospital, including appropriating two dormitories and schoolrooms and being fed by the Hospital. However, this was seemingly tolerated by the other governors and by the British parliament, which, far from curtailing the Foundling Hospital, facilitated its growth in its final thirty years.

Counting the Cost

Supporters of the Foundling Hospital saw value in having a large proselytising institution in Ireland to instil 'the principles of Loyalty to their king, and attachment to the Protestant religion and constitution of the country'.[1] Among them, optimism had been high following the enquiry of 1797 that through reform of its operations, the mortality rate could be kept to a low level. The surgeon, John Creighton, had been open about mortality rates, and these had been published by the Hospital up to 1809, but notably these did not include deaths of children while with country nurses. Based on these figures, Wakefield had made a reasoned plea to parliamentarians and administrators for the Hospital's closure, but had been ignored, and few figures had been made public since then.[2] Thus the figures published in 1826 , by a parliamentary commission that inspected the Hospital in 1824 and 1825, come as something of a shock.

From these we learn that there were 52,150 admissions from June 1796 to January 1826. Of these, 14,613 died in the Hospital, before being given to country nurses. A further 25,859 were notified as having died while with country nurses. To this we must add a further 1,052 deaths among older children, giving a total of 41,524 notified deaths out of 52,150 admissions, with only 10,626 recorded survivors.

When presented with this information – showing death rates for this period that were much higher than had previously been widely known – far from taking immediate action, the parliamentary commissioners did not even publish the details for nearly another year.[3] Instead, they quibbled over the figures. This was because of the 25,859 deaths notified in the country, there were no 'dead certificates' for 9,622 of them. But this was in an era before the introduction of formal death certification. (Even the term 'dead certificates' was novel, and localised to the Foundling Hospital.) The only 'dead certificates' provided were by the nurses to the Hospital in order to collect any unpaid wages. But obtaining these meant the nurse first paying a visit to the local Anglican clergyman and applying for the certificate. This then had to be brought to the Hospital in person by the nurse – in many cases a round trip of two days or more on foot – followed by an 'examination on oath' at the Hospital.[4] The only incentive for a nurse to go to these lengths would be to collect any unpaid wages. In most cases where a certificate had not been provided, the Hospital pointed out, it had simply not been worth the nurse's while to make this arduous journey to present the certificate and collect whatever wages were due. Depending on how soon after the last annual payment the death took place, these could be very small. In addition, the first month's wages were paid in advance, so no wages would be due for any child dying within its first month with a nurse, by far the period of highest mortality.[5] In these circumstances, it is impressive that nurses had gone to these lengths in 16,237 cases. But the commissioners chose to believe that in the case of 'uncertified' deaths, these children had not in fact died, but were cases where children had been retained by their nurses.

However, there was one piece of information that would strongly indicate whether the child had died or been withheld by a nurse, and that was the age at which the child disappeared off the books. There was no need for a nurse, who wished to retain a child, not to bring it for payment in the early years, as there was no chance of it being drafted. As we have seen, drafting was happening later and later as the Hospital strained under growing numbers. Often it didn't happen before the age of 7 or 8, or even 10. In addition we know that infant mortality is naturally much higher in the first year than subsequently. (Separately, figures from 1791 show that of all children dying in the care of country nurses, 77 percent had died by the end of the first year, and 92 percent by the end of the second.) Therefore a pattern that showed the majority of deaths occurring in the early years would strongly counter the notion that these figures were due to infants being withheld. The register, Thomas Finlay, was clear that a large proportion of the 9,000 had been struck off the books in their early years.[6] Based on his examination of the books, he informed the commissioners, he had 'taken a memorandum of the numbers of those children whom I suppose to have been detained from affection.'[7] The commissioners chose either not to look at Finlay's evidence, or to exclude it from their report.[8] After 'the most attentive consideration of the views which he has suggested' they rejected his evidence. To do otherwise, they believed, 'would fix upon the system of the institution such a waste and destruction of infant life' – an institution, which, after all, had been supported and funded by the British parliament for decades.[9]

In fact, the commissioners were broadly supportive of the continuation of the Hospital, lavishing praise on the Magees. Indeed, they expressed deep regret at the death of Mrs Magee in 1824, while failing to express similar sentiments about the deaths of the 31,902 infants that they didn't dispute (let alone the 9,622 that they did). They advised minor alterations only. The main change they recommended was that all foundlings should be dispatched to Protestant nurses from the outset. This would mean the children would not need to be drafted back to the Hospital to be imbued with the Protestant faith. But the revelations of the nakedly sectarian objective of the institution, and the suffering inflicted on children in its pursuit, must have caused disquiet in some quarters.

In 1829 Catholics achieved a measure of political reform under the Roman Catholic Relief Act, which removed many of the restrictions imposed on them, despite the opposition of kings George III and IV. Following this, the Foundling Hospital must have been even more of an embarrassment and the numbers must have constituted a rebuke to the imperial parliament.

Finally, in June 1829 a select committee of the British House of Commons, basing its advice on the evidence of the 1826 Report but clearly differing with its authors as to conclusions, recommended to the governors 'that from and after 1 January 1830, all further admissions to the Foundling Hospital should cease'.[10] A few months later the newspapers carried the following historic announcement:

Foundling Hospital, Dublin, Sept. 24, 1829
The Governors of the Foundling Hospital hereby give notice that, pursuant to the order of his Excellency the Lord Lieutenant, the Hospital will be finally closed against the Admission of Deserted Infants on the First day of January 1830; from which day no infant can, on any account, be received into the Foundling Hospital, Dublin.

By Order,
T. Finlay, Registrar[11]

The *Morning Register* – an advocate of Catholic Emancipation – in reporting the order, saw it as a symbol, or foretelling, of the end of the ascendancy, likening the latter, in a piece of doggerel, to an illegitimate child abandoned by the authorities.[12]

Admissions ceased in 1831, apart from a single orphan transferred from the Lying-in Hospital, where its mother had died – possibly the last ever admission. Drafting also appears to have ceased sometime within the next few years, so that by 1836, the great hall and its vast barrack-like wings were almost empty, 'occupied solely by the reduced staff and officers ... with temporary accommodation for such of the children (seldom more than twenty to thirty at a time) as it is found necessary' to remove temporarily from country nurses or apprenticeships.[13]

Thousands of country nurses in their distinctive dress no longer flocked annually to the Hospital to receive payment – a feature of Dublin life for over 100 years. A couple of years earlier a system of inspectors had been introduced.[14] Four inspectors now toured the relevant parishes to vouch for the care of the children, and payment was processed through the local Anglican minister. But the Hospital was still a huge administrative operation with over 4,500 children on its books – 2,000 at nurse in the country and over 2,500 in apprenticeships.

Even as the buildings lay virtually empty there were urgent calls for the premises to be converted to use as a workhouse amid claims they 'would soon be filled with applicants from the famishing poor' because of 'extensive indigence, famine and disease' in the country.[15] Under the Irish Poor Relief Act, the Foundling Hospital was invested in the Poor Law Commissioners from 1839, although the Hospital was still run by the governors, who reported to the commissioners. The commissioners decided the premises should be converted to use as a workhouse, completing the circle begun in 1704.

And so, in September 1839, after over a century of occupancy at its iconic James's Street site, alternative premises for the Foundling Hospital were obtained at 49 Cork Street, where Edward Atkinson, a sailcloth manufacturer, had sail lofts and a rope warehouse.[16] The buildings were converted, for the sum of £200, to provide accommodation for the six remaining officers and the small number of children passing through, in addition to a boardroom for the governors. (Later 52 Cork Street.)[17]

As the numbers of foundlings dwindled, the officers and Board of Governors were eventually replaced by the post of Inspector of Foundlings. This role became the responsibility of the Governor of the House of Industry until, in turn, that office itself was abolished. Around this time, the foundlings cease to be clearly identifiable as a group in the records, and were subsumed into the vast mass of humanity dealt with by the Poor Law Commissioners, as famine and further poverty swept over Ireland.

The foundlings re-emerge briefly from obscurity in two reports by William Wodsworth, the assistant secretary of the Local Government Board for Ireland and now 'Inspector of Foundlings', in 1874 and 1875. Forty-four years after the Hospital's closure, there were still a small number of ageing foundlings receiving support because of physical or mental disability. It was Wodsworth's responsibility to supervise and inspect the care of these, still being provided by 'nurses' in the country. By now they were reduced to just fifty-four 'helpless, deformed, or otherwise afflicted foundlings' aged from 44 to 83 years of age. Wodsworth, a dedicated public servant, managed to visit most of them, 'arriving unexpectedly at various hours of the day and going straight into the places of abode of the foundlings'.[18]

He found that several of them had not been visited for some years by any official. Two foundlings, 'Thomas Brooks, a dwarf, and Catherine Henlon, extremely delicate', were found to be 'in a miserable and wretched condition, located in a lone, remote and dilapidated dwelling, without fire or light; the woman who had them in charge having gone away to another part of the country, and her newly married son and his wife, neglecting, and, I fear, possibly ill-treating, these helpless persons. The only other occupant of the place besides themselves … was a ferocious, half-starved cur, who needed vigorous repression.' Wodsworth arranged for the pair to be resettled in more comfortable homes.

In another case Wodsworth 'found it necessary to take immediate and active steps to remedy what I saw to be neglect of a poor blind and epileptic creature' in the care of a woman 'who at one time had as many as eighteen foundlings under her charge'. But Wodsworth was able to ensure better accommodation for her with the assistance of 'the kind and benevolent clergyman of the parish whose attention I … drew to the case'.[19]

However, in most cases Wodsworth found that the foundlings were well cared for. In many cases they were regarded as a member of the family. One female foundling had spent fifty-six years in the same household and had 'reared two generations' of the family. In some cases foundlings were working or 'aiding in farming operations'. The foundlings were shown 'a degree of kindness and attention which it would be hard to find for them elsewhere'. The small annual allowance of £2 to £8 was not enough 'to account for the kind treatment which they generally receive'.[20]

In his role as Inspector of Foundlings, Wodsworth seems also to have been contacted by able-bodied former foundlings, desperate to find out about their origins. He was 'much struck by the feeling of painful wonderment and anxiety existing with many of them as to whom their parents might have been. There seemed to be a void in the heart upon the subject, aching to be filled.' One had become 'the chief of the Detective Police, in one of the most important of the English towns'. Another foundling, 'an old gentleman, comes periodically for information as to his age and the particulars of his early youth. He has fine, well-cut aristocratic features, and has saved £1,200 in service as a butler, and cannot quite make up his mind what to do with it.' Another, though completely blind, 'for many years earned nearly a living by stone-breaking' and was remarkable for his industry as well as 'the wonderful precision of his blows'. He had also 'been a pedlar at times, and knew every road, boreen, and by-path in Wicklow,' before his case 'attracted the attention of a nobleman in his neighbourhood, whose benevolence has aided in smoothing the later years of his path in life'.[21]

According to Wodsworth, it was 'the interest aroused by many of these cases that first led me to read and search the records of this ancient institution'.[22] At the time these records amounted to 100 volumes of minutes, registers and 'mortality books'.[23] He went on to write a slim volume about the history of the Hospital, which contains a small amount of valuable information that has not survived elsewhere.

Over the following years the numbers of foundlings continued to dwindle until the last-known survivor of this 'vast legislative and administrative mistake', as Wodsworth deemed it, an elderly woman, died in 1911, 181 years after the first admission.[24]

Appendix I – Admissions and Mortality

Admissions

The aim of this section is to calculate the total number of children admitted to the Foundling Hospital. Annual admission figures can be found for 82 out of 100 years in the Foundling Hospital's own reports, provided to parliament. These amount to 112,128. These figures can be seen in Table A.

However, no admission figures are reported for sixteen years in total: 1744 to 1751, 1774 to 1780 and 1827. Estimating the admissions for these years would allow us to estimate total admissions for the entire period of the Foundling Hospital's operation.

In order to take account of the gradual rise in admissions, estimates have been calculated as follows for the eight-year period 1744 to 1751: admissions for the five years prior to 1744 (excluding the exceptional year of 1741 when admissions doubled – see below) were averaged (result: 558). Admissions for the five years after 1751 were also averaged (result: 662). An average was then take of these two figures (610) and this was used as the estimated average admission for the eight years in question. Therefore total estimated admissions for the eight years was 610 × 8 = 4,880. The same method was used to calculate estimated admissions for 1774 to 1780. Total estimated admissions for this period was 9,625. The estimated total was then calculated as in Table 1, below.

Table 1. Admissions to Foundling Hospital, Dublin

Reported admissions	112,128
Estimated Admissions 1744 to 1751	4,880
Estimated admissions 1774 to 1780	9,625
Estimated admissions 1827	450
Total Estimated Admissions	127,083

An annual breakdown of all admissions is available in Table A.

Admission trends

As can be seen from Figure 1, while there are fluctuations from year to year, the trend of admissions is generally upwards from the date of opening of the Hospital, with an apparent acceleration taking place from the 1760s and continuing until the early nineteenth century.

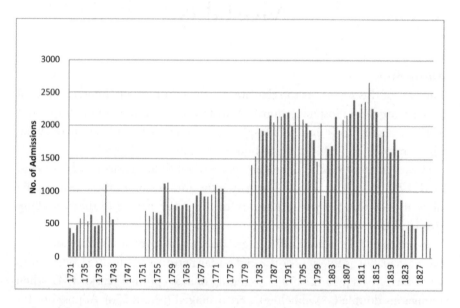

Fig. 1: Admissions to foundling hospital: Years for which annual figure available.[1]

Some of this increase can be accounted for by population growth. In addition, within the overall trend several spikes can be seen. The most prominent early spike occurs in 1741 when 1,102 children were admitted – nearly double the previous year's intake (see Table A). This coincided with the major famine of 1741 when as much as 16 per cent of the population may have lost their lives.[2] Viazzo, in interpreting spikes in abandonment to the Spedale degli Innocenti foundling hospital in Florence in the seventeenth century, writes of 'crisis abandonment' analogous to 'crisis mortality' as a feature of subsistence crises. These had disappeared by the eighteenth and nineteenth centuries in Florence.[3]

The reason for the pronounced peak in admissions in 1757 and 1758 has yet to be uncovered. However, this coincided with a 'partial famine' accompanied by an influenza epidemic and with the beginning of the Seven Years War.[4] For as yet unknown reasons, admissions began to fall in 1794 and did not begin to rise again until 1802. (The apparent spike in 1800 is an artefact caused by a change in the accounting period.)

A key influence on admission numbers was, of course, policy – that of the institution or wider policy. As seen, a peak admissions figure of 2,664 occurred in 1813. The change in legislation in 1814 (detailed in the text) did not have a dramatic impact on numbers.[5] Although admissions started to decline, they remained high, hovering around 2,000. The next change to the legislation was in 1820,[6] allowing closure of the Hospital to admissions from the country during the winter months.[7] This had some impact, but the change that had most effect of all was the imposition, in 1822, on the parishes, of a £5 charge, payable for each infant on admission.[8] The result was dramatic. From 1,640 admissions in 1821, admissions had plummeted to 419 by 1823. The hospital was finally closed to admissions in 1830.

Mortality

Regarding the Dublin Foundling Hospital, of the few authors who touch on the subject, most cite mortality figures relating to specific periods of its operation. In part because they refer to different periods, these vary widely – e.g. from 25 to 90 per cent. In addition, the rates cited overwhelmingly refer to deaths within the Hospital itself – that is, during the usually brief period lasting days, or in a minority of cases, weeks, while the infant waited to be assigned to a wet nurse, rather than the entire period during which the child was in the care of the Hospital. Figures cited in the text quantify the death rate over the entire duration of the child's contact with the Foundling Hospital, including with the wet nurses who were contracted by the Hospital to provide care for the infants under its governance.

Figures are available for three distinct periods: 1730 to 1737, 1791 to 1796, and 1796 to 1826. Cumulatively this allows us to calculate mortality rates for 42.5 of the 100 years during which the Hospital accepted foundlings, and for approximately 55 per cent of all admissions.

Period	Deaths per thousand admissions
1730 to 1737	800[9]
1791 to 1796	790[10]
1796 to 1826	796 (610)[11]

Details of admissions and deaths from 1796 to 1826 are shown in Table B.

If we accept the assertion of the parliamentary commissioners of 1826, that all of the 9,622 infants for whom 'dead certificates' had not been provided were still alive, this would yield a mortality rate of 610 deaths per thousand admissions. Extrapolating this rate to admission periods for which total death rates are not known yields a total mortality figure of 82,947 (while a further 18,000 or more disappeared from the records).

Applying the perhaps more realistic rate of 790 deaths per thousand admissions would yield an estimated total mortality of 100,395 among children admitted to the Foundling Hospital.

Comparative Mortality Rates

Historians know surprisingly little about infant and child mortality rates before the advent of censuses in the nineteenth century.[12] Researchers here are forced to rely on fragmentary parish records. Nevertheless, Tait manages to calculate infant mortality rates (IMRs) for a number of parishes in Ireland based on careful analysis of the surviving registers.[13] At fewer than 100 deaths per thousand births, these are low in comparison with English and continental European rates of the time.[14] For example, Levene notes that the IMR peaked in London at 450 per thousand in the 1740s and subsequently fell to 250 per thousand by the 1770s and was 'probably well under 200 by the end of the century'.[15] The following table contains a selection of infant mortality rates for various regions and periods.

Table 2. Infant Mortality Rates (Deaths Per Thousand Live Births [IMR]).[16]

Location	Period	IMR
Ireland	1680–1705	71–84.9
London	1740s–1800	<200–450
Tuscany	1720–1840	250–350
Northern Italy	1670–1800	256–313
Southern Italy	1660–1840	153–274
Geneva	1641–1790	239–300
England & Wales	1701–1851	150–180

Comparison with other foundling hospitals

Precise comparison with mortality rates in foundling hospitals in other countries is difficult, if not impossible, due to the different methodologies used in compiling the figures. Often, insufficient information is given in the sources cited to allow direct comparison. Without re-examining the primary sources for each of these hospitals, it is hardly possible to determine whether the figures are comparable; nevertheless, some figures will be given to allow a tentative, qualified comparison.[17]

Table 3. Mortality Rates in Foundling Hospitals[18]

Location of foundling hospital	Deaths per thousand admissions
Paris	503–841
Lyons	337
Rheims	639
Rouen	791–946
London	520–666 (This figure includes deaths in first year only)
Florence	600–800
Cadiz	697
Zaragoza	865

Potential factors reducing the Foundling Hospital infant's chances of survival included maternal poverty and malnutrition, very young maternal age, reduced duration of maternal breast-feeding, prolonged travel to and from the Hospital, and exposure to new disease environments, both in the Hospital and in the nurse's community. The poor women employed as nurses were probably often malnourished and engaged in hard physical labour, reducing their chances of successful feeding. Some may not even have been lactating. On the other hand Bardet, in examining wet nurses working for the Paris foundling hospital maintains it was social prejudice that caused these women to be blamed for the poor health and low survival rate of the infants, while the real cause lay in the conditions of the children's abandonment – time spent on the street in whatever town they were abandoned in, followed by a long trip to Paris, followed by a wait in the Foundling Hospital. Fildes came to a similar conclusion in her detailed study of wet nurses attached to the London Foundling Hospital, concluding that occasional high death rates there were a reflection of the state of health of the infant when given to the nurse.[19]

Table A. Annual Admissions to the Dublin Foundling Hospital[20]

Year	Admissions	Year	Admissions	Year	Admissions	Year	Admissions
1731	430	1756	635	1781	1390	1806	2094
1732	356	1757	1113	1782	1529	1807	2148
1733	481	1758	1136	1783	1964	1808	2191
1734	576	1759	800	1784	1919	1809	2385
1735	666	1760	792	1785	1900	1810	2207
1736	531	1761	780	1786	2150	1811	2332
1737	643	1762	792	1787	2051	1812	2368
1738	461	1763	809	1788	2144	1813	2664
1739	478	1764	791	1789	2134	1814	2257
1740	617	1765	820	1790	2187	1815	2216
1741	1102	1766	936	1791	2192	1816	1831
1742	676	1767	1011	1792	1998	1817	1915
1743	558	1768	924	1793	2205	1818	2210
1744	n/a	1769	923	1794	2253	1819	1598
1745	n/a	1770	949	1795	2101	1820	1792
1746	n/a	1771	1094	1796	2037	1821	1640
1747	n/a	1772	1042	1797	1929	1822	873
1748	n/a	1773	1045	1798	1780	1823	419
1749	n/a	1774	n/a	1799	1453	1824	486
1750	n/a	1775	n/a	1800	2041[21]	1825	511
1751	n/a	1776	n/a	1801	933[22]	1826	450
1752	692	1777	n/a	1802	1656	1827	n/a
1753	627	1778	n/a	1803	1697	1828	476
1754	683	1779	n/a	1804	2140	1829	555
1755	676	1780	n/a	1805	1934	1830	148

Table B. Admissions to the Dublin Foundling Hospital and Deaths 1797 to 1826[23]

Year	No. of admissions	Died in infant nursery	Died in the country	Grown children died in the country	Grown children died in the infirmary
1797	1929	1438	253		8
1798	1780	934	270		14
1799	1453	662	315		13
1800	2041	479	477		26
1801	933	296	1298		6
1802	1656	441	562	5	22
1803	1697	561	1524		17
1804	2140	752	727		22
1805	1934	350	923	18	21
1806	2094	470	1093		75
1807	2148	486	1292	5	15
1808	2191	537	892	6	56
1809	2385	597	1286	5	33
1810	2207	565	1391	2	29
1811	2332	721	1093	21	31
1812	2368	870	1063	15	20
1813	2664	964	1098	18	26
1814	2257	843	1327	10	17
1815	2216	771	1075	14	24
1816	1831	264	1081	22	16
1817	1915	266	1328	26	19
1818	2210	350	954	3	14
1819	1598	243	1108	23	21
1820	1792	222	816	14	17
1821	1640	230	823	14	17
1822	873	113	455	28	15
1823	419	48	386	10	43
1824	486	20	288	6	64
1825	511	59	300	29	47
1826	450	52	361	28	

Appendix II – Letters

Amongst the Foundling Hospital records William Wodsworth found a collection of letters 'accidentally preserved from a general destruction of documents'. They show 'the anguish of the mothers at parting with their children'. Many were written on behalf of the women by local clergymen, who administered the system at parish level. Wodsworth transcribed twenty of them in his *Brief History* and the majority are reproduced below. It is not clear what criteria Wodsworth used for selecting this sample, therefore we don't know how representative they are. They date from a single brief period: 1815 to 1817. For the likely fate of the children in question, readers should consult Table B.

To the Governors of the Foundling Hospital
James's Street.

Killyman

May 9th 1816

Gentlemen,

The bearer of this is a poor woman whose child was taken to your Hospital without her consent and left there on the 7th of September 1812. She still retains her maternal affection for her offspring and would be very glad to recover it. She is willing to pay any expense attending the getting her child back and says she is very able to maintain it. Her name is Mary Ward and her child's name is Mary.

I hope you will have the goodness to consider her case and if possible let her have her child.

I am gentlemen
Your obedient servant
Ch[arles] Caulfield
Rector of Killyman

✳ ✳ ✳

May 2nd , 1817.

My Dear Sir,

The bearer Hannah Carroll wishes to get a child out of the Foundling Hospital, which was put in on Thursday last. It is her own child and the father is able to support it. There was a gross deception practised on me, or I would not have given a note of admission for it. The real father paid a poor miserable creature to pass for him – Do in the business whatever you think proper.

Your ob᛫ ser.

L. W. Hepenstal.

✳ ✳ ✳

To
The Governors of the Foundling Hospital,
James's Street,

Dublin
Larrha House

19ᵗʰ July 16

Sir,

The bearer, "Hessy Harte" has came to me & admits herself to be the mother of the child called "Charlotte Fielding" & sent by me to you as Minister of Larrha of which having arrived with you and its treatment I have got no account which surprises me. Now she is desirous to get this child back but whether it can be done you are best judge and will act as is right on the occasion. I told her I was not competent to advise her but if she gave security for taking care of the child and bringing it up right I supposed you would return it to her.

She is a Catholic.

Your Obedient Servant
Da[vid]˙ Price

✳ ✳ ✳

To
The Governors of the House of Industry

July 1816

Annie McCloughry the bearer of this certificate is mother to the male infant named Thomas McManus received into the House of Industry by my recommendations on the 23rd of May.* The child had been deserted by his father in Granard and under the conviction that there was no person able to support him I had him sent to Dublin. His mother who resides in a distant parish, hearing that he had been deserted by his father has now come forward and offered to maintain him herself. She has brought a certificate to me from her parish clergyman of her being mother to the child and I think that if the Governors are pleased to have him restored to her she will take due care of him.

Henry L. Webb
Minister
Parish of Granard

*The child was mistakenly sent to the House of Industry and subsequently transferred to the Foundling Hospital.

✳   ✳   ✳

To
The Governors of the Foundling Hospital
Dublin

Newry

October 23rd, 1816

Gentlemen,

I am induced to take the liberty of addressing you on behalf of the bearer Letty Spires whose child was transmitted from hence on the 15th day of October & received into the Hospital in Dublin on the 17th inst. under the following circumstances. The mother Letty Spires was married to a soldier in the 61st Regiment of foot whilst quartered here. The regiment is gone to the West Indies & she left behind without any provision for herself or child. Having sent the child to the paternal grandfather by way of extorting from [him] a support for the child he, unknown to her, sent [it off] to the Foundling Hospital. She is now most anxious to recover possession of her child & under the circumstances which I have detailed I trust that you will have the goodness to direct that she may receive it again.

I have the honour
to remain
Gentlemen
your very obedient
& humble servant
C.W. Campbell
Vicar of Newry.

✳   ✳   ✳

Rev. Annesly Bailie,
Foundling Hospital,
Dublin.

Laul Glebe,
Down.

29 Jan, 1817

Sir,

There was a female child named Ann Magee sent to the Foundling Hospital in the month of September in the year 1811 from the townland of Ballywooden otherwise Turkish in the parish of Laul. Father's name James Magee, mother's name I forget, but think it was Ann Keown, the carrier's name Mary Baxter – the father of the child died lately & his father & mother who are rich & comfortable wish to get the child back again – I do not know whether the Governors ever consent to return a child but think it would be a very happy circumstance for the child if they would accede to the old people's wishes in this case – the grandfather's name is Patrick - & the bearer's name who is to get the child Henry Shanon.

I take the present opportunity of requesting you will give my best wishes to Mrs. Bailie and remember me to all friends.

Yours very sincerely,
Edmond Custis

✳   ✳   ✳

Debby Doran of Morne, parish of Kilkeel and county of Down whome her child was taken from forsibly and sent to Dublin on the eight of May inst – 1817 – its name was William Marimon Edged five months or better the bearer its distress mother through the goodness of the gentlem concern'd in rearing such children hopes will grant it to her again.

✳   ✳   ✳

Curratown,
22nd July, 1816

I know the bearer Catherine Carolan to have had a child taken from her this day by Thomas Keenan the father of it, with intent to send it to the Foundling Hospital. She has applied to me to recommend her to the Board to get the nursing of it again which I think if approved she will take very good care of.

J. W. Charlton JP,
Co. Meath.

✳   ✳   ✳

To the Governors of the
Foundling Hospital
Dublin

Creggan, Dundalk
July 10th, 1815

Gentlemen,

The bearer of this (who is the mother of a female child received at the Hospital the 5th of July) repents very much having given up the child to the father of it, & wishes to rear it herself. Her family have consented to her doing so, & have agreed to assist her, & the poor creature seems to be so wretched since she parted with her child that I have been induced to comply with her request, & write to say that I hope you will have no objection to give her back her child – I told her that probably it has been sent to the County Wicklow or Carlow, 50 miles from Dublin - she is prepared to go any distance for it.

I enclose the letter received by the person who left the child at the Hospital by which you can ascertain where it is now.

& am your very faithful
humble servant,
Henry Stewart.

✱ ✱ ✱

To the Right Honourable and Honourable the Governors and Governesses of the Foundling Hospital

The Humble Petition of Rose Trench most humbly sheweth –

That your Petitioner had the misfortune to be seduced by a person of the name of Thomas Stockdale under a promise of marriage during the time petitioner did live in the Phoenix Park in the service of her Grace the Duchess of Richmond – That said child which petitioner bore to said Stockdale was sent to nurse, where he remained for a considerable time till the nurse demanded her wages when the said Stockdale took the child and under an assumed name of John Johnson sent him to the Foundling Hospital, tho' very well able to keep said child.

May it therefore please this honourable Board to take petitioners case into consideration and grant said child to her, and petitioner faithfully promises that she will take all the motherly care in her power of the child, and petitioner will for ever pray.

Rose Trench

✱ ✱ ✱

To the Rev. Mr. Hawkesworth.

The petition of Bridgett Kearney humbly sheweth –

Your petitioner did on the 17ᵗʰ of April leave her child in the Foundling Hospital to be reared, she being at the time poor and unable to support her.

She now is informed by letter from her brothers who were serving in the army that a remittance is to be made her to enable her to support herself and child, she humbly begs your reverence will relieve her anxiety by giving her an order to have the child restored she will ever pray for your long life and welfare.

Petitioner begs leave to remark that the parish has lost nothing by the conveyance of the child (Bridgett Lynott). She has applied herself to Dr Creighton who desired to have your letter with the return that was sent from the Hospital, and that the child would be restored to her by paying 16s 3d which petitioner is ready to pay.

To the Foundling Hospital

Tuam, 4ᵗʰ August, 1817

Indorsement

If not contrary to the rules of the Foundling Hospital, Mr Hawkesworth would venture on the liberty of recommending the petition to the notice of the Governors. Inability to support her infant compelled the poor woman to resort to the Hospital, nor did she, when she had determined on this step, expose her child, as she might have done, leaving it to the care of the parish. On the contrary, the poor creature travelled one hundred miles that she might herself resign a charge she was no longer able to support. Being now in better circumstances she entreats of the Governors to return the child, and Mr Hawkesworth hopes there can exist no rule in so good an institution against restoring an infant to the bosom of a mother, from which (in this instance) it is evident that poverty alone could ever have torn it.

Head Governess of the Foundling Hospital
James' St.

February 25th, 1817

Madam,

I certify the bearer [Mary Clarendon] to be the mother of Thomas Clarendon which she herself left in your school 12 months the 15th day of last November, was actuated by distress to do so in consequences of her husband leaving the country to seek employment elsewhere; he is now returned, treats her with all manner of ill nature, and says until such time as she produces the child she shall not be a single farthing the better of him, as it is the only child she ever had. She is informed that you hesitate giving out any child without a payment of 15 s which she says is utterly impossible for her to produce at present. I imagine you will not hesitate giving it as I suppose you are overloaded with them, and particularly as she says his father is able to support him.

Jane Walker,

Tuesday morning, 9 o'clock.

∗ ∗ ∗

To Rev. Annesly Bailie, etc. Etc.
Foundling Hospital.

Drumcondra
Feb. 19, 1817

Sir,

As Mrs. Guinness's illness has prevented me from seeing Mr. Guinness,[*] I take the liberty of writing to you myself to request that you will have the goodness to obtain permission from the Board for an infant named Cath. Kelly (recommended some time back by Mr. Guinness) to be restored to its parents. The child was sent to the Hospital without the knowledge of her parents, who we thought deserted her, but who it now appears had no such intention, but are able and willing to maintain her.

I remain sir,
your obedient humble servant,
Augusta Kiernan.

[*Probably Arthur Guinness, one of the Governors.]

∗ ∗ ∗

Glebe, near Keady,
June 9th, 1817

To the Governors and Governesses of the Foundling Hospital, Dublin.

The bearer – Bridget McCullogh – is mother of the child sent by me to the Hospital on 12th May last. It is named by me, in my letter of that day, John – supposed to be the child of John Wilson of Parish of Tyhollan [in the] county of Monaghan & Bridget McCullogh of Tullinene & same – sent by Catherine Hamilton of Ishenigin & same parish.

Since then I find the father's real name is Francis (not John) Wilson, but everything else is correct in my letter.

I also find that this Francis Wilson is a very wealthy man – the mother of the child is a Roman Catholick – & a poor young woman – she was servant to this man who debauched her (and without her knowledge) had the child sent away by imposing on me – through the means of an apothecary of his own name – George Wilson – of Keady.

I received the letter from the Hospital announcing the arrival of the child there – which letter, I gave to Dr. Wilson of Keady some days ago, on a promise of his returning it, but he has not – only says that he will next week – and as the mother is almost distracted at the loss of her child – and is a person who, I believe, never had any improper connexion with any man except this Wilson, and will give security to take care of her child – if it can be done with propriety – it will make her very happy to get her child again. If the Governesses will have the condescension to permit her to speak to them – I believe they will grant her request. At any rate if the child is alive she may be permitted to see it or informed how it is. I am certain the child would be better in every particular under the care of the Hospital than elsewhere and I have advised the mother all I could to let it remain so – but as circumstances are I can't avoid giving her this letter. I mean to have the father prosecuted for the maintenance of the child & for the damages, the mother can prove against him.

I have the honour to remain
your most obedient ser[t],
E. Robarts
Rector of the parish of Keady,
Diocese of Armagh.

* * *

To Revd Annsley Bailie

Thursday,
March 6th, 1817

The Governors of the Foundling Hospital are most earnestly entreated by the mother of the child named Arthur Wellington (admitted there on the first of October 1815) to restore him to her, as she is now perfectly able to support him, & most anxious to get him from the situation, she having been forced to allow of his being placed there. Circumstances of a pecuniary nature obliged her to separate from his father above three months before he was born, & for the satisfaction of her friends who at that time supported her & his infant sister (since dead of water on the brain) she consented to his going there, these circumstances no longer existing she prays and begs the Governors not to hesitate in giving him to her. She is willing if necessary to swear to the truth of this statement.

Note – Arthur Wellington is recorded as having been restored to his parent.[*]

[*The only one of these cases to be so recorded.]

✷   ✷   ✷

Rev^d. A. Bailie.

Newtown Glebe
June 3rd 1816

Sir,

The bearer Elizabeth Smith takes a child by name Elizabeth Handy to the Foundling Hospital. It is the daughter of an unfortunate girl who wishes to swear it to a young man of the name of Kelly who also was ready to swear and came before a neighbouring justice to swear it was not his. Both parties were willing to make affidavits but the magistrate would not take either. She is totally unable to support it. Under such circumstances I trust it may be admitted as otherwise she will go about with it. I shall thank you to give the bearer a receipt. Tho' she is a person I know will take all due care of it, it will be more satisfactory.

Your most obedient servant
Henry Rochfort

✷   ✷   ✷

To Mr. Bayley

Sir

On the 17th of March 1815 I was nurse in the house & on ye 18th a child was brought in by the name of Mary Hanning of which I am the mother. Your goodness will I hope excuse the liberty I have taken in troubling you as my future happiness depends on your granting if possible my request the father having promised to marry me if I can produce the child your kindness will be gratefull remember'd by

Sir your humble servt
Margaret Downey.

Being in the utmost distress at the time and not having any means of support for myself & infant was the only reason of my parting with it and the father not now knowing where it is and wishing to provide for it hope you will consider my situation.

Rathfarnham,
Nov. 19th 1816

Sir,

The bearer Ally Byrne had a child put into the Foundling Hospital in the month of March last. She has been since married to the father of it and they say they are both able and willing to take care of the child. In that case you will give the mother the child, if the thing is usual.

Your humble servant,

Henry MacLean

Bibliography

Manuscript Sources

Corbet, Robert, 'A Diary of the Weather and Winds For 19 Years Commencing with AD 1716 and Concluding with 1734 Exactly Observed and taken at the City of Dublin' (Transcription by Dublin City Archive).

Irish Architectural Archive (RIAI Murray Collection 0092/046 – 0570).

King Letters (TCD, MS 1995-2008/414).

Marsh's Library (MS Z3.1.1 (144–149)).

National Archives.

National Library of Ireland, (Lane papers, MS 8645/1 – 3).

Public Record Office of Northern Ireland.

Primary Printed Sources

Anon., *A Letter to a Friend in the Country concerning The Work-House* (Dublin, n.d.).

Anon., *The Case of the Foundlings of the City of Dublin; humbly recommended to the consideration of the Parliament* (Dublin, 1730).

Board of Governors, *Rules for Conducting the Education of the female children in the Foundling Hospital,* (Dublin, 1800).

Boulter, Hugh, *Letters written by his excellency Hugh Boulter, D.D. Lord Primate of All Ireland, &c. to several ministers of state in England and some others.* 2 vols (Oxford, 1770).

Bray, Thomas, *A Memorial Concerning the Erecting in the City of London or the Suburbs thereof, an Orphanotrophy or Hospital for the Reception of Poor Cast-Off Children or Foundlings* (n.p., n.d.).

Brownlow, John, *Memoranda; or Chronicles of the Foundling Hospital including memoirs of Captain Coram* (London, 1847).

Bulkeley, Richard, *Proposal for the future easing of this city and kingdom from the great burden of the poor* (University of Nottingham Library, Bentinck papers).

Burtchaell, G.D. & Sadleir, T.U., eds., *Alumni Dublinenses* (Dublin, 1935).

Cary, John, *An Essay on the state of England in relation to its trade, its poor, and its taxes, for carrying on the present war against France* (Bristol, 1695).

Cary, John, *An Account of the Proceedings of the Corporation of Bristol, in execution of the Act of Parliament for the better employing the poor of that City* (London, 1700).

Collis, John, *A National Credit for a National Use* (Dublin, 1705).

Collis, John, 'Proposals for the Taking in Boys into the King and Queen's Workhouse in Strand-street near Capel-street, Dublin' (Dublin, 1690).

Dublin Almanac and General Register of Ireland for the year of our Lord, 1847

Dublin Courier

Dublin Gazette

Dublin Morning Register

Faulkner's Dublin Journal

Foundling Hospital, Dublin, *The Report of the committee appointed to enquire into the complaint of Thomas Adderley* (Dublin, 1758).

Foundling Hospital, Dublin, *Answer of the Governors of the Foundling Hospital to a memorial of the Lord Mayor, sheriffs, commons and citizens of Dublin to the Lord Lieutenant* (Dublin, 1816).

Foundling Hospital, London, *An Account of the Hospital for the Maintenance and Education of Exposed and Deserted Young Children* (London, 1796).

Gentleman's and London Magazine and Monthly Chronologer (London, 1756).

Gilbert, John, & Gilbert, Rosa, eds., *The Manuscripts of the Marquis of Ormonde preserved at the Castle, Kilkenny*, 3 vols (London, 1895).

Gilbert, John, ed., *Calendar of Ancient Records of Dublin* (CARD).

Griscom, John, *A Year in Europe*, 2 vols (New York, 1824).

Hanway, Jonas, *An Earnest appeal for mercy to the children of the poor* (London, 1766).

Harvey, William, 'Tentamen medicum inaugurale, de venenis' (MD thesis, Edinburgh University, 1774).

Hawkesworth, J., ed., *The Works of Jonathan Swift, D.D., Dean of St. Patrick's, Dublin*, 18 vols (London, 1784).

Hibernian Journal

Lyons, John Charles, *The Grand Juries of the County of Westmeath*, 2 vols (Ledestown, 1853).

New Monthly Magazine, Vol. IX, January to June 1818 (London, 1818).

Probate Record and Marriage Licence Index 1270–1858.

Pue's Occurrences

Redington, Joseph, ed., *Calendar of Treasury Papers* (London, 1889).

Rocque, John, *Exact Survey of the city and suburbs of Dublin, with the division of the parishes reduc'd from the large plan in four sheets* (Dublin, 1756).

Rocque, John, *Survey of the City, Harbour, Bay and Environs of Dublin on the same Scale as those of London, Paris & Rome* (Dublin, 1757).

Saunders's News-Letter

Shaw, W. Arthur, *Calendar of Treasury books and papers, 1729–1745: Preserved in the Public Record Office* (London, 1900).

Sheridan, Thomas, ed., *The works of the reverend Jonathan Swift DD, Dean of St Patrick's*, 19 vols (London, 1801).

Southern Reporter and Cork Commercial Courier

Stamford Mercury

Stoyte, Francis, *Workhouse Dublin: The Report of the Lord Mayor* (Dublin, 1705).

Swift, Jonathan, *A Short View of the State of Ireland* (Dublin, 1727).

Treble Almanack (Dublin, 1832).

Underwood, Michael, *Treatise on Diseases of Children* (London, 1789).

Vernon, John, *Remarks on a paper, entituled, An Abstract of the State of the Work-House, for maintaining of the poor of the city of Dublin* (Dublin, 1716).

Warder and Dublin Weekly Mail

Watson Stewart, John, *The Gentleman's and Citizen's Almanack* (Dublin, 1797).

Wodsworth, W.D., *A brief history of the ancient foundling hospital of Dublin from the year 1702* (Dublin, 1876).

Wolveridge, James, *Speculum matricis hybernicum, or, The Irish midwives handmaid catechistically composed by James Wolveridge, M.D.; with a copious alphabetical index* (London, 1670).

Young, Arthur, *A Tour made in Ireland with general observations on the present state of that kingdom* (Dublin, 1780).

Parliamentary Sources

Annual Report of the Local Government Board for Ireland, being the third report under 'The Local Government Board (Ireland) Act', 35 & 36 Vic., c. 109, HC, 1875. [C. 1221].

Charitable Institutions (Dublin), HC 1842 (389), xxxviii, 165.

Eighth Report from the Governors of the Board of Education in Ireland, HC 1810 (193), x, 269.

House of Industry and Foundling Hospital: Accounts. House of Commons (London, 1828).

Irish Legislation Database, Queen's University, Belfast.

Journals of the House of Commons of the Kingdom of Ireland, 8 vols (Dublin, 1753).

Journals of the House of Commons of the Kingdom of Ireland, 19 vols (Dublin, 1796 to 1801).

Journals of the House of Lords of the Kingdom of Ireland, 8 vols (Dublin, 1779).

Law Commission, *Statute Law Repeals: Nineteenth Report* (London, 2012).

Report from the Select Committee on the Irish Miscellaneous Estimates, (June 1829). HC 1829 (342) iv, 127.

Second Report of the Commissioners for inquiring into the Condition of the Poorer Classes in Ireland, (1836). HC 1837 (68) xxxi, 587.

Statutes at large passed in the Parliaments held in Ireland, 8 vols (Dublin, 1765).

Third Report of the Commissioners of Irish Education Inquiry, HC 1826–7, [C 13], xiii, 1.

Twentieth Report of the Commissioners for Auditing Public Accounts in Ireland, HC 1831–2, [C 75] p.50.

Secondary Sources

Andrews, Donna, *Philanthropy and Police: London Charity in the Eighteenth Century* (Princeton, 1989).

Aries, Philippe, *Centuries of Childhood: A Social History of Family Life* (New York, 1962).

Bardet, Jean-Pierre, Corinne Dufour and Jacques Renard, 'The death of foundlings: a tragedy in two acts', in Alain Bideau, Bertrand Desjardins and Héctor Pérez-Brignoli, eds., *Infant and Child Mortality in the Past* (Oxford, 1997).

Barnard, T.C., 'Reforming Irish Manners: The Religious Societies in Dublin during the 1690s', *The Historical Journal*, Vol. 35, No. 4 (Dec. 1992), pp.805–38.

Bayley Butler, Beatrice, 'Lady Arbella Denny, 1707–1792', in *Dublin Historical Record*, Vol. 9, No. 1 (Dec. 1946–Feb. 1947).

Bright, J. Franck, *A History of England*, 3 vols (New York, 1880).

Burton, Nathanael, *History of the Royal Hospital, Kilmainham* (Dublin, 1843).

Butcher, E.E., ed., *Bristol Corporation of the Poor: selected records 1696–1834* (Bristol, 1932).

Cameron, Charles, *History of the Royal College of Surgeons in Ireland* (Dublin, 1886).

Collins, Robert, *A short sketch of the life and writings of the late Joseph Clark Esq., M.D.* (London, 1849).

Cousins, Mel, 'The Irish Parliament and relief of the poor: the 1772 legislation establishing houses of industry', in *Eighteenth-Century Ireland/Iris an dá chultúr*, Vol. 28 (2013), pp. 95–115.

Cox, Catherine, 'Institutional space and the geography of confinement in Ireland, 1750–2000', in Thomas Bartlett, Brendan Smith, Jane Ohlmeyer and James Kelly, eds., *The Cambridge history of Ireland*, 4 vols (Cambridge 2018).

Crossman, Virginia, *Poverty and the Poor Law in Ireland, 1850–1914* (Liverpool, 2013).

Cunningham, H., 'The employment and unemployment of children in England, c. 1680–1851', in *Past and Present*, No. 126, pp.115–50.

D'Alton, John, *The History of the County of Dublin* (Dublin, 1838).

De La Tocnaye, *A Frenchman's Walk through Ireland* (Dublin, 1917).

Dease, William, *Observations on the different methods of treating the venereal disease* (Dublin, 1779).

Dickson, David, *Dublin: the making of a capital city* (London, 2014).

Dickson, David, ed., *The Gorgeous Mask: Dublin 1700–1850* (Dublin, 1987).

Dictionary of National Biography (London, 1885–1900), Vol. 58. Source: Wikisource.

Dudley, Rowena, 'The Dublin Parishes and the Poor: 1660–1740', in *Archivium Hibernicum*, Vol. 53 (1999), pp. 80–94.

Fildes, Valerie, 'The history of infant feeding 1500–1800' (PhD thesis, University of Surrey, 1982).

Fildes, Valerie, *Breasts, Bottles and Babies: A history of infant feeding* (Edinburgh, 1986).

Fildes, Valerie, *Wet Nursing: a history from antiquity to the present* (Oxford, 1988).

Fitzgerald, Patrick, 'Poverty and vagrancy in early modern Ireland 1540–1770' (PhD thesis, Queens University Belfast, 1994).

Fitzpatrick, William, *Ireland Before the Union* (Dublin, 1867).

Fleetwood, J., *The History of Medicine in Ireland* (Dublin, 1983).

Fleming, David, and Logan, John, eds., *Pauper Limerick: the register of the Limerick House of Industry 1774–93* (Dublin, 2011).

Geary, Laurence, *Medicine and Charity in Ireland 1718–1851* (Dublin, 2004).

Gilbert, J.T., *A History of the City of Dublin*, 3 vols (Dublin, 1854).

Gourdon, Vincent, 'Should abandoned children be baptised? The French case, the sixteenth to the early twentieth century', in Nicoleta Roman, ed., *Orphans and Abandoned Children in European History: sixteenth to twentieth centuries* (Oxon, 2018).

Hayton, David, 'Moral Reform and Country Politics in the Late Seventeenth-Century House of Commons', in *Past & Present*, No. 128 (Aug. 1990), pp.48–91.

Hayton, David, *The Anglo-Irish Experience, 1680–1730: Religion, Identity and Patriotism* (Woodbridge, 2012).

Hindle, S., 'Waste' Children? Pauper apprenticeship under the Elizabethan poor laws, c. 1598–1697', in P. Lane, N. Raven and K.D.M. Snell, eds., *Women, Work and Wages in England, 1600–1850* (Woodbridge, 2004).

Hitchcock, Timothy, *Down and Out in Eighteenth-Century London* (London, 2004).

Hitchcock, Timothy, King, Peter and Sharpe, Pamela, eds., *Chronicling Poverty: The Voices and strategies of the English poor, 1640–1840* (London, 1997).

Hitchcock, Timothy, *The English Workhouse: a study in Institutional poor relief in selected counties, 1696–1750* (Ph.D. thesis, University of Oxford, 1985).

Hufton, Olwen, *The Poor of Eighteenth-Century France, 1750–1789* (Oxford, 1974).

Inglis, Brian, 'The Freedom of the Press in Ireland 1784–1842' (PhD thesis, Trinity College Dublin, 1950).

Johnston-Liik, Edith Mary, *History of the Irish Parliament 1692–1800*, 6 vols (Belfast, 2002).

Kelly, James, '"This iniquitous traffic": The Kidnapping of Children for the American Colonies in Eighteenth-Century Ireland', in *The Journal of the History of Childhood and Youth*, Vol. 9, No. 2 (Spring 2016).

Kelly, James, 'Infanticide in 18th-century Ireland', in *Irish Economic and Social History*, xix (1992), pp.5–26.

King, Sir Charles Simeon, ed., *A Great Archbishop of Dublin William King D.D.* (London, 1908).

King, Steven, and Tomkins, Alannah, eds., *The Poor in England 1700–1850: an economy of makeshifts* (Manchester, 2003).

Lady Llanover, ed., *The Autobiography and Correspondence of Mary Granville, Mrs Delany*, 3 vols (London, 1861).

Levene, Alysa, 'The estimation of mortality at the London Foundling Hospital, 1741–99', in *Population Studies*, Vol. 59, No. 1, 2005, pp.87–97.

Levene, Alysa, *Childcare, Health and Mortality at the London Foundling Hospital 1741–1800* (Manchester, 2007).

McClure, Ruth, *Coram's Children: the London Foundling Hospital in the Eighteenth Century* (Yale, 1981).

McEntee, Don and Corcoran, Michael, *The Rivers Dodder and Poddle* (Dublin, 2016).

McGuire, James and Quinn, James, eds., *Dictionary of Irish Biography*, 9 vols (Cambridge, 2009).

Meldrum, Tim, 'London Domestic Servants from Depositional Evidence, 1660–1750: Servant-Employer Sexuality in the Patriarchal Household', in Tim Hitchcock, Peter King and Pamela Sharpe, eds., *Chronicling Poverty: The Voices and strategies of the English poor, 1640–1840* (London, 1997).

Moody, T.W. and Vaughan, W.E., eds., *A New History of Ireland* (Oxford, 1986).

O'Carroll, Joseph, 'Contemporary Attitudes Towards the Homeless Poor 1724–1775' in David Dickinson, ed., *The Gorgeous Mask: Dublin 1700–1850* (Dublin: Trinity History Workshop), pp. 64–85.

Ó Ciosáin, Niall, *Ireland in official print culture, 1800–1850* (Oxford, 2014).

Ó Ciosáin, Niall, *Print and popular culture in Ireland 1750–1850* (Dublin, 2010).

Pullan, Brian, 'Catholics, Protestants, and the Poor in Early Modern Europe', in *Journal of Interdisciplinary History*, xxxv:3 (Winter, 2005), pp.441–456.

Quane, M.A., 'A Dublin Hospital in 1788–89', in *Journal of the Irish Medical Association* (1965).

Raughter, Rosemary, 'A Natural Tenderness: The Ideal and the Reality of Eighteenth-Century Female Philanthropy' in M.G. Valiulis and Mary O'Dowd (eds.) *Women in Irish History* (Dublin, 1997).

Raughter, Rosemary, ed., '"My Dear lady C": Letters of Lady Arbella Denny to Lady Caldwell 1754–1777', in *Analecta Hibernica*, No. 41 (2009).

Risse, G., *Hospital life in Enlightenment Scotland* (Cambridge, 1986).

Robins, Joseph, *The Lost Children, A Study of Charity Children in Ireland 1700–1900* (Dublin, 1980).

Rogers, Nicolas, 'Carnal knowledge: illegitimacy in eighteenth-century Westminster', in *Journal of Social History*, Winter 89, Vol. 23, pp.355–375.

Sadler, S.H., *Infant feeding by artificial means* (London, 1896).

Sheridan, Thomas, ed., *The works of the Rev. Jonathan Swift D.D., Dean of St. Patricks Dublin*, 19 vols (Edinburgh, 1801).

Sherwood, Joan, *Infection of the innocents: wet nurses, infants and syphilis in France 1780–1900* (McGill-Queen's University Press, 2010).

Slack, Paul, *From Reformation to Improvement: Public welfare in early modern England* (Oxford, 1999).

Smuts, M., 'Organized violence in the Elizabethan monarchical republic' in *History*, Vol. 99, Issue 336 (July 2014).

Sonnelitter, Karen, '"To unite our temporal and eternal interests": Sermons and the charity school movement in Ireland, 1689–1740', in *Eighteenth-Century Ireland / Iris an dá chultúr*, Vol. 25 (2010).

Sonnelitter, Karen, *Charity Movements in Eighteenth-Century Ireland* (Woodbridge, 2016).

St. John Joyce, Weston, *The Neighbourhood of Dublin* (Dublin, 1921).

Tait, Clodagh, 'Some sources for the study of infant and maternal mortality in later seventeenth-century Ireland', in Elaine Farrell, ed., *She Said She Was in the Family Way: Pregnancy and infancy in modern Ireland* (London, 2012).

Ulbricht, Otto, 'The debate about foundling hospitals in Enlightenment Germany: Infanticide, illegitimacy, and infant mortality rates', in *Central European History*, 18(3/4): pp.211–256.

van Leeuwen, Marco H.D., 'Logic of Charity: Poor Relief in Preindustrial Europe', in *The Journal of Interdisciplinary History*, Vol. 24, No. 4 (Spring 1994), pp.589–613.

Viazzo, P.P., Bortolotto M. and Zanotto, A., 'Five centuries of foundling history in Florence: changing patterns of abandonment, care and mortality', in C. Panter-Brick and M.T. Smith, eds., *Abandoned Children* (Cambridge, 2000).

Wagner, Gilian, *Thomas Coram, Gent., 1668–1751* (Woodbridge, 2004).

Warburton, J., Whitelaw, J. and Walsh, R., *History of the City of Dublin*, 2 vols (London, 1818).

Wickes, Ian G., 'A history of infant feeding, part II: Seventeenth and eighteenth centuries', in *Archives of Disease in Childhood*, Vol 28, Issue139 (June 1953), pp. 232–240.

Wills, James, ed., *Lives of Illustrious and Distinguished Irishmen*, 3 vols (Dublin, 1840).

Wilson, Rachel, *Elite Women in Ascendancy Ireland 1690–1745* (Woodbridge, 2015).

Woods, James, *Annals of Westmeath Ancient and Modern* (Dublin, 1907).

Endnotes

Inscription

1   Warburton, J., Whitelaw, J. and Walsh, R., *History of the City of Dublin*, 2 vols (London, 1818), i, p.585. The King James Bible has it as 'he who doeth unto the least of these, my brethren, he doeth unto me'.

Prologue

1   Irish Architectural Archive, RIAI Murray Collection no. 0092/046.0615.
2   *Journals of the House of Commons of the Kingdom of Ireland*, ('Commons Journals') 19 vols (Dublin, 1796 to 1801), xvii, Appendix, pp.ccxlviii, ccxli.
3   *Commons Journals*, xvii, Appendix, p.ccxlviii.
4   Warburton et al, i, p.583 et seq.
5   Irish Architectural Archive, RIAI Murray Collection.
6   *Walkers Hibernian Magazine*, January 1783 (Dublin, 1783), p.3.
7   Warburton et al, i, p.588.
8   *Commons Journals*, xvii, Appendix, p.ccxlviii.
9   *Dublin Evening Post*, 11 May 1797.
10   *Commons Journals*, xvii, Appendix, p.ccxliii.
11   Ibid., Appendix, p.cclxi.
12   See for example M. A Quane, 'A Dublin Hospital in 1788–89', *Journal of the Irish Medical Association* (1965).
13   *Commons Journals*, xvii, Appendix, p.cclxi.
14   Ibid., Appendix, p.ccxlviii.
15   Ibid., Appendix, p.ccxliii.
16   Later this was confirmed to be 'simple water with tincture of opium, at the mercy of the head nurse tender herself to pour in what she pleased' (*Third Report of the Commissioners of Irish Education Inquiry*, [C 13], H.C. 1826–7, xiii, 1, p.74).

Chapter 1

1   James Wills, ed., *Lives of Illustrious and Distinguished Irishmen*, 3 vols (Dublin, 1840), Vol. iii, p.414.
2   John Gilbert, ed., *Calendar of Ancient Records of Dublin* (CARD) (Dublin, 1894), Vol. vi, p.90. (Spelling and punctuation of quotations may occasionally be altered for clarity.)

3   Timothy Hitchcock, *Down and out in eighteenth-century London* (London, 2004), pp.24, 25.

4   33 Henry VIII s.1 c.15; Patrick Fitzgerald, 'Poverty and vagrancy in early modern Ireland 1540–1770' (PhD thesis, Queens University Belfast, 1994), p.5.

5   Ibid., p.6.

6   Ibid., p.8.

7   Ibid., p.9.

8   Ibid., p.12.

9   M. Smuts, 'Organized violence in the Elizabethan monarchical republic', in *History*, Vol. 99, Issue 336, July 2014, pp.433–34.

10   Fitzgerald, p.14.

11   Ibid., p.268.

12   Rowena Dudley, 'The Dublin Parishes and the Poor: 1660–1740', in *Archivium Hibernicum*, Vol. 53 (1999), p.81.

13   Ibid.

14   Fitzgerald, p.22.

15   *The Manuscripts of the Marquis of Ormonde preserved at the Castle, Kilkenny*, 3 vols (London, 1895), i, pp.156, 181.

16   CARD, Vol. vi, p.218.

17   Ibid., p.219.

18   P. Slack, *From Reformation to Improvement* (Oxford, 1999), p.66; H. Cunningham, 'The employment and unemployment of children in England, c. 1680–1851', in *Past and Present*, No. 126, pp.115–50.

19   S. Hindle, "Waste' Children? Pauper apprenticeship under the Elizabethan poor laws, c. 1598–1697', in P. Lane, N. Raven, K.D.M. Snell, eds., *Women, Work and Wages in England, 1600–1850* (Woodbridge, 2004), p.18.

20   John Collis, *Proposals for the Taking in Boys into the King and Queen's Workhouse in Strand-street near Capel-street, Dublin* (Dublin, 1690).

21   Collis, *Proposals*, 1690.

22   National Archives (UK), MSS CO 391/10; Timothy Hitchcock, 'The English workhouse: a study in institutional poor relief in selected counties, 1696–1750' (PhD Thesis, Oxford, 1985), p.26.

23   John Collis, *A National Credit for a National Use* (Dublin, 1705), p.4. All dates are given in New Style.

24   CARD, Vol. vi, p.179.

25   Irish Legislation Database, Queen's University, Belfast.

26   Collis, *A National Credit for a National Use*, p.4.

27   See Slack, *From Reformation to Improvement*, p.85, for details of the legal aspects of the London Corporation of the Poor.

28   Ibid.

29   The same John Cary who was instrumental in the destruction of the Irish woollen trade.

30   Hitchcock (Ph.D. thesis), p.14.

31   Ibid., pp.17–19.

32   9 & 10 William III, c.35.

33   John Cary, *An Account of the Proceedings of the Corporation of Bristol, in execution of the Act of Parliament for the better employing the poor of that City* (London, 1700).

34   N.L.I., Lane papers, MS 8645/1.

35 John Vernon, *Remarks on a paper, entituled, An Abstract of the State of the Work-House, for maintaining of the poor of the city of Dublin* (Dublin, 1716), p.11.

36 Rachel Wilson, *Elite Women in Ascendancy Ireland 1690–1745* (Woodbridge, 2015), p.148.

37 Slack, p.47.

38 David Hayton, 'Moral Reform and Country Politics in the Late Seventeenth-Century House of Commons', in *Past & Present*, No. 128 (Aug. 1990), pp.48–91, at pp.67–8. Hayton found a strong association between the existence of reform societies in certain cities in England, and the subsequent formation of corporations in those cities.

39 T.C. Barnard, 'Reforming Irish Manners: The Religious Societies in Dublin during the 1690s', in *The Historical Journal*, Vol. 35, No. 4 (Dec., 1992), pp.805–38, at p.818.

40 Richard Bulkeley, 'Proposal for the future easing of this city and kingdom from the great burden of the poor' (University of Nottingham Library, Bentinck papers, MS Pw A 2326).

41 2 Anne c.19; *The Statutes at large passed in the Parliaments held in Ireland*, 8 vols (Dublin, 1765), iv, p.62.

42 Ibid.

43 Ibid.

44 Ibid.

45 Ibid.

46 CARD, Vol. v, p.208.

47 Thomas Sheridan, ed., *The works of the reverend Jonathan Swift DD, Dean of St Patrick's* (London, 1801) Vol. IX p.419. (*A Proposal for Giving Badges to the Beggars in all the Parishes of Dublin, 1737*).

48 2 Anne c.19.

49 2 Anne c.6.

50 Vernon, p.2.

Chapter 2

1 Nathanael Burton, *History of the Royal Hospital, Kilmainham* (Dublin, 1843), p.21. This theory is discounted by some.

2 King Letters (TCD, MS 1995-2008/414).

3 Wilson, p.148.

4 CARD, vi, p.342.

5 Francis Stoyte, *Workhouse Dublin: The Report of the Lord Mayor* (Dublin, 1705).

6 Vernon, pp.1, 11.

7 Ibid., p.12.

8 'Order for Collecting Poor-Money 1706', Marsh's Library (MS Z3.1.1 (143)).

9 Stoyte, 1705.

10 King Letters (TCD, MS 1995-2008/1164).

11 'The Case of Nicolas Peters Gent and Dorcas Peters als. Suttle his wife', Marsh's Library (MS Z3.1.1 (152)).

12 Vernon, p.2.

13 'Statement concerning admissions to the workhouse during the years 1706 to 1710', Marsh's Library (MS Z3.1.1 (153)).

14 Ibid.

15   Ibid.

16   Sir William Fownes to Dr Swift, 9 Sept. 1732, in J. Hawkesworth, ed., *The Works of Jonathan Swift, D.D., Dean of St. Patrick's, Dublin*, 18 vols (London, 1784), xvi, p.411.

17   Marsh's Library (MS Z.3.1.1 (153)).

18   Ibid.

19   Vernon, p.2.

20   Ibid., p.3.

21   Wodsworth, W.D., *A brief history of the ancient foundling hospital of Dublin from the year 1702* (Dublin, 1876), p.3.

22   Wodsworth, 1876, p.3.

23   Vernon, p.4.

24   Ibid.

25   Ibid., p.6.

26   Ibid., p.10.

27   Ibid., p.6.

Chapter 3

1   John D'Alton, *The History of the County of Dublin* (Dublin, 1838), p.90. (Eliza, meanwhile, had died).

2   CARD, vii, p.6 (with thanks to Turtle Bunbury at www.turtlebunbury.com).

3   Vernon, p.2.

4   Ibid., p.1.

5   Ibid., p.5.

6   Ibid., p.3.

7   Ibid., p.4.

8   'Accounts of A Workhouse (Dublin) AD 1706 with considerations to the Lord Archbishop 1708 by John Vernon,' Marsh's Library (MS Z3.1.1 (144)).

9   Vernon, p.5.

10   Warburton, et al, *History of the City of Dublin*, i, p.227.

11   Vernon, p.6.

12   Ibid., p.7.

13   Dickson, David, *Dublin: the making of a capital city* (London, 2014), p.123.

14   *A New History of Ireland*, Vol. iv, p.5.

15   See also Chapter 11.

16   Vernon, p.9.

17   Ibid., p.10.

18   2 G 1 c. 17.

19   *Journals of the House of Commons of the Kingdom of Ireland*, 8 vols (Dublin, 1753), viii, p.974. This was not the first parliamentary enquiry into the workhouse – there is reference to a 1719 enquiry. However, the report of that enquiry appears not to have been printed, and so does not survive. (Ibid., Vol. iv, p.518 [17 July 1719]); David Hayton, *The Anglo-Irish Experience 1680–1730*, p.193.

20   Dickson, p.130.

21 McGuire, James, Quinn, James, eds., *Dictionary of Irish Biography*, 9 vols (Cambridge, 2009), i, p.672.

22 *Commons Journals (1753)*, viii, p.974.

23 E.g. see letter to Archbishop King recommending appointment of one Matthews as Master in 1708 (TCD, MSS 1995-2008/1301)

24 E.g. see. Board of Governors, *Rules for Conducting the Education of the female children in the Foundling Hospital*, (Dublin, 1800), pp.10, 11.

25 *Journals of the House of Commons of the Kingdom of Ireland*, 8 vols (Dublin, 1753), Commons Journals (1753), viii, p.978.

26 Robert Corbet, 'A Diary of the Weather and Winds For 19 Years Commencing with AD 1716 and Concluding with 1734 Exactly Observed and taken at the City of Dublin' (Transcription by Dublin City Archive) p.215.

27 CARD, Vol. 7, p.322.

28 Irish Legislation Database.

29 'A List of the Poore in the City Workhouse 1725/6,' Marsh's Library (MS Z3.1.1 (148)).

30 The practice of employing inmates as nurses, 'washers' and servants is confirmed in Vernon, p.2.

31 Marsh's Library (MS Z3.1.1 (149)).

32 Ibid.

33 *Commons Journals (1753)*, viii, p.980.

34 Sir William Fownes to Dr Swift, 9 Sept. 1732, in J. Hawkesworth, ed., *The Works of Jonathan Swift, D.D., Dean of St. Patrick's, Dublin*, 18 vols (London, 1784), xvi, p.411.

35 1 G II c. 2.

36 'The Governors of the workhouse of the city of Dublin.'

37 Thomas Sheridan, ed., *The works of the Rev. Jonathan Swift D.D., Dean of St. Patricks Dublin*, 19 vols (Edinburgh, 1801), ix, p.415.

38 Jonathan Swift, *A Short View of the State of Ireland* (Dublin, 1727).

39 Jonathan Swift, 'A proposal for giving badges to the beggars in all the parishes of Dublin', in Thomas Sheridan, ed., *The works of the Rev. Jonathan Swift D.D., Dean of St. Patricks Dublin*, 19 vols (Edinburgh, 1801), ix, pp.415–6.

40 CARD, Vol. 7, p.502; Vernon, p.5.

Chapter 4

1 *Journals of the House of Lords of the Kingdom of Ireland*, 8 vols (Dublin, 1779), iii, p.115.

2 Anon., *The Case of the Foundlings of the City of Dublin* (Dublin, from internal evidence this was published between January and April 1730), p.1.

3 Also known as syrup of meconium, 'meconium' being a Greek word for opium. Meconium is also the term used to describe the early stools of a newborn, they having the same dark greenish colour.

4 *Lords' Journals*, iii, p.115. The remaining two infants had been returned to their mothers shortly after they were found.

5 Ibid.

6 Ibid.

7 'Letter of Archbishop King to his Clergy 23 Feb 1722/3', quoted in Anon., *The Case of the Foundlings of the City of Dublin; humbly recommended to the consideration of the Parliament* (Dublin, 1730), p.2.

8 Ibid.

9 *Lords' Journals*, iii, p.108.

10 William Fitzpatrick, *Ireland Before the Union* (Dublin, 1867), p.80.

11 *Lords' Journals*, iii, p.115.

12 Ibid., p.116.

13 Ibid.

14 James Kelly, 'Infanticide in 18th-century Ireland', in *Irish Economic and Social History*, xix (1992), pp.5–26.

15 Ibid., p.7.

16 Ibid., p.11.

17 Ibid.

18 Ibid., p.9.

19 Ibid., p.8.

20 6 Anne, c. 4; *The Statutes at large passed in the Parliaments held in Ireland*, 8 vols (Dublin, 1765), iv, p.120.

21 Nevertheless, Kelly identifies only fourteen confirmed executions for the crime between 1721 and 1800.

22 Tim Meldrum, 'London Domestic Servants from Depositional Evidence, 1660–1750: Servant-Employer Sexuality in the Patriarchal Household', in Tim Hitchcock, Peter King, Pamela Sharpe, eds., *Chronicling Poverty: The Voices and strategies of the English poor, 1640–1840* (London, 1997), p.52. For a purported change in attitudes to sexuality and marriage in eighteenth-century London see Timothy Hitchcock, 'Unlawfully begotten on her Body: Illegitimacy and the Parish poor in St Luke's Chelsea', Ibid., pp.71, 72. For a discussion of theories behind the rise in illegitimacy in the eighteenth century see Nicolas Rogers, 'Carnal knowledge: illegitimacy in eighteenth-century Westminster', in *Journal of Social History*, Winter 89, Vol. 23, pp.355–375.

23 Meldrum, 'London Domestic Servants', p.52.

24 Ibid.

25 Anon., *The Case of the Foundlings of the City of Dublin*, p.5.

26 Ibid.

27 Ibid., p.2.

28 Ibid., p.3.

29 73x8x5/2

30 Anon., *The Case of the Foundlings of the City of Dublin*, p.3.

31 Ibid., p 4.

32 Ibid., p 7.

33 In Biblical imagery, the raven, though worthless and reviled, was still fed by God.

34 *Lords Journals*, iii, p.112 (22 December 1729).

35 Anon., *The Case of the Foundlings of the City of Dublin*, p.7.

36 Ibid., p 8.

37 This is clear from internal evidence within the document.

38 *An Act for the better enabling the Governors of the Workhouse of the City of Dublin to provide for and employ the poor therein, and for the more effectual punishment of*

vagabonds, and also for the better securing of and providing for lunatics and foundling children. By convention it will be referred to as the 1729 Act.

39   Thomas Bray, *A Memorial Concerning the Erecting in the City of London or the Suburbs thereof, an Orphanotrophy or Hospital for the Reception of Poor Cast-Off Children or Foundlings* (n.p., n.d.), published in 1728 or 1729 according to McClure, *Coram's Children*, pp.21, 276.

40   McClure, *Coram's Children*, pp.42, 43. The Amsterdam orphanage, the *Aalmoeseniers Weeshuijs der Stadt Amsterdam*, took in foundlings but was not a dedicated foundling hospital.

41   Timothy Miller, *The Orphans of Byzantium: Child Welfare in the Christian Empire* (Washington, 2003), pp.52–60.

42   There was a strong association with education and particularly musical education, with the Constantinople orphanotropheion famous for the quality of its choir. The word 'Conservatory' comes from '*conservatorio*', the latin word for a girls' orphanage where the girls were to be 'conserved' from the vices of the street.

43   Fildes, *Wet Nursing*, pp.127–8.

44   Ulbricht, 'The debate about foundling hospitals', p.213.

45   Ibid.

46   Ibid.

47   Boulter to Bishop of London, 5 May 1730, in Hugh Boulter, *Letters written by his excellency Hugh Boulter, D.D. Lord Primate of All Ireland, &c. to several ministers of state in England and some others*, 2 vols (Oxford, 1770), ii, p.10.

48   *Annual Report of the Local Government Board for Ireland, being the first report under 'The Local Government Board (Ireland) Act', 35 & 36 Vic., c. 109*, [C. – 794.], H.C., 1873, p.53; Wodsworth, *A brief history*, p.11.

49   In the sense of converting a group or population. Clearly the 'conversion' of newborn children does not arise.

50   The earliest breakdown of the geographical origin of the children admitted comes from 1789, when 1,188 out of 2,144 admissions (55 per cent) were from outside Dublin (*Commons' Journals*, xiv, Appendix ccciii, ccci).

51   Irish Architectural Archive, RIAI Murray Collection 0092/046 – 0570.

Chapter 5

1   *Lords Journals*, iii, p.430, Appendix ix. In addition, older children were taken in to the nursery. See Table A, Appendix.

2   Examples include Paris, Rouen and Caen (Bardet, 'The death of foundlings', p.247); Florence (Viazzo et al, 'Five centuries of foundling history', p.74); Fildes, *Wet Nursing*, p.144; Fildes, Thesis, p.289.

3   Clodagh Tait, 'Some sources for the study of infant and maternal mortality in later seventeenth-century Ireland', in Elaine Farrell, ed., *She said she was in the family way': Pregnancy and infancy in modern Ireland* (London, 2012), p.67.

4   Fildes, Thesis, p.471; Fildes identifies this work as occurring at the start of a new wave of midwifery texts in English in the 1670s, largely based on the work of continental writers.

5   Wolveridge, James, *Speculum matricis hybernicum, or, The Irish midwives handmaid catechistically composed by James Wolveridge, M.D.; with a copious alphabetical index* (London, 1670).

6   Wolveridge, *Speculum*, pp.140–153.

7   Fildes Thesis, p.469; Wickes, 'History of infant feeding', part II, p.239.

8   Wolveridge, *Speculum*, p.152.

9   Wickes, 'History of infant feeding', part II, p.235.

10 Ibid.

11 Ibid., p.236.

12 Ibid.

13 Ibid.

14 Fildes, Thesis, p.208.

15 Although the process had something in common with the distribution of piece-work to self-employed contractors which was common in the textile industry, and with which many of the Governors would have been familiar.

16 *Dublin Evening Post*, 10 August 1734.

17 *Pue's Occurrences*, 10 August 1734.

18 *Lords Journals*, iii, p.427.

19 *Commons Journals*, (1782), iv, p.178.

20 Ibid., 2 October 1717.

21 *Commons Journals*, (1782), v, p.597.

22 Joseph Redington, ed., *Calendar of Treasury Papers* (London, 1889), Vol. 6, (1720–1728), Volume 267, (1728). Part 1 p.541; 'Volume 247: January 9–June 30, 1724', Vol. 6, (1720–1728), pp.257–276. British History Online, www.british-history.ac.uk/cal-treasury-papers/vol6/pp257-276 [accessed 15 February 2018].

23 South Dublin County Council, *Corkagh Park* (Dublin, 2001).

24 Shaw, W. Arthur, *Calendar of Treasury books and papers, 1729–1745: Preserved in the Public Record Office* (London, 1900), 1735–38, p.82.

25 Wagner, Gilian, *Thomas Coram, Gent., 1668–1751* (Woodbridge, 2004), p.69.

26 Intriguingly, Francis had a business partnership with Thomas Coram, later founder of the London Foundling Hospital (1739).

27 *Lords Journals*, iii, pp.423–30. Unless otherwise specified the majority of the information in the following account comes from the 'Report of the Committee appointed to enquire into the state of the Workhouse of this City laid before the House on 21st March 1737/8.'

28 The number of Assistants was increased from nine to 'fifteen or more' in the 1727 legislation, a quorum being five.

29 *Commons Journals*, vi, Appendix ccccxiv.

30 *Lords Journals*, iii, p.429.

31 E.g. as cited by sir Frances Bond Head in relation to French hospitals and by Mrs Guthrie in relation to the St Petersburg and Moscow foundling hospitals in the nineteenth century. Wodsworth, *A brief history*, pp.7, 9.

32 *Lords Journals*, iii, p.430, Appendix ix.

33 Wickes, 'A history of infant feeding', part iv, p.419.

34 Fildes, Thesis, pp.220–9.

35 Wickes, 'A history of infant feeding', part ii, p.238.

36 Michael Underwood, *Treatise on Diseases of Children* (London, 1789), cited in Wickes, 'A history of infant feeding', part iii, p.336.

37 Fildes, Thesis, pp.311–12.

38 *Lords Journals*, iii, p.430, Appendix ix.

39 *Lords Journals*, iii, p.429.

40 9 G II c. 25.
41 Ibid..
42 Ibid.
43 Ibid.
44 Wodsworth, p.4.
45 *Lords Journals*, iii, p.429.
46 Ibid.
47 *The New Monthly Magazine and Universal Register*, Vol. 9 (January–June 1818), p.311.
48 *Dublin Gazette*, 17 January 1738.
49 *Lords Journals*, iii, p.430, Appendix viii.
50 Wodsworth, p.4.
51 Lords Journals, iii, p. 430, Appendix v.
52 Ibid.
53 Ibid.
54 Ibid., Appendix viii.
55 'Rules and Orders directing the Regulation of the Workhouse, Dublin', *Lords Journals*, iii, p.430, Appendix xi.
56 *Lords Journals*, iii, p.430, Appendix xi.
57 Ibid.
58 Ibid.
59 Wodsworth, p.27.
60 Ibid.
61 Ibid.
62 *Lords Journals*, iii, p.428.
63 Ibid.
64 Ibid.
65 Ibid.

Chapter 6

1   *Dublin Gazette*, 17 January 1738; *Stamford Mercury*, 2 February 1738.
2   *Dublin Evening Post*, 17 January 1738; *Dublin News-Letter*, 17 January 1738.
3   *Dublin Gazette*, 17 January 1738.
4   Ibid.
5   Ibid., 14 Feb 1738, 14 March 1738.
6   *Lords Journals*, iii, p.430.
7   *Dublin Gazette*, 17 January 1738.
8   Ibid.
9   *Lords Journals*, iii, p.430, Appendix x.
10 Later corrected to sixty-one in written testimony. Ibid.
11 *Lords Journals*, iii, p.429.
12 Ibid., p.430.
13 Ibid., p.427.
14 In 1731 legislation had been introduced (5 G II c.14.) transferring the task of collection from churchwardens to collectors employed by the Workhouse on commission of 6*d* for every 20*s* collected.
15 *Lords Journals*, iii, p.428.
16 Ibid., p.425.

17   Ibid., p.430, Appendix ix. A mortality rate of 800 per 1,000 admissions.
18   Dublin Evening Post, 3 Jan 1741.
19   Dublin Gazette, 24 Mar, 1741.
20   Dublin Evening Post, 3 Jan 1741.
21   Dickson, David, *Arctic Ireland*, (Belfast, 1997) pp. 16-17.
22   .Dublin Evening Post, 3 Jan 1741.

Chapter 7

1   *Commons Journals* vi, Appendix cv; Wodsworth, W.D., *A Brief History of the Ancient Foundling Hospital of Dublin from the year 1702* (Dublin, 1876), p.28. Dates are given in new style.
2   Gilbert, J.T., *A History of the City of Dublin*, 3 vols (Dublin, 1854), i. pp.165, 167, 170.
3   Wodsworth, p.28.
4   This institution was variously referred to as 'the workhouse', the 'workhouse and foundling hospital' and the 'foundling hospital'. All three terms will be used depending on the era referred to and the context.
5   Wodsworth, p.28.
6   *Commons Journals*, vi, Appendix cv.
7   Wodsworth, p.29.
8   Ibid.
9   Ibid..
10   Ibid.
11   *Commons Journals*, vi, Appendix cv.
12   Wodsworth, p.29.
13   Wodsworth, p.30.
14   *Probate Record and Marriage Licence Index* 1270–1858, p.707.
15   Sir William Fownes to Dr Swift, 9 Sept. 1732, in J. Hawkesworth, ed., *The Works of Jonathan Swift, D.D., Dean of St. Patrick's, Dublin* (18 vols., London, 1784), xvi, p.411.
16   Dr Knox's testimony, *Commons Journals*, vi, Appendix xcviii.
17   *Commons Journals*, vi, Appendix c.
18   *Commons Journals*, vi, Appendix ci.
19   'Mr Pursell's pleasure garden', *Commons Journals*, vi, Appendix xci, xcix.; Rocque's map of 1756 shows a walled garden adjoining the Bedlam yard. See plate section.
20   *Commons Journals*, vi, Appendix xcix.
21   Ibid., Appendix cii.
22   Ibid., Appendix cv.
23   Ibid., Appendix c.
24   T.W. Moody and W.E. Vaughan, eds., *A New History of Ireland*, 9 vols (Oxford, 1986), iv, p.95.
25   Ibid., p.97.
26   Ibid., p.96.
27   *Commons Journals* (1753), vii, p.433. 21 November 1743.
28   Thomas Sheridan, ed., *The works of the Rev. Jonathan Swift D.D., Dean of St. Patricks Dublin*, 19 vols (Edinburgh, 1801), ix, p.415.
29   *Commons Journals*, vi, Appendix ciii.
30   Ibid., Appendix civ.

Chapter 8

1   Ibid., Appendix cvi.
2   Ibid., Appendix c.
3   Rocque, John, *Survey of the city and suburbs of Dublin, with the division of the parishes reduc'd from the large plan in four sheets* by (Dublin, 1757).
4   *Pue's Occurrences*, Saturday, 18 June 1757; Rocque, 1757.
5   *Gentleman's and London Magazine and Monthly Chronologer* (London, 1756), Vol. xxv, (November 1756), p.608.
6   *Commons Journals*, vi, Appendix xcvi, xcviii.
7   Ibid., Appendix xcvi.
8   Foundling Hospital Dublin, *The Report of the committee appointed to enquire into the complaint of Thomas Adderley* (Dublin, 1758).
9   Ibid.

Chapter 9

1   Irish Architectural Archive, Murray Collection, No. 54.
2   *Commons Journals*, vi, Appendix xcvii.
3   The Rev Dr Charles Cobbe, Archbishop of Dublin, was a Governor.
4   Foundling Hospital Dublin, *The Report of the committee appointed to enquire into the complaint of Thomas Adderley* (Dublin, 1758).
5   Anon. *A Letter to a Friend in the Country concerning The Work-House* (Dublin, n.d.).
6   *Commons Journals*, vi, Appendix xcvii.
7   St. John Joyce, Weston, *The Neighbourhood of Dublin* (Dublin, 1921), p.453; Don McEntee and Michael Corcoran, *The Rivers Dodder and Poddle* (Dublin, 2016), p.60.
8   *Commons Journals*, vi, Appendix xcvi.
9   Ibid., Appendix xcviii.
10   *Lords Journals*, iii, p.430, Appendix vi.
11   'One pint of stirabout is made of 4 ounces of oatmeal, boiled thick with water, and seasoned with a little salt.' 1774 Rules.
12   *Commons Journals*, vi, Appendix c, cii.
13   Ibid., Appendix xcvii.
14   *Pue's Occurrences*, 26 November 1757.
15   E.g. in December 1757 there were said to be 2,022 with country nurses. *Commons Journals*, vi, p.114.

Chapter 10

1   *Commons Journals*, vi, Appendix xcvi to ciii. Unless otherwise specified the information in this chapter comes from this source.
2   Old Kilmainham Gaol.
3   This is not the same William Hawker, who as parliamentary clerk had been ordered to audit the Grueber's accounts in 1738.
4   1763 edition.
5   Foundling Hospital Dublin, *The Report of the committee appointed to enquire into the complaint of Thomas Adderley* (Dublin, 1758).
6   Ibid.

7   *Commons Journals*, vi, p.97.
8   Ibid., p.100.
9   Ibid., Appendix xcvii.
10   Ibid., Appendix c.
11   Ibid., p.113.
12   Wodsworth, p.29.
13   *Pue's Occurrences*, 28 November to 2 December 1758.

Chapter 11

1   *Dublin Courier*, Friday, 4–7 April 1760.
2   Irish Architectural Archive Murray Collection No. 36.
3   *Dublin Courier*, Friday, 4–7 April 1760.
4   Beatrice Bayley Butler, 'Lady Arbella Denny, 1707–1792', in *Dublin Historical Record*, Vol. 9, No. 1 (Dec. 1946–Feb. 1947).
5   Ibid.
6   See E.g. Bayley Butler, p.3; Rosemary Raughter, ed. '"My Dear lady C": Letters of Lady Arbella Denny to Lady Caldwell 1754–1777', in *Analecta Hibernica*, No. 41 (2009), p.142.
7   Wodsworth, p.31.
8   Lady Llanover, ed., *The autobiography and correspondence of Mary Granville, Mrs Delany* 3 vols (London, 1861), iii, pp.155, 208, 286, 548.
9   *Dublin Courier*, 28 to 30 April 1760.
10   William Henry, *The Cries of the Orphans. A Sermon preached in the Parish church of St Michael on Sunday April 27th* (Dublin, 1760).
11   See Karen Sonnelitter '"To unite our temporal and eternal interests": Sermons and the charity school movement in Ireland, 1689–1740', in *Eighteenth-Century Ireland / Iris an dá chultúr*, Vol. 25 (2010), pp.62–81 on the multiple functions of charity sermons.
12   The onset of the Seven Years War may partly explain the sudden jump in admissions from 635 in 1756 to 1,113 and 1,136 in 1757 and 1758. (*Commons Journals*, ix, Appendix vi, p.ccxi). See also Chapter 3.
13   *Universal Advertiser*, 10 March 1759, cited in Kelly, J., 'Infanticide in Eighteenth Century Ireland', in *Irish Economic and Social History*, Vol. 19 (1992).
14   *Faulkner's Dublin Journal*, 1 May 1759, cited in ibid.
15   Kelly, J., p.13.
16   *Commons Journals*, vii, p.lxxxiii. Rev John Worrall, the Dean's Vicar of St Patrick's, became a friend of Swift's, looked after his garden, and supervised the choirs in both cathedrals. (Bardon, Jonathan, *Hallelujah* (Dublin, 2015)).
17   *Commons Journals*, ix, Appendix xviii, p.ccxxi.
18   I G II c. 27.
19   This page only survives because a plan of the new chapel is drawn on the back. Irish Architectural archive ref. 0092/046.0599.
20   *Dublin Courier*, 28 to 30 April 1760.
21   Ibid., 2 to 5 May 1760.
22   Ibid., 28 to 30 April 1760.
23   *Commons Journals*, ix, Appendix ii, p.cciii.
24   *Dublin Courier*, 28 to 30 April 1760.
25   *Commons Journals*, vi, p.ccccxiv.

26 Ibid., p.ccccxiv.
27 Ibid., ix, Appendix ccix; Wodsworth, p.29. However. Wodsworth describes a different state of affairs. He refers to a report produced in 1769 that calculated Pursell's total embezzlement as £529 10s 9d. This report maintained that Pursell had deliberately contrived to structure the accounts to make it seem that 'one "Touchey", the clerk' – presumably Fauchey the Foundling Clerk – had been responsible (Wodsworth, p.29).
28 *Commons Journals*, vi, p.ccccxiv
29 *Pue's Occurrences*, 19 August 1758.
30 *Commons Journals*, vi, p.114.
31 Ibid., p.143.
32 Ibid., vii, p.27.
33 Ibid., vii, p.lxxxvii.
34 Which they mistakenly dated to the 1759 session of parliament. *Commons Journals*, vii, p.214.
35 *Commons Journals*, 11 November 1771.
36 Made by Alexander Gordon of Temple Bar. *Dublin Historical Record*, Vol. 9, No. 1, p.7.
37 *Dublin Courier*, 17 October 1760; *Dublin Historical Record*, Vol. 9, No. 1 (Dec. 1946–Feb. 1947), p.7.
38 Wodsworth, p.34.
39 *Commons Journals*, vii, p.334.
40 Ibid., xvii, Appendix cclxxvii.
41 *Dublin Historical Record*, Vol. 9, No. 1 (Dec. 1946–Feb. 1947) p.7.
42 Ibid.
43 The awarding of 'premiums' for exemplary behaviour was probably borrowed from the Dublin Society, where the practice was well established.
44 *Commons Journals*, vii, p.334.
45 Ibid., p.214.
46 Ibid., Appendix lxxxvii.
47 *Dublin Courier*, 23 to 25 April 1764.
48 Ibid.
49 Ibid. *Commons Journals*, vii, p.335.
50 *Dublin Courier*, 25 to 27 July 1764.
51 Irish Architectural Archive, RIAI Murray Collection No. 36.
52 *Dublin Courier*, 1 to 3 August 1764.
53 *Dublin Courier*, 7 to 9 May 1764.
54 See PRONI T3019/6080 21-05-1770
55 *Dublin Courier*, 10 to 12 December 1764.
56 Wodsworth, p.26.
57 Although Wodsworth has them in blue with red collars and cuffs, he was not an eyewitness and both the *Dublin Courier*, above, and the *Hibernian Magazine*, January 1783, have them in green with red cuffs. It's possible green was changed to blue in the wake of the 1798 rebellion. At this time, from the 1772 seal and the above accounts the girls' uniform seemed to consist of a green jacket bodice laced down the front to the waist, with short skirts overlying the petticoat, a long bibless apron gathered and tied at the waist, elbow-length sleeves with scarlet cuffs. The neck opening was covered with a neck handkerchief, and on the head was worn a simple cap or pinner.
58 *Commons Journals*, vi, p.ccccxiv.
59 Ibid., vii, p.216.

60   Ibid., p.334.
61   Ibid., Appendix lxxxii.
62   *Dublin Courier*, 4 to 7 April 1760.
63   PRONI Ref T2915/11/35
64   It was this child, John Henry Viscount Fitzmaurice, in whose honour a few years
      earlier a communion cup had been donated to the Hospital 'when he entered it
      at the age of two years,' according to the inscription (Wodsworth, p.34); 'My Dear
      Lady C', *Analectica Hibernica*, No. 41 (2009) p.137.
65   *Commons Journals*, 11 November 1771.
66   PRONI reference D562/2747 Letter to Lady Massarreene, 5 May 1772.
67   Ibid.
68   *Commons Journals*, 11 November 1771.
69   Ibid.
70   11 & 12 George III c.11.
71   See bond for Lucy Bligh, Irish Architectural Archive, RIAI Murray Collection,
      0092/046.0599 (verso).
72   *Commons Journals*, vii, p.335; A leading advocate for the creation of nationwide
      'Houses of Industry' was Dean Richard Woodward.

Chapter 12

1   *Hibernian Journal*, 5 to 7 July 1773.
2   DIB, Vol. 2, p.123.
3   There is no record of how the child fared following Hely's consultation.
4   Father of the future revolutionary. Separately, Emmett later solicited for the job of
      physician to the Foundling Hospital. Given his known liberal sympathies, had he
      been successful, the history of the institution might have turned out differently
      (*Saunders's News-Letter*, 10 October 1774).
5   *Hibernian Journal*, 23 to 26 April 1773.
6   Letter to Dr Robert Emmett dated 4 October 1772 published in *Hibernian
      Journal*, 5 to 7 July 1773.
7   If true, this would represent an inversion of the normal protocol.
8   *Pue's Occurrences*, 3 May, 1757.
9   *Hibernian Journal*, 22 to 24 December 1773.
10   Ibid., 19 to 21 April 1773
11   Governors of the Foundling Hospital and Workhouse, *Rules, Ordinances, Bye-Laws
      and Regulations* (Dublin, 1774).
12   Ibid.
13   *Saunders's News-Letter*, 9 to 12 September 1774.
14   Ibid., 23 to 26 September 1774.
15   Ibid., 19 to 21 October 1774.
16   *Hibernian Journal*, 21 July 1780.
17   Wodsworth, pp.34, 36.
18   *Commons Journals*, vii, p.214.
19   Ibid., Appendix lxxxvii.
20   Ibid., vii, Appendix ccccxiv.
21   Ibid., ix, Appendix ccxxi.
22   See E.g. Hanway, *An Earnest Appeal for Mercy to the Children of the Poor*
      (London, 1766).

23   James Kelly, '"This iniquitous traffic":The Kidnapping of Children for the American Colonies in Eighteenth-Century Ireland', in *The Journal of the History of Childhood and Youth*, Vol. 9, No. 2 (Spring 2016), p.240.

24   *Commons Journals*, ix, Appendix ccxix.

25   Ibid., ix, Appendix ccxxi.

26   Wodsworth, p.35.

27   Bayley Butler, p.8.

28   *Saunders's News-Letter*, 28 July 1778.

29   Ibid., 21 June 1779.

30   Ibid., 12 June 1782.

31   Commons Journals, ix, Appendix cccxciv.

32   Wodsworth, p.35.

33   *Commons Journals*, xii, p.314. Regulation of the carriage trade was transferred to the commissioners of police.

34   *Commons Journals*, ix, Appendix cciii to ccix.

35   Ibid.

36   Ibid., xi, p.31.

37   Sonnelitter, *Charity Movements*, p.122.

38   *An Account of the Hospital for the Maintenance and Education of Exposed and Deserted Young Children* (London, 1796), p.32. The London Foundling Hospital reverted to its highly selective approach to admissions, accepting only a relatively small number.

Chapter 13

1   *Commons Journals*, xvii, Appendix ccxlviii.

2   Ibid., and ccxli.

3   E.g. *Freeman's Journal*, 4 April 1797.

4   *Freeman's Journal*, 6 April 1797.

5   Ibid., 4 April 1797.

6   Ibid., 6 April 1797.

7   Ibid., 12 April 1797; *The Parliamentary Register* (Dublin, 1801), Vol. 17, p.467; *Freeman's Journal*, 13 April 1797.

8   E.g. *Freeman's Journal*, 29 April 1797.

9   *Parliamentary Register*, Vol. xvii, p.467.

10   Ibid., Vol. xi, p.257.

11   The name was probably pronounced 'Blacqueer' by contemporaries (just as, for example, D'Olier Street was pronounced 'D'Oleer Street') – one of his nicknames was 'Queerblack'.

12   DIB.

13   James Woods, *Annals of Westmeath Ancient and Modern* (Dublin, 1907), p.30. Whether true or not, it was a rumour that attached to Blaquiere in his lifetime.

14   DIB.

15   Johnston-Liik, Edith Mary, *History of the Irish Parliament 1692–1800*, 6 vols (Belfast, 2002), iii, p.203.

16   *The Parliamentary Register*, Vol. xvii, p.467.

Chapter 14

1. *Freeman's Journal*, 18 April 1797.
2. *Commons Journals*, xvii, Appendix ccxl.
3. Ibid., xiv, Appendix ccc.
4. Ibid., cccvi.
5. Ibid.
6. Ibid., xvii, Appendix cclx.
7. *The Parliamentary Register*, Vol. 17, p.476.
8. *Freeman's Journal*, 18 April 1797.
9. *The Parliamentary Register*, Vol. 17, p.477.
10. *Freeman's Journal*, 18 April 1797
11. Ibid., 20 April 1797.

Chapter 15

1. *Commons Journals*, xvii, Appendix cclxi. However, nurses in the infant nursery were paid £5 – indicating that they were possibly wet nurses.
2. E.g. a letter from Thomas English to the Chief Secretary, 20 May 1797 indicating that in his Armagh parish up to sixty foundlings were conveyed to Dublin in one year. National Archives State Papers OP/27/9.
3. *Third Report of the Commissioners of Irish Education Inquiry*, [C 13], H.C. 1826-7, xiii, 1, p.73.
4. *Commons Journals*, xiv, p.ccc.
5. George Sigmond, *Lancet*, 1836, p.631.
6. Ibid.
7. *Commons Journals*, xvii, Appendix cclii.

Chapter 16

1. *Freeman's Journal*, 22 April 1797; *Commons Journals*, xvii, Appendix ccxlviii. The other two visitors were John Hewitt and Town Major Henry Sirr. The fifth remains unnamed.
2. *Commons Journals*, xvii, Appendix ccxl.
3. 'Extract from the Bye-laws' [of the Foundling Hospital] *Commons Journals*, xvii, p.cclix.
4. Probably reproduced as *Commons Journals*, xvii, Appendix iv, p.ccxlix.
5. Fleetwood, J., *The History of Medicine in Ireland* (Dublin, 1983), p.110.
6. *Freeman's Journal*, 29 April 1797.

Chapter 17

1. *Freeman's Journal*, 4 May 1797.
2. Ibid., 4 May 1797.
3. *Commons Journals*, xvii, Appendix cclxxvii.
4. *Freeman's Journal*, 4 May 1797.
5. Ibid., 9 May 1797.
6. *Commons Journals*, xvii, Appendix cclxvii.

7   *Freeman's Journal*, 9 May 1797.
8   *Commons Journals*, xvii, Appendix ccliii.
9   Probably a reference to the case reported in the *Hibernian Journal*, 2 September 1795.
10   *Freeman's Journal*, 9 May 1797.
11   *Dublin Evening Post, 9 May 1797.*
12   Ibid.
13   Burtchaell, G.D., and Sadleir, T.U., eds., *Alumni Dublinenses* (Dublin, 1935), p.378.
14   Risse, G. *Hospital life in Enlightenment Scotland* (Cambridge, 1986).
15   Harvey, William, 'Tentamen medicum inaugurale, de venenis' (MD thesis, Edinburgh University, 1774), p.4.
16   In his testimony in 1797 Harvey indicates that he has worked in the Hospital for twenty years. Perhaps prior to his appointment he worked in some acting capacity, or perhaps he was simply vague about the date.
17   Cameron, Charles, *History of the Royal College of Surgeons in Ireland* (Dublin, 1886), p.300.
18   Collins, Robert, *A short sketch of the life and writings of the late Joseph Clark Esq., M.D.* (London, 1849), p.80.
19   Ibid.
20   *Freeman's Journal*, 13 June 1797; Brian Inglis, 'The Freedom of the Press in Ireland 1784–1842', (PHD thesis, Trinity College Dublin, 1950), p 137.
21   *Freeman's Journal*, 11 May 1797; *Commons Journals*, xvii, Appendix vii, p.ccli.
22   *Freeman's Journal*, 11 May 1797.
23   *Dublin Evening Post*, 11 May 1797.
24   *Freeman's Journal*, 11 May 1797.

Chapter 18

1   *Freeman's Journal*, 13 May 1797.
2   Ibid.
3   Ibid.
4   Ibid.
5   Joan Sherwood, *Infection of the innocents: wet nurses, infants and syphilis in France 1780–1900* (McGill-Queen's University Press, 2010), p.45.
6   Ibid., p.7.
7   *Commons Journals*, xvii, Appendix ccxlii.
8   Sherwood, p.48.
9   Ibid.
10   *Commons Journals*, xvii, Appendix ccxlii.
11   Fildes Thesis, pp.288, 292; Sadler, S.H., *Infant feeding by artificial means* (London, 1896), p.179.
12   Dease, William, *Observations on the different methods of treating the venereal disease* (Dublin, 1779), p.24.
13   Sherwood, pp.49–54.
14   *Commons Journals, xvii*, Appendix cclxxii, cclxxiii.
15   *Freeman's Journal*, 23 May 1797.
16   *Dublin Evening Post*, 1 June 1797.
17   *Freeman's Journal*, 23 May 1797

18   De La Tocnaye, *A Frenchman's Walk through Ireland* (Dublin, 1917), pp.252, 255, 258.
19   *Freeman's Journal*, 8 June 1797.
20   Ibid..
21   Ibid.
22   Warburton et al, Vol. i, p.584.
23   *Freeman's Journal*, 15 June 1797.
24   Ibid.
25   Ibid.
26   Ibid.
27   Ibid.
28   Ibid. The Black Cart was used to round up vagrants and beggars for incarceration in the House of Industry. The allegation was that it was only active when the Committee of Supply was sitting in parliament to decide on its allocation of funds.
29   Ibid.
30   Irish Legislation Database.
31   *Dublin Evening Post*, 20 June 1797.
32   James Woods, *Annals of Westmeath, Ancient and Modern* (Dublin, 1907), p.29; John Charles Lyons, *The Grand Juries of the County of Westmeath*, 2 vols, (Ledestown, 1853) i. One of the judges was none other than the Honourable John Toler, the Solicitor General.
33   John Charles Lyons, *The Grand Juries of the County of Westmeath from the year 1727 to the year 1853*, 2 vols (Ledestown, 1853), i. Woods, pp.22–29.
34   Johnston-Liik, iii, p.203.
35   J. Franck Bright, *A History of England*, 3 vols (New York, 1880), iii, p.1200.

Chapter 19

1   *Commons Journals*, xvii, Appendix cclxxvii.
2   Ibid.
3   John Watson Stewart, *The Gentleman's and Citizen's Almanack* (Dublin, 1797), p.140.
4   John F. Fleetwood, *The History of Medicine in Ireland* (Dublin, 1983), p.138.
5   *Saunders's News-Letter*, 5 July 1797.
6   *Third Report of the Commissioners of Irish Education Inquiry*, H.C. 1826-7 [C 13], p.71.
7   Ibid., p.73.
8   Ibid., p.73.
9   Ibid., p.74.
10   Ibid.
11   Wodsworth, p.45.
12   Ibid.
13   Ibid.
14   *Third Report of the Commissioners of Irish Education Inquiry*, H.C. 1826-7, [C 13], xiii, 1, p.73. ('*Third Report*').
15   Ibid.
16   *Eighth Report from the Governors of the Board of Education in Ireland*, p.207. HC 1810 (193), x, 269. ('*Eighth Report*'). Although we only know this because forty-nine died 'subsequent to the 4th week'.

17 Ibid., p.210.
18 *Eighth Report*, p.208.
19 Ibid., p.211.
20 Ibid., p.199.
21 *Commons Journals*, xvii, Appendix div.
22 Ibid., Appendix dxxiii.
23 Ibid., Appendix dcxciii.
24 38 G III c. 35. In 1800 the Chancellor of the (Irish)Exchequer was added to the Governors, bringing the total to ten (40 G III c. 33.).
25 *Eighth Report*, p.205.
26 *Ibid.*, p.177.
27 Ibid., p.201.
28 Ibid., p.212.
29 Ibid., pp.171–2.

Chapter 20

1 *Eighth Report*, p.213.
2 Ibid.
3 Ibid., p.173.
4 RIAI Murray Collection, Irish Architectural Archive.
5 *Eighth Report*, p.174.
6 Ibid. Mortality figures show a spike in the deaths of 'grown children' in 1806 and 1808.
7 Ibid.
8 Edward Wakefield, *An account of Ireland Statistical and Political*, 2 vols (London, 1812), ii, p.427.
9 Ibid., p.431.
10 Ibid., p.431.
11 *Dictionary of National Biography* (London, 1885–1900), vol. 58, p.449. Source: Wikisource.
12 Wakefield, ii, p.435.
13 *Eighth Report*, p.178.
14 Ibid., p.180.
15 Ibid.
16 *Third Report*, p.145.
17 Wakefield, p.436.
18 *Third Report*, p.148.
19 Foundling Hospital, Dublin, *Answer of the Governors of the Foundling Hospital to a memorial of the Lord Mayor, sheriffs, commons and citizens of Dublin to the Lord Lieutenant* (Dublin, 1816), p.22.
20 Ibid., p.27.
21 Ibid., p.22.
22 Ibid., p.29.
23 Ibid., p.41.
24 *The Dublin Foundling Hospital Act 1814* (54 George III c.128.); Law Commission, *Statute Law Repeals: Nineteenth Report* (London, 2012), p.141.
25 *Answer of the Governors*, p.10.

26   Ibid., p.3.
27   Ibid., p.7.
28   *Third Report*, p.148.
29   3 Geo.IV c.35, '*Dublin Foundling Hospital Act 1822*.'

Chapter 21

1   John Griscom, *A Year in Europe*, 2 vols (New York, 1824), p.317.
2   *New Monthly Magazine*, Vol. ix, January to June 1818 (London, 1818), p.311.
3   Wodsworth, p.6.
4   By contrast, the registers of the *Spedale degli Innocenti* in Florence listing every admission for five hundred and fifty years still survive.
5   *Third Report*, pp.94–5.
6   Ibid., pp.87–8.
7   Ibid., p.89.
8   Ibid., p.91.
9   Ibid., p.97.
10   Ibid., p.111.
11   Ibid., p.117.
12   Ibid., p.91.
13   Part of the Foundling Hospital from 1824. See below.
14   *Eighth Report*, p.189; *Third Report*, p.61.
15   *Saunders's News-Letter*, 26 July 1810; *Third Report*, p.152.
16   *Third Report*, p.61.
17   Ibid., p.44.
18   *Report of George Nicholls on institutions in Dublin receiving grants from public funds* (London, 1842), pp.5, 6.
19   *Third Report*, p.127.
20   Ibid., p.7.
21   Ibid., p.34.
22   Ibid., pp.51, 63.

Chapter 22

1   *Third Report*, p.55.
2   Ibid., p.5.
3   Board of Governors, *Rules for conducting the education of the female children in the Foundling Hospital* (Dublin, 1800), p.5.
4   *Third Report*, p.8.
5   Warburton et al, i, p.588.
6   Board of Governors, *Rules for conducting the education of the female children in the Foundling Hospital* (Dublin, 1800), p.11.
7   *Eighth Report*, p.178.
8   John Carr, *The Stranger in Ireland* (Philadelphia, 1806), p.315.
9   Warburton et al, i, p.584.
10   *Rules* (1800), p.17.
11   Warburton et al, i, p.585.
12   Ibid.

13   *Rules* (1800), p.5.
14   Although this was to change in later years. See Chapter 23.
15   *Eighth Report*, p.190.
16   Ibid., p.190.

Chapter 23

1   *DIB*, Vol. 6, p.252.
2   *Dictionary of National Biography 1885–1900*, Vol. 35, p.314, retrieved from Wikisource, 13 December 2017.
3   Ibid., *Dublin Weekly Register*, 5 January 1822; Wakefield, Edward, *An account of Ireland, statistical and political*, 2 vols (London, 1812), ii, p.469.
4   *Third Report*, pp.23, 41.
5   *Morning Register*, 12 August 1825.
6   Ibid., 23 August 1825.
7   *Third Report*, p.33.
8   Ibid., pp.42, 143.
9   Ibid., p.81.
10   Ibid., p.43.
11   Ibid., p.42.
12   Ibid., p.64.
13   Ibid.
14   Ibid., p.66.
15   Ibid., p.60.
16   Ibid., p.65.
17   Ibid., p.32.
18   Ibid., p.66.

Chapter 24

1   *Third Report*, p.36.
2   Ibid., p.18.
3   Ibid., p.34.
4   Ibid., p.156.
5   Under Magee the ten-member Board of Governors came to consist of two archbishops, one bishop, four other clergymen including Archbishop Magee's son, and only three non-clergymen (House of Commons, *House of Industry and Foundling Hospital: Accounts* (London, 1828), p.6.)
6   *Third Report*, p.156.
7   Ibid., p.7.
8   Ibid., p.28.
9   Ibid., pp.140–1.
10   *Dublin Morning Register*, 6 August 1825.
11   *Third Report*, p.140.
12   *Southern Reporter and Cork Commercial Courier*, 15 August 1826; *Saunders's News-Letter*, 3 August 1826.
13   *Third Report*, p.77.
14   *Saunders's News-Letter*, 4 August 1829 and 26 August 1829.

15   *Third Report*, pp.37, 45.
16   Ibid., p.68
17   Ibid., p.56.
18   Ibid., p.32.
19   Ibid., p.7.
20   Ibid., p.7
21   Ibid., p.52.
22   Ibid., p.63.
23   Ibid., p.35.
24   Ibid., p.46.

Chapter 25

1   *Eighth report*, p.186.
2   Wakefield, pp.423, 435.
3   The commissioners received the bulk of the figures probably in November 1824, and certainly no later than December 182 (*Third Report*, pp.19, 23).
4   Third Report, p.29.
5   Ibid.
6   *Commons Journals*, xiv, Appendix ccciv. Third Report, p. 6.
7   Third Report, p.30.
8   One of the Governors, Rev. John Pomeroy, also disagreed that there were many foundlings alive and well in the countryside (*Third Report*, p.59).
9   Ibid., p.6.
10   House of Commons, *Report from the select committee on the Irish miscellaneous estimates* (June 1829). HC 1829 (342) 4 127.
11   E.g. *Evening Packet and Correspondent*, 15 October 1829.
12   *Morning Register*, 5 October 1829.
13   *Second Report of the Commissioners for inquiring into the Condition of the Poorer Classes in Ireland* (1836) HC 1837 (68) xxxi, 587, p.6.
14   Probably 1834; see 'Report of George Nicholls on Institutions in Dublin receiving grants from public funds'; *Charitable Institutions (Dublin)*, House of Commons, 1842, p.8. HC 1842 (389), xxxviii, p.165.
15   *The Warder and Dublin Weekly Mail*, 6 May 1837.
16   *Charitable Institutions (Dublin)*, House of Commons, 1842, p.8. HC 1842 (389), xxxviii, p.165; *The Treble Almanack* (Dublin, 1832).
17   *The Dublin Almanac and General Register of Ireland for the year of our Lord, 1847* (Dublin, 1847), p.328.
18   *Annual Report of the Local Government Board for Ireland, being the third report under 'The Local Government Board (Ireland) Act', 35 & 36 Vic., c. 109*, HC, 1875. [C. 1221], p.50.
19   Ibid., p.52.
20   The rents of the property belonging to the Foundling Hospital were still being collected and used to defray the expenses of the foundlings, along with a parliamentary grant.
21   Wodsworth, pp.iii, iv.
22   Ibid., p.iv.
23   *Freeman's Journal*, 26 October 1876; Wodsworth, pp.5–6.

24   *Annual Report of the Local Government Body for Ireland (39th Report)* (HC 1911 [5847] xxxiii, 1), p.xxvi.

Appendix

1   Sources: *Lords Journals*, iii, p430, Appendix ix; *Commons Journals*, iv, 21 November 1743, ccxxv; *Commons Journals*, vi, 12 May 1760, ccccxiv; *Commons Journals, ix, Appendix ccxi*, 13 November 1773; *Commons Journals*, xiv, 24 March 1791, Appendix ccci; *Commons Journals*, xvii, 3 May 1797, Appendix ccliii; *Reports from the Commissioners of the Board of Education in Ireland* (1813), viii, p.171, 172; *Third Report of the Commissioners of Irish Education Enquiry* (1826), pp.148–152; *History of Dublin*; Warburton et al, i, p.591; *Twentieth Report of the Commissioners for auditing Public Accounts in Ireland* [C 75] HC (1831-2), p.50.

2   D. Dickson, C. Ó Gráda and S. Daultrey, 'Hearth tax', cited in Mary E. Daly, 'Famine and Famine Relief, 1740–2000', in E.F. Biagini and M.E. Daly, eds., *The Cambridge Social History of Modern Ireland*, p.39.

3   Viazzo et al, 'Five centuries of foundling history', p.77.

4   C. Ó Gráda, 'Famine in Ireland 1300–1900' (UCD 2014), pp.10, 33.

5   Statutes at Large 54 Geo.3 c.128 'Dublin Foundling Hospital Act 1814'.

6   Ibid., 1 Geo.4 c.29 'Dublin Foundling Hospital Act 1820'.

7   E.g. *Dublin Evening Post*, 21 April 1821, admissions further suspended until 20 August 1821; ibid., 25 October 1823 – Closure to admissions 'from the country parts of Ireland' from November 1823 to May 1824.

8   3 Geo.4 c.35 'Dublin Foundling Hospital Act 1822'.

9   See Chapter 6. 'An Account of Foundling Children received from parishes, and how disposed of at nurse abroad, and in the nursery in the Workhouse, from 25 March 1730 to 25 December 1737, distinguishing the number received each year', *Lords Journals* iii, p.430, Appendix ix.

10   However, in the same period, an additional 2,847 were 'struck off the books', meaning the mortality rate is in fact likely to have been higher. *Commons Journals*, xvii, Appendix cclxvii.

11   Breakdown available in Table B; *Third Report of the Commissioners of Irish Education Inquiry*, pp.148–152; For the response of the parliamentary commissioners carrying out this inquiry to these figures, focussing on the absence of 'dead certificates' for 9,752 of them, see ibid., p.29.

12   Tait, 'Some sources for the study of infant and maternal mortality', p.55.

13   The infant mortality rate (IMR) is the number of deaths in the first year of life per thousand live births.

14   Tait, p.69.

15   Levene, *Childcare, health and mortality*, p.49.

16   Sources: Bideau, *Infant and Child Mortality in the Past*, pp.18, 19, 25, 79; Tait 'Some sources for the study of infant and maternal mortality', p.69; Levene, ibid.

17   Readers are referred to Levene for a detailed discussion of infant mortality rates including the statistical phenomenon of 'left truncation'.

18   Viazzo, P.P., Bortolotto M., and Zanotto, A., 'Five centuries of foundling history in Florence: changing patterns of abandonment, care and mortality', in C. Panter-Brick and M.T. Smith, eds., *Abandoned Children* (Cambridge, 2000), p.86; Fildes, *Wet-nursing*, pp.155–157; Wickes, p.238. Levene, *Childcare, health and mortality*, p.50.

19   Levene, *Childcare, health and mortality*, p.60. Bardet, 'The death of foundlings', p.
      248. Fildes, Wet Nursing, p. 184.
20   *Lords Journals*, iii, p.430, Appendix ix; *Commons Journals*, iv, 21 Nov 1743, ccxxv;
      Commons Journals, vi, 12 May 1760, ccccxiv; *Commons Journals*, ix, Appendix ccxi,
      13 Nov 1773; *Commons Journals*, xiv, 24 Mar 1791, Appendix ccci; *Commons
      Journals*, xvii, 3 May 1797, appendix ccliii; *Reports from the Commissioners of
      the Board of Education in Ireland*, (1813), viii, p.171, 172; *Third Report of the
      Commissioners of Irish Education Enquiry* (1826), pp.148–152; *History of Dublin*,
      Warburton et al, i, p.591; *Twentieth Report of the Commissioners for auditing Public
      Accounts in Ireland* [C 75] HC (1831–2), p.50.
21   Eighteen months total. (The start of the accounting year changed to January.)
22   Six months total.
23   *Third Report of the Commissioners of Irish Education Inquiry*, pp.148–152.

Index